Visualizing the I

Visualizing the Nation

Gender, Representation, and Revolution in Eighteenth-Century France

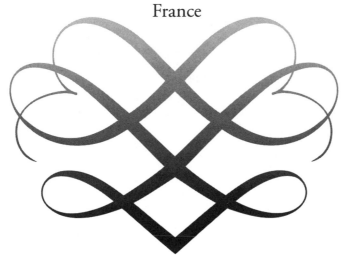

Joan B. Landes

CORNELL UNIVERSITY PRESS
Ithaca and London

First published 2001 by Cornell University Press
First printing, Cornell Paperbacks, 2003

Printed in the United States of America

Library of Congress Cataloging-in-Publication Data

Landes, Joan B., 1946–
    Visualizing the nation : gender, representation, and revolution in eighteenth-century France / Joan B. Landes
        p. cm.
    Includes bibliographical references and index.
    ISBN 0-8014-3811-X (cloth : alk. paper)—ISBN 0-8014-8848-6 (pbk. : alk. paper)
    1. France—History—Revolution, 1789–1799—Art and the revolution.
2. Art, French. 3. Art—Political aspects—France. 4. Nationalism and
art—France. 5. Sex role in art. 6. Allegories. 7. Body,
Human—Symbolic aspects—France—History—18th century.   I. Title.
    N6846 .L344 2001
    704.9'424'094409033—dc21

                                    2001000203

Cornell University Press strives to use environmentally responsible suppliers and materials to the fullest extent possible in the publishing of its books. Such materials include vegetable-based, low-VOC inks and acid-free papers that are recycled, totally chlorine-free, or partly composed of nonwood fibers. For further information, visit our website at www.cornellpress.cornell.edu.

        3 5 7 9   Cloth printing   10 8 6 4 2
    1 3 5 7 9   Paperback printing   10 8 6 4 2

RAVEN

USED BOOKS

52-B JFK STREET
HARVARD SQUARE
617. 441. 6999

OPEN 7 DAYS A WEEK
MONDAY–THURSDAY 10AM–9PM
FRIDAY & SATURDAY 10AM–10PM
SUNDAY 11AM–8PM

SPECIALIZING
IN SCHOLARLY
USED BOOKS.

Contents

Illustrations

Acknowledgments

In the writing of this book I have incurred many debts—personal, institutional, and intellectual. This project was generously supported by the Swedish Collegium for Advanced Study in the Social Sciences in Uppsala, Sweden, which afforded me the privilege of a semester leave in a wonderful collegial environment with excellent research facilities and staff. I was also fortunate to have spent three equally remarkable months at the Humanities Research Centre of the Australian National University, another very special institution. I am particularly grateful to Björn Wittrock and Bo Gustafsson of SCASSS and Iain McCalman of the HRC for their support. I have no doubt that this would have been a very different, and far less successful, book without the stimulation born of interdisciplinary conversation and cross-cultural friendship that my stay at these institutes made possible. The Pennsylvania State University provided valuable funding for the final stages of my research, as did Hampshire College at its inception. In addition, I was fortunate to have been a participant in an National Endowment for the Humanities Summer Institute on "Image and Text in the Eighteenth Century," directed by Michael Fried and Ronald Paulson, which encouraged me in my initial forays into the world of early modern visual culture.

I am deeply grateful for the incisive critiques and astute advice of friends and colleagues who read this manuscript. Patrice Higonnet deserves special mention, for his generous support and suggestions throughout several stages of this project. Mary Sheriff's visual and theoretical insights were a tremendous aid in allowing me to clarify my most basic arguments. Lynn Hunt, Marie-Hélène Huet, and Jeremy Popkin shared their special wisdom about eighteenth-century France. Doris Sommer prompted me to think harder about visual regimes, as well as the link between visuality, allegory, and nationalism. Guido Ruggiero and Jeffrey Alexander provided me with the chance to frame my arguments for students of the "beginning" and the "end" of modernity. Jeff was an unflinching supporter at a crucial stage of this project. Jack Censer offered helpful advice on the intricacies of acquiring prints; Lise Andriès, Carole Pateman, Barbara Caine, and Rico Franses provided welcome responses to different parts of this project. Sura Levine, with whom I cocurated the 1989 exhibition "Representing Revolution: French and British Images, 1789–1804" at the Mead Art Museum of Amherst College, was an invaluable guide to the joys and frustrations of art research, and an essential intellectual partner in the earliest stages of this book project. I am grateful for the generous participation of Dr. Fritz Daguillard in our exhibition, a fellow spirit in navigating the intersections of art, politics, and culture in revolutionary times. I have spent many happy hours in the museums of Paris and Stockholm with Francine Fatoux and Ulla Wikander, and at North American museums with Heather McPherson. Ulla Wikander shared my enthusiasm for European gender history. Maria Pia Lara, Nan Woodruff, and Judy Kroll have been steady friends and important partners in dialogue, at home and abroad.

I have been extremely fortunate to be able to present my work in many different locales. As a student of the public sphere, I learned in practice the *frisson* that results from a good—and challenging—conversation. At the outset of the project I was privileged to present a special lecture to the Association for Eighteenth-Century Studies and a keynote address to the Consortium on Revolutionary Europe, 1750–1850. Later on, I had the opportunity to deliver plenary addresses at the Swedish Historical Society, the George Rudé Seminar in French History and Civilisation, and the Nineteenth-Century French Studies Colloquium. I was pleased to participate in the "Intimate Encounters Symposium: Love and Enlightenment" at the Hood Museum of Art of Dartmouth College, the conference on "The Culture of the Terror in the French Revolution" at Brown University, and the conferences on "Women and the French Revolution" and "Discourses of Civil Society," both at the University of California at Los Angeles. I also had the chance to present aspects of this book at conferences of the American Historical Association and the Society for French Historical Studies. I am grateful to Tim Raser, Doris Kadish, Laura Mason, Richard Rand, Sara Melzer, Leslie Rabine, Jeffrey Alexander, and the other organizers of these events. In addition, I owe a special thanks to my hosts and audiences at numerous universities and colleges, especially for raising probing questions that greatly enriched my thinking: the University of Minnesota, Minneapolis; Harvard University; Australian National University; the University of Melbourne; the University of Sydney; Macquarie University; Victoria University of Wellington; the University of Auckland; the University of California, Irvine; Williams College; the University of Wisconsin, Madison; California State University at Fullerton; the University of Arizona; the University of Kansas, Lawrence; the Universities of Stockholm, Lund, and Umea, Sweden; the State University of New York at Stony Brook; the Universities of Utrecht, Groningen, and Amsterdam, the

Netherlands; Sarah Lawrence College; the University of Waikato, New Zealand; the University of Massachusetts, Boston; Amherst College; the University of North Carolina, Chapel Hill; and the University of Chicago.

This book would not have been possible without the encouragement and support of John Ackerman, editor extraordinaire and warm adviser. I also thank the librarians at the Bibliothèque Nationale, the Musée Carnavalet, the Library of Congress, the Art Institute of Chicago, the New York Public Library, the Carolina Rediviva Library of Uppsala University, and the Pattee Library of the Pennsylvania State University. I was fortunate to have had the research assistance on this project of two exceptionally talented graduate students, Jennifer Davis and Sarah Goodfellow. I am also grateful to the many undergraduate and graduate students at my own campuses and elsewhere who have pushed me to develop my ideas in fruitful directions. Paul Harvey, Benedicte Monicat, Julia Simon, and Christine Clark-Evans cheerfully answered my linguistic queries. At Penn State, my colleagues in history, women's studies, and early modern studies have provided a welcome space for the kind of cross-disciplinary exploration that is at the heart of this study, as did previously our brave band of cultural studies faculty at Hampshire College.

Chapter 2 of this book is adapted from "Representing the Body Politic: The Paradox of Gender in the Graphic Politics of the French Revolution," by Joan B. Landes, from *Rebel Daughters: Women and the French Revolution*, edited by Sara E. Melzer and Leslie W. Rabine, copyright © 1992 University of California Humanities Research Institute. Used by permission of Oxford University Press, Inc. Parts of this material also appeared earlier in "Political Imagery of the French Revolution," in *Representing Revolution: French and British Images*, 1789–1804 (Amherst, Mass.: Mead Art Museum of Amherst College, 1989), 13–21.

Unless otherwise indicated, all translations in this book are my own.

This book is dedicated to Theodore Norton, whose constant love, patience, and above all confidence in me helped make it possible, and to our daughter, Eleanor, another believer!

Visualizing the Nation

Introduction

In politics the body changes. Once individual, it becomes collective; once
material, it becomes ideal; once an unconscious and involuntary condition,
it becomes a conscious and voluntary state.
—Anne Norton, *Reflections on Political Identity*

T HIS IS a book about bodies—how they are pictured and how these
pictures communicate political and social meanings. The bodies that
matter are gendered bodies within the popular arts of the French Revolution. I argue that representations of women within popular imagery promoted the ideals of French republicanism and contributed to individuals'
self-understanding as citizens of the nation-state. The 1790s were a time of dramatically changing expectations and newly differentiated roles for men and
women in both the intimate and public arenas. The redefinition of femininity
and masculinity in this period was deeply embedded in the process by which
courtly culture was repudiated and femininity associated with its most deca-
dent and corrupt features. In looking at public imagery, I am interested in how
images valorized certain personal behaviors and repudiated others in relation
to collective ideals. But images can just as often make trouble, disrupt as well
as secure desired identifications. In the revolutionary context, representations
of the female body risked approving what was being disapproved: the affecta-
tion and sensuality of femininity in Old Regime culture, as well as the independent agency of women in republican society. Thus, while I investigate the
ways in which visual culture influences gender ideology, I do not see this as a
seamless process. I ask how representations of bodies both constitute and
transgress the boundaries between the material and immaterial, the conscious
and the unconscious, the personal and the political, the individual and the

I

collective. What is certain is that, as Ann Norton claims, "in politics the body changes."[1] In revolutionary France, such changes were part and parcel of the process by which the newly forged nation-state imposed its demands on the individual subject.

The nation is a greedy institution—economically, physically, and emotionally. It is the object of a special kind of love—one whose demands are sometimes known to exceed all others, even to the point of death. I argue that the feminine iconography of the nation encouraged citizens in their productive political passions, that its body worked to consolidate passionate attachments to home and homeland. Liberty, Republic, and La Patrie ("the fatherland") may look like antique goddesses and share a comforting affinity with the female saints of Roman Catholicism. However, as Doris Sommer explains, "Unlike the competitive comparisons between nationalism and religion, the interchangeability between nation and sex. . . is mutually reinforcing. And it is possible, through their overlapping analogies to religion, to see sex and nation helping each other to displace earlier attachments."[2] It is well appreciated that a nation-state's political legitimacy is founded on consent, not just on force, but less often acknowledged is how visual imaginings may be part of the process by which a citizen learns to love an abstract object with something like the individual lover's intimacy and passion.

This is accordingly a book about visual ways of knowing. It reflects the ever-widening interest in visual evidence in the humanistic and scientific disciplines. My sources are drawn from revolutionary print culture in the years between 1789 and 1795—engravings, etchings, illustrated newspapers, and broadsides—in French and American collections.[3] I began serious research on revolutionary imagery in preparation for an exhibition on French and British artists of the French and Haitian Revolutions, which I cocurated with the art historian Sura Levine in 1989. Our search for domestic sources for loan objects—to avoid borrowing from French collections in the year of that country's bicentennial—led us initially to the notable collections of the New York Public Library and major museums with rich holdings in eighteenth-century French art. But what turned out to be the greatest treasure trove for us—the holdings of the Library of Congress—were then incompletely cataloged and little known, even among specialists in the field. I virtually stumbled on them in 1988, following up a hunch by the curator of European drawings at the Baltimore Museum of Art. I mention this to indicate how quickly the situation has changed, as marked by the publication of new works on revolutionary imagery and the featuring of visual sources at the numerous celebrations and conferences devoted to the bicentennial of the French Revolution.[4]

In at least two senses, this study has strong company. First, I share the pre-occupation of so many of today's cultural historians and theorists with issues of the body and forms of embodiment, on the one hand, and with grammars of representation, on the other.[5] As I have already indicated, the bodies under investigation here are distinguished by their sexual and gender attributes. I emphasize the power of gendered imagery in helping (negatively) to destroy the icons and symbols of Old Regime state and society and (affirmatively) to create a new citizen body within a republican nation-state. Second, I propose that the visual domain is more than a mirror reflecting real events or an illustration of deeper intellectual trends, the keys to which are to be found in the study of words and texts. In contrast, I look to images as vehicles for the exchange of ideas and the making of political arguments. I agree with Antoine de Baecque that it is possible "to interpret the Revolution on the basis of its images" and with Barbara Stafford's caution against (what she terms) "an entrenched antivisualism pervading western neoplatonizing discourse from the Enlightenment forward."[6] In staking out a claim for visual cognition, however, I do not mean to underestimate the interaction that exists between pictures and texts. As W. J. T. Mitchell reminds us, "All media are mixed media, and all representations are heterogeneous."[7]

The problems posed by female representations of and in the nation developed from the convulsive changes that shook France at the close of the eighteenth century. To abbreviate a long and complicated series of developments, the Revolution can be said to mark the passage from monarchical government to the institutions of the modern nation-state. As the traditional narrative goes, previously subjects of the crown, "Frenchmen" now became citizens of the nation. By a radical inversion, society's members declared themselves the authors and source of society in place of the king. Despite the inevitable abstraction inherent in such a proclamation, it must be stressed that society so construed is not just an abstract universal, for its members constitute a specific national community. As one commentator explains, "As the bearer of a sovereign power, the society uncovered is always a particular society, a nation, with an identity of its own. And this nation, because it is supposedly constituted by the unanimous accord of the contracting parties [in the contract constituting society], must necessarily appear as unified and, assuming the accord was reached without deception, as just."[8] The words of Article 3 of the Declaration of the Rights of Man and Citizen underscore the implicit premises of the contractual theory of national sovereignty: "The source of all sovereignty resides essentially in the nation. No body, no individual can exercise authority that does not explicitly proceed from it."[9]

Leaving aside for the moment the important question of whether women and their bodies were ever intended to be part of the sovereign body of the nation, we can at least agree that the move from being a subject (a person *subject to* the superior, uncontestable will of the monarch) to a citizen (the *bearer of* independent [natural] rights and the source of all sovereignty) could not have left unaffected anyone's sense of self. As evidence of that change, the revolutionaries mandated the use of the familiar *tu* in favor of the formal *vous* form of address and substituted the universal term *citoyen* for the privileged title *monsieur*. In the heady atmosphere of revolutionary change, it was not unusual for French republicans, like their most utopian forebears during the Enlightenment, to conceive of themselves as "citizens of the world." However, such cosmopolitan aspirations proved to be an (as yet) fanciful wish. More impressive is the decided weight of nationalism as the seemingly permanent condition of rights-bearing individuals.[10] In France as elsewhere in modern society, nationalism as a political sensibility was accompanied by the fashioning of new identities in such intimate domains as the self, the body, sexuality, and sexual difference. Even the choice of everyday articles of clothing became for citizens a matter charged with political significance.[11]

As it turned out, to be a *citoyenne* ("citizeness") was not quite the same thing as being a citizen. Despite the proclamation of the rights of man in 1789, the institution of universal manhood suffrage in 1792, and the abolition of slavery in 1794, as well as important reforms in civil and family law that benefited women, women remained second-class members of the nation, deprived of fundamental political rights.[12] The Constitution of 1791 categorized all women as "passive citizens" (along with the majority of men, whose status was a function of their economic position). Nor was their constitutionally inferior status to improve with the more democratic climate that followed with the declaration of the Republic. Even in the democratic Constitution of 1793, which eliminated the distinction between active and passive citizenship, women were still denied equal political status. In this respect, they were not merely victims of Old Regime customs and practices. For notwithstanding other differences that separated women, all women now shared a common position before the law because of their gender, which eerily confirmed Jean-Jacques Rousseau's claim that "everything depended fundamentally on politics."[13] Nonetheless, politically active women did not retire willingly from the revolutionary public sphere; they had to be expelled. On 9 Brumaire Year II (30 October 1793), the National Convention outlawed all clubs and popular societies of women.[14] Subsequently, the Paris Commune upheld Pierre Gaspard Chaumette's proposal to bar women from its sessions as well.[15] The new legal definition of citizenship meant that all women—but especially those who asserted their rights by participating in popular insurrections and demanding a broader role in the political arena—occupied an ambiguous status vis-à-vis the sovereign. In the words of Dominique Godineau, they were "*citoyennes* without citizenship."[16]

Sex, it happens, mattered a great deal, and so did morality. And in both arenas, women were expected to behave differently from the way men did. What is more, good behavior was not just a private matter; private morality was intimately tied to public virtue and state interest. Unhampered sexuality was seen as a threat to the republican body politic, and women's unlicensed sexuality and untempered enthusiasms were thought to imperil state and civil order. As the Jacobin deputy André Amar proclaimed in his defense of the motion before the Convention to ban women's clubs in the fall of 1793, the different roles appropriate to the two sexes followed directly from their separate natures: "This question," he insisted,

> is related essentially to morals, and without morals, no republic. . . . Their [women's] presence in popular societies. . . would give an active role in government to people more exposed to error and seduction. Let us add that women are disposed by their organization to an over-excitation which would be deadly in public affairs and that interests of state would soon be sacrificed to everything which ardor in passions can generate in the way of error and disorder. Delivered over to the heat of public debate, they would teach their children not love of country but hatreds and suspicions.[17]

The etymological and historical connections between the terms *citizenship* and *civility* help to clarify the extent to which membership in the nation called for good governance of both the self and the city. As George L. Mosse has so brilliantly argued, decent and correct manners and morals, as well as a proper attitude toward sexuality, were intimately connected with the development of modern nationalism.[18] And female propriety, chastity, and fidelity, along with monogamy, all became tropes of civilized or virtuous nationhood.

Visual evidence from the period reveals a great deal about the fashioning of new cultural and political identities, as well as the way in which manners and morals occupied the French citizenry's attention. Especially striking about such evidence is the sheer abundance of female representations within the immense corpus of revolutionary iconography. Whether in the guise of an allegory of the nation (Republic, Liberty, *La Patrie*) and its most elevated values (freedom, equality, nature, truth), on the one hand, or in the contemptible shape of a female caricature, on the other, women's bodies were everywhere to be found in public imagery circulating within the new political culture. On the surface, this explosion of images would not be so remarkable were it not for republicans' preoccupation with maintaining women in their proper place. Increasingly, good governance and good morals were associated with domesticity; and domesticity came to mean women's restriction to the domestic sphere and domestic tasks, in lieu of their full participation in the nation's public life.[19] Surely, revolutionary visual culture is paradoxical in its insistent public "showing" of the female body while upholding a gendered discourse of female domesticity and male publicity.

The chapters of this book reflect my continuing concern with gendered forms of representation in French revolutionary political culture. I retain a skeptical interest in public-sphere theory as an explanation of the rise of modern political liberty, democracy, and gender equality. In previous work I challenged the universality of Jürgen Habermas's classical model of the public sphere from the standpoint of gender relations. Here I aim to redress what increasingly appears to be a one-dimensional view of modern French political culture, from which I do not exempt myself: stated baldly, the notion that culture amounts to the sum of so many printed words on a page. Yet this influential idea is a by-product of eighteenth-century historians' emphasis on the foundational role of language and political discourse in accounting for the demise of the Old Regime. Indeed, my earlier work described the decisive historical passage from French absolutism to bourgeois society as an opposition between the old and new forms of representation, "between the iconic spectacularity of the Old Regime and the textual and legal order of the bourgeois public sphere."[20]

In this book I hope to complicate this argument. Although texts and their readers did have an enormous weight in the new political culture, it would be wrong to imply for that reason that images or other aspects of the Old Regime's performative and visual culture diminished in importance. For example, notwithstanding the growing weight of print culture, Jeffrey Ravel insists on the popularity of theater and theatrical metaphors across the shift from Old Regime to revolutionary culture.[21] In a parallel fashion, I am interested in the graphic arts of the Revolution as a vehicle by which political arguments were made and power was mediated and constituted in both visual and textual domains. While respecting interpenetrating visual and verbal conventions, I suggest that analysis of visual representations can advance our understanding of the articulation, promotion, and dissemination of political arguments.

This last claim may seem surprising, or even beside the point, given the large number of publications concerning revolutionary imagery that have appeared in the past two decades. For historians, attention to visual sources was spurred initially by Maurice Agulhon's pathbreaking studies of the female allegory of Republic, and by Lynn Hunt's many exciting interrogations of visual evidence, including her influential account of Hercules as a symbol of the radical revolution in the context of the "crisis of representation" caused by the monarchy's collapse and the Republic's birth.[22] Marina Warner and Madelyn Gutwirth have looked at female imagery in the period.[23] James A. Leith has examined the role of propaganda in revolutionary culture and the Revolution's impact on the built environment (real and imagined).[24] Michel Vovelle's monumental efforts, in conjunction with the Bicentennial, to introduce to a wider public the vast store of revolutionary iconography preserved in France's great library and museum collections has multiplied the visual evidence available for historical reflection, as have Antoine de Baecque and Claude Langlois's studies of revolutionary and counterrevolutionary caricature and Rolf Reichardt's appreciations of revolutionary imagery.[25]

Nevertheless, there is a difference, as de Baecque insists, between "conferring on representations not only the capacity to express meaning, but also the status of a mode of understanding." Accordingly, I share de Baecque's desire "to hold together two different ways of doing history, two strategies that were too easily opposed to one another in the 1980s." As I have stated, I warmly endorse his call "to interpret the Revolution on the basis of its images" and regard his interventions as pivotal in moving toward the kind of history of representations I am attempting in this study. However, it is instructive to consider the manner in which de Baecque (a historian of images) describes Vovelle's efforts, given Vovelle's stature as a student of the revolutionary image, and to note the contrast de Baecque draws between Vovelle's work and that of François Furet, the influential exponent of linguistic or discourse analysis. Even in the most expert hands, the historian of images implies, the study of images has had to take second place to textual analysis—the former counting as illustration, not interpretation:

> While François Furet brilliantly explored the domain of interpretation, offering in his *Penser la Révolution* and in the *Dictionnaire critique de la Révolution français* a sort of "box of thoughts" from which we have all drawn eagerly, Michel Vovelle preferred to respond by placing himself on another terrain, in the "field" as it were, examining new archival sources (particularly images) and new approaches to the event ("men-

talités," cultural practices, lexicology, content analysis, geopolitical cartography). The first *interpreted* events, ceaselessly exploring the Revolution as a means to understanding modern political thought; the second *illustrated* them, taking the narrative of the Revolution in all its forms: printed, pictorial, discursive) to be the best vehicle for representing history, focusing on the need of men and women to "figure" politics, to "draw up an image" of their own history.[26]

De Baecque's point can be enlarged in that linguistic and discourse analysis in revolutionary studies continued to hold a privileged position over other modes of interpretation and evidence. De Baecque's recent work, *The Body Politic: Corporeal Metaphor in Revolutionary France, 1770–1800* (originally titled *Le Corps de l'histoire*), affirms this emphasis, although it is exemplary in suggesting the interchange that occurred between the metaphoric language of pamphlets and texts and the visual images drawn to describe the new political society. In both the textual and visual domain, he asserts that there existed a similar repertoire of figures: the degeneracy of the nobility, the impotence of the king and the virility of the republic, the bleeding wounds of republican martyrs, and the spectacle of laughter accompanying attacks on real and metaphorical bodies. In terms of the program of visual interpretation that de Baecque announces in his *Representations* article, however, his splendid 1988 study of revolutionary caricature, *La Caricature révolutionnaire,* and his many articles on visual imagery better approximate his call for an interpretation of the Revolution on the basis of its images. Even so, there is room for expansion, for none of his efforts has focused centrally on the role of gender relations in revolutionary political culture.[27] While sharing de Baecque's orientation, I nevertheless view my analysis as a complementary effort.

Similarly, my interest in the role of visual cognition and the interplay between gender and nationalism sets this study apart from Madelyn Gutwirth's valuable inquiry into verbal and visual representation in eighteenth-century France. Gutwirth sees the Revolution as a moment in a longer struggle over taste and value, in which women's advancement in society is resisted and an unquestioned male supremacy restored. Her story is both stylistic and political, one in which "misogyny [is used] as an arm of polemics."[28] Like the literary and visual artists she studies, she, too, uses metaphor to analogize women's fateful decline—or "twilight"—by the end of the eighteenth century.[29] A narrative of women's decline in the passage from old to new regimes, however, fails to address the differently constituted subjectivity of women and men in the new Republic. In addition, I am interested in the possibilities for both normative and subversive readings of visual representations, as well as the multivalent properties of the image. Rather than speculate on the sources of sexual repression or the diminished erotic aura of female goddesses, I place passion at the center of my exploration of patriotism. I ask how the depiction of the nation as a desirable woman may have eroticized men's bond to that nation.

Agulhon's classic study of republican imagery pointed the way toward the last of these questions, at least insofar as a personified image of the nation helped to anchor national attachments. Agulhon also legitimized initial research into the problem of the female representation of Republic. However, Agulhon's work predated the important infusion of feminist approaches into revolutionary and Old Regime studies, as well as revolutionary studies' recent "critical turn" toward problems of representation.[30] For example, Hunt's 1983 study of the masculine imagery of popular radicalism suggested the need for a more expanded appreciation of gender relations in revolutionary culture, which she advanced in *The Family Romance of the French Revolution*. Like Agulhon, Hunt has understood the benefit of examining visual sources in the study of revolutionary culture.

By calling attention to these contributions, however, I hardly mean to suggest that visual studies now occupy center stage in the study of history. Despite their growing appreciation of images, historians as a group remain skeptical of the value of visual evidence. What could be more awkward than to ask a specialist in written documents to prioritize visual media? But disciplinary specialization is not the only barrier to a fuller acknowledgment of the "knowingness" of visual communication. Nor are historians alone in privileging the text over the image. Prejudices abound on behalf of the text—deemed to be a "higher," more durable monument to civilization—and against the image, ranked "lower" because more fleeting and impressionistic in its effects. Barbara Stafford attributes such biases to the "linguistic turn" in contemporary thought:

> The totemization of language as a godlike agency in western culture has guaranteed the identification of writing with intellectual potency. Ferdinand de Saussure, the early twentieth-century founder of structuralism, strengthened the biblical coupling of meaning with naming by formulating the opposition of signifier/signified. These verbalizing binaries turned noumenal and phenomenal experience into the product of language. Not only temporal but spatial effects supposedly obeyed an invisible system, the controlling structure of an inborn ruling *écriture*. . . . Most damagingly, Saussure's schema emptied the mind

of its body, obliterating the interdependence of physiological functions and thinking. It is not surprising that, up to now, an educational economy materially based on language has either marginalized the study of images, reduced it to a subaltern position, or appropriated it through colonization. In most American university curricula, graphicacy remains subordinate to literacy. Even so-called interdisciplinary "visual culture" programs are governed by the ruling metaphor of reading. Consequently, iconicity is treated as an inferior part of a more general semantics.[31]

The paradigm shift responsible for what is often called "the new cultural history" is wholly implicated in what Stafford and others have referred to as "the linguistic turn."[32] Keith Michael Baker's definition of political culture exemplifies well how philosophers Michel Foucault and Jürgen Habermas influenced the fashioning of the discursive approach to revolutionary history. Following Habermas, Baker has sought to account for the invention of public opinion in Old Regime society, and to explain its role in reshaping politics and the sources of legitimization. Like Foucault, he argues that human identity and action are linguistically constituted.[33] Political culture is, Baker writes,

> the set of discourses or symbolic practices by which . . . claims are made. It comprises the definitions of the relative subject-positions from which individuals and groups may (or may not) legitimately make claims one upon another, and therefore of the identity and boundaries of the community to which they belong. It constitutes the meanings of the terms in which these claims are framed, the nature of the contexts to which they pertain, and the authority of the principles according to which they are made binding. It shapes the constitutions and powers of the agencies and procedures by which the contestations are resolved, competing claims authoritatively adjudicated, and binding decisions enforced. Thus political authority is, in this view, essentially a matter of linguistic authority; first, in the sense that political functions are defined and allocated within the framework of a given political discourse; and second, in the sense that their exercise takes the form of upholding authoritative definitions of the terms within that discourse.[34]

For Baker, there is no such thing as nondiscursive social realities. Instead, reality is always constituted through different discursive practices or language games. He borrows this particular perspective on the Revolution, and the eighteenth century more generally, from François Furet's influential 1978 polemic against Marxist historians of the French Revolution, *Penser la Révolution française*. Furet argued that the Revolution must be understood as "a political phenomenon, a profound transformation of political discourse involving powerful new forms of political symbolization."[35] But where Furet saw the Revolution as exceptional in the power it gave to discourse, Baker insists that social and political arrangements are never outside of language. Not just the Revolution, he writes, but all "social and political changes are themselves linguistic."[36]

This emphasis on language derived from Foucault and Furet led Baker, like so many other French historians, to an enlarged appreciation of Habermas's 1962 account of the rise of the liberal public sphere, *Strukturwandel der Öffentlichkeit*—translated into French in 1978 and into English in 1989.[37] Habermas attempted a social-historical analysis of the changing meanings associated with the terms *public*, *public opinion*, and *publicity* from antiquity through medieval, early modern, and modern society. He argued that the rise of liberal parliamentary regimes in eighteenth-century Europe was a product of the free exchange of opinion about governmental affairs between private individuals. For Habermas, the liberal public sphere—as a political and cultural phenomenon—resulted from the expanded dissemination of printed texts: "[The] zone of continuous administrative contact [between state authorities and private subjects] became 'critical' . . . in the sense that it provoked the critical judgment of a public making use of its reason. The public could take on this challenge all the better as it required merely a change in the function of the instrument with whose help the state administration had already turned society into a public affair in a specific sense—the press."[38] Overall, Habermas's public is a discursive phenomenon, a printed affair. Although he appreciated that the printing press also played a role in the dissemination of reproducible images, Habermas generally regarded pictures and visual culture as features of the Old Regime, which came to be supplanted by texts and their readers in the formation of a critical and oppositional liberal public sphere.[39]

For discourse theorists, words are the medium in which critical discussion occurs. Defenders of textual supremacy will want to know whether there is a visual equivalent of dialogue or debate, or whether pictures can satisfy the requirements of a rational politics on Habermas's model. In response, the visualist might challenge the claim that all knowledge—not least critical ways of knowing—is tied to texts, or that political authority is entirely a matter of linguistic authority. She might ask whether the linguistic model can account for the link between perception and thought, or between the body and the mind.

She might insist on conceiving spectatorship as a thought-provoking, attentive activity and not just "empty gaping."[40] Moreover, even when the discourse theorist has admitted the ubiquity of the image, the visualist will want to be on guard against any impulse to degrade the image in favor of the word. And if the status of the image is granted, it will be necessary to know how to describe the relationship between an image and a text. Philip Stewart, a student of book illustration, suggests a fruitful point of departure—that there is nothing innocent about an image. Even in the medium of the illustrated literary text, Stewart challenges the assumption that the image is only a reflection of an original textual source:

> The confrontation of an image *with* a text embodies, along with complementarity, a sort of defiance: a challenge to its mastery, an assertion of a coequal viewpoint. In certain ways it might be helpful to think of illustration as being "against" rather than "to" the text, probing its tacit ambiguities if not its weaknesses. Even more interesting, at times, are the tricks it can play with metaphor; for although both image and text can of course be metaphoric, they cannot always—and perhaps cannot usually—adopt each other's metaphors and thus are tempted to substitute, literalize, or otherwise transmogrify the metaphors they feed upon in the other medium.[41]

It is interesting that Stewart chooses the metaphor of embodiment to introduce the confrontational relationship between the image and the text. In a broader sense, I find the issue of embodiment compelling. Thus, I submit that by attending to visuality, we are in a better position to appreciate the embodied nature of representation—even in the revolutionary age, when, in principle, bodily metaphors seem to have lost their prior significance as a vehicle for the palpable manifestation of monarchical power. Yet despite the dramatic shift that occurred from the sanctified body of the king to the abstract notion of the nation, the representatives of the new nation struggled with the problem of how to incorporate—and embody—the people's sovereignty. In the process they redeployed an older allegorical political imagery that drew bodies, and not least female bodies, more impressively than ever into the public sphere.[42] The Republic was certainly constituted in and through a discourse on gender relations, as I have argued in earlier work. But I now believe it is necessary to go further and explore how images worked sometimes independently and sometimes in tandem with words to affect the preferred sexual positions of men and women in the new society.

Methodologically, we have a great deal to learn from the graphic arts about the central issues of the Revolution—whether it be the principle of individual freedom, the new definition of the nation as a popular sovereign body, or the celebration of virtue and the condemnation of vice. In this book, I am chiefly concerned with the role played by images of the female body in the constitution of national identity, democratic equality, and political liberty, and in shaping the manners and morals that accompanied national identity in republican France. Admittedly, all scholarship tends to distort the wider landscape in order to clear a view for its particular subject matter. So much is well understood. Yet given the growing weight of evidence on the role of women and gender relations, along with the sheer amplitude of iconography of the female body in the revolutionary period, one would have to be almost intentionally ignorant to continue to treat such topics as of only incidental importance. By attending to the specific dynamics of gender, I aim to further our appreciation of the revolutionary imagination. In the process, I hope to demonstrate some of the mechanisms by which individuals were constituted (politically as well as socially) as gendered subjects.

I have chosen to present images that primarily underscore the influence of allegory and caricature—the two leading genres that graphic artists used during the Revolution.[43] Given that at least six thousand engraved images produced between 1789 and 1799 are held in public collections, I make no claim to completeness.[44] Nor are my selections based on some quantitative measure of thematic contents. With respect to allegory, no amount of counting is necessary to prove the obvious: the predominance of feminine imagery within the allegorical corpus. This is widely acknowledged. Less well understood is whether and how the fact of so many representations of women mattered, and if so, in what ways. As for caricature, neither revolutionaries nor their opponents would have considered women as such as a topic of the same importance as, say, the clergy and the aristocracy or the sansculottes and the Jacobins. But caricaturists did feature women to satirical effect, and I am interested in how the trope of gender figured in their bag of tricks. Because of the heightened political circumstances of the period and the sometimes hasty manner of their execution, many of the works I consider are unsigned. Their anonymity greatly compounds the difficulty of ascertaining how many (if any) of the artists in this period were women. Limited documentation makes a study of artistic provenance untenable for the present.

Among the many allegorical renderings of the taking of the Bastille, I am aware of one signed work by a female artist—Roze Le Noir's etching *Hunting the Great Beast*.[45] Although *Hunting the Great Beast* is by no means a refined work, it was one of the most often reproduced and visually striking allegorical renderings of the taking of the Bastille. In addition, two women engravers, *Citoyenne* Rollet and Marie-Adelaide Boizot, appear to have participated in the movement against slavery. Rollet engraved a copy of George Morland's *Execrable Human Traffic*, an English antislavery image that was published in France to accompany the 1794 decree abolishing slavery; Boizot, the sister of the well-known sculptor Louis-Simon Boizot, was the possible engraver of the paired abolitionist images *Moi libre aussi*, one male and one female.[46] The example of Marie-Adelaide Boizot, like the female engravers discussed by the nineteenth-century sociologist Julies Renouvier in his study of revolutionary art, confirms the value of family connections. That so many of these women were engravers rather than painters (especially of the highest genre, history painting) is also noteworthy. They include Mme (*Citoyenne*) Montalant, Sophie Janinet (later Mme Giacomelli, daughter of the celebrated color engraver Jean-François Janinet), Angélique Briceau (born into an artistic family and the wife of the artist Louis-Jean Allais), Marguerite Hémery (wife of the engraver Nicolas Ponce), Thérèse-Eleonore Lingée (daughter of the artist Hémery, sister of Marguerite Hémery, wife of the engraver Charles-Louis Lingée, and later wife of another artist, Lefebvre).[47]

In addition to family ties, an egalitarian reform movement that flourished for a few years in the early stages of the Revolution facilitated women's participation in the arts. For the reformers, as Nicolas Mirzoeff explains, "equality meant giving women artists equal status, modernizing art training, ending the powerful cliques like that of [Jacques-Louis] David's studio, and declaring all artistic genres equal." Among the important participants in this movement was the painter Adélaïde Labille-Guiard. Mirzoeff concludes, however, that by 1793 it was clear that although the Académie Royale de la peinture et de la sculpture [Royal Academy of Painting and Sculpture] had been abolished, its policies of artistic practice, including the exclusion of women, had survived.[48]

Despite the achievements of certain individuals and the possibilities for gender and artistic equality presented by early revolutionary reforms, it is important to recall the barriers that precluded eighteenth-century women from competing at the highest artistic levels.[49] Women could neither draw after nature nor attend the highest schools of artistic learning. According to Mary Sheriff, "Modesty dictated that women not look at the nude male body, which is what study after nature means in this context. Posing the male model was the only life drawing sanctioned in the Academy, and the practice was basic to [Charles Claude Flahaut, comte de la Billarderie] d'Angiviller's conception of history paintings as subjects depicting the male body in heroic art." Not only were girls disadvantaged in the finer points of practice, but they were deprived of knowledge in subjects thought essential to history painting: geography, history, literature, anatomy, and perspective. As Sheriff explains, "This exclusion exemplifies the general situation in France where young men and women were educated separately and learned different kinds of subjects and skills thought 'convenable' to their sex. Women's modesty prohibited women from occupying the same learning space as men, and it also forbade them from learning the same subjects. . . . [I]ntellectual work was deemed dangerous for women, because it could damage their health and, most frightening of all, impair their reproductive capacities."[50] Strong objections of this kind were raised, for example, in a tempestuous response to the first truly postrevolutionary Salon in 1791, after some women were beginning to paint from live models. Unnerved by the absolute havoc caused by "daughters turning to the study of the art of painting," a critic remarked that "young girls [were] susceptible to all impressions, exposed to all seductions, thrown among and confused with a mass of boys, drawing entirely naked men amongst them and exposed to all their attitudes." He claimed that "the models sometimes display in the most apparent manner the impression that the young girls have on them, and I have seen them forced to leave their pose and stand to one side in order to let their nature regain its state of calm."[51] This critic perceived a complete overturning of the gender order, an inverted world in which "naturally" reasonable men lose their control, women are mixed and even confused with boys, powerful female impressions overwhelm all those present, and women study—that is, gaze at—men instead of being their objects.

The denial to women of the requisite education, including access to live models needed to excel in the most elevated genres, relates directly to the problem of the representation of the female body in revolutionary art. First, this is an empirical question concerning who it is that draws the female body. Second, it raises a decisive theoretical issue: Who is doing the looking, and for whose pleasure or consumption is the image produced? As Simone de Beauvoir asserted in *The Second Sex*, "Representation of the world, like the world itself, is the work of men; they describe it from their own point of view, which they confuse with the absolute truth."[52] Art critic John Berger's pointed critique of the representation of the nude in Western art extends Beauvoir's unsettling claims directly to the visual domain. In an admittedly sweeping gesture, Berger distinguished between a man's and a woman's look: "*Men act* and *women appear*. Men look at women. Women watch themselves being looked at. This determines not only most relations between men and women but also the relation of women to themselves. The surveyor of woman in herself is male:

the surveyed female. Thus she turns herself into an object—and most particularly an object of vision: a sight."[53]

For Berger, with few exceptions, the act of representation occurs within the public workings of power. The nude in particular is a construction of female sexuality that signifies not only a man's desire but his position of ownership and power. Moreover, both men and women are caught within the look—which, to use a vocabulary unavailable to Berger at the time of his writing, is gendered male. Or, as the British film critic Laura Mulvey stated in her highly influential 1975 psychoanalytic discussion of cinema, structurally the narrative film posits a male gaze and a female object: "In a world ordered by sexual imbalance, pleasure in looking has been split between active/male and passive/female. The determining male gaze projects its phantasy onto the female figure which is styled accordingly. In their traditional exhibitionist role, women are simultaneously looked at and displayed, with their appearance coded for strong erotic and visual impact so that they can be said to connote *to-be-looked-at-ness.*"[54]

The empirical fact of who paints or engraves a particular work, to return to our initial concern, would appear to be less important on this account than the seeming evacuation of the woman's point of view as a consequence of the conventions surrounding the representation of the body in Western art. As Foucault contended, the body is a crucial site for the exercise and regulation of power. The production of knowledge concerning the body and its self-regulation are manifestations of power.[55] Commenting on the female body as representation, Lynda Nead further points to the dilemma of "woman playing out the roles of both viewed object and viewing subject, forming and judging her image against cultural ideals and exercising a fearsome self-regulation, through the individual exercising control over the self." Thus, women's subordination is reflected not only in the way in which they are represented, but also in the effects such representations have on their own self-image: how women are framed and how they participate in framing themselves through the containment of femininity and female sexuality. Men's power over women is in this respect reflected by the manner in which "the body is seen as image, according to a set of conventions, and woman acts both as judge and executioner."[56]

Such critical perspectives on the representation of the body have provoked still further questions. Not content to concede to men all power as representing subjects, feminists have been prompted to interrogate the "female gaze;" asking not only does it matter when women artists rather than men depict male or female nudes, but what happens when a woman looks back. Just as the gaze need not be normalized as masculine, we might want to investigate how women have wielded the gaze in a subversive or oppositional fashion.[57] Of course, the largely anonymous nature of the works under review prevent us from ascertaining how a particular female artist might have betrayed or re-worked the canonic rules of representation. Nevertheless, by retaining the pos-sibility of an oppositional reading—or "making"—of an image, we might avoid the pitfalls created by an oversimplified application of the theoretical structure that posits the gaze as male and places woman in the eternal feminine position of passive object of representation. To do so does not deny the con-siderable power men have wielded over image-making or the extent to which the woman's body has been made to signify a certain meaning in relation to truth and power, on the one hand, or to pleasure and desire, on the other.

Furthermore, the representation of women and their bodies is not without ambiguity; nor is the image without its own measure of authority. As Richard Leppert, following Marcia Pointon, writes of the female nude, "The very act of picturing her, and not something else, marks the power her body possesses over her male counterpart." Along with the image's ability to inscribe relations of power embedded in the wider social context, "the female nude occupies a space that is inevitably open to contestation, hence that space is profoundly ambiguous."[58] Pictures of nudes are not alone in conveying this sort of ambi-guity. The same processes are at work in the plentiful images of fully and par-tially clothed female figures that populated the revolutionary visual sphere. Beyond who is doing the looking, I would affirm that the work of art is a site of contestation; that a work of art has instability and excesses within it. In the graphic arts of the Revolution, therefore, the bedeviling emphasis on female images offers a useful point of departure for thinking not only about consoli-dations of identity but also about identity's fragility. In subsequent chapters I explore the power that the female image had in relation to the formation of na-tional as well as gender identity, but I do so within a broader discussion of how images functioned as complex vehicles for the communication of critical ideas and how arguments over the role of the image in revolutionary culture were re-lated to suspicions about the impact of femininity or women in the cultural sphere.

What, then, of the problem of female figuration in the Revolution gener-ally? The reasons advanced for female allegory are easily reprised, and all de-serve our full consideration: the grammatical gender of abstract nouns in French, Latin, and Greek; the Catholic veneration of the Virgin Mary; the role of female patron saints in religious practice and popular festivity; the impor-tance of goddesses, as personifications of various virtues, within classical myth; and, perhaps most important, the crisis in representation caused first by the adoption of a constitutional monarchy and subsequently by the fall of the French monarchy. However, it is not enough to question why the revolutionaries turned to female allegory or to enumerate the precedents in prerevolutionary culture that might have inclined them to readopt a female likeness of the nation or its central values. Rather, it is crucial to inquire into the effects of the national body's femininity—that is, by the surprising feminine face of the aggressively masculine version of revolutionary French nationalism. Not only does the national body's sexuality and gender position deserve a fuller explanation, so, too, does the foregrounding of heterosexual relations despite the existence of homosocial or fraternal impulses in the fashioning of the new body politic.

Although the new female representations may have resembled ancient goddesses, they no longer signified the partiality and privileges that constituted the old order of authority. Following Samuel Taylor Coleridge and the Romantics, we can define allegory as a personified abstraction constructed to fit an established prior meaning, for the most part restricted to the best educated members of the polity. For example, the figure of Strength in Cesare Ripa's early-seventeenth-century *Iconologia* is represented as an armed lady with big bones and a stalwart chest. Similarly, the text accompanying the figure of Charity in Hubert François Gravelot and Charles Nicolas Cochin's *Iconologie* explains that she is a seated woman surrounded by children, one nursing on her breast. She holds in her other hand a flaming heart, and an open purse spilling coins indicates Charity's diverse meanings of helping those in need. In contrast, the new allegories of the nation during the Revolution could be thought of as symbols, naturally evoking a sense of the whole.[59] Thus, the female body of Liberty or *La Patrie* does not exclude but invites even women's identification with the project of nationalism. Women, like men, were constituted as political subjects in the new nation, not only through the practice of republican motherhood but also in and through the complicated processes of visual identification with iconic representations of virtue and nationalism.

I do not want to belabor this point or to revive an outdated distinction in literary theory. Certainly both symbols and allegories have a duality of meaning, and they both encompass a polysemous representation of one thing by another. Unlike Coleridge, I would not condemn allegory for its didacticism and praise symbols for their natural and organic character. To the contrary, a great deal of didacticism was associated with revolutionary symbolism. Many of the allegorical productions of the Revolution, based on aspirations for greater accessibility and immediacy already incorporated in Gravelot and Cochin's *Iconologie*, are known to suffer nevertheless from the same kind of abstruseness and overcoding that provoked trenchant criticisms of allegory by enlightened authors earlier in the century. As for the claim of nature or the natural, that fiction is central to virtually all of the schools of thought that we associate with the birth of modern society—liberalism, republicanism, nationalism, and romanticism. However, there is one restricted sense in which the Romantic contrast between allegory and symbol may prove useful for our effort to distinguish republican visual regimes from their Old Regime counterparts. What marks the new regime is an ability to invite a kind of individual participation in the universal or collective whole.

By serving the principle of universality within the democratic order of legitimation, the female body performs a critical function. First, the representation of the nation as a man would have been incompatible with the republican attack on monarchy, given that the entire system of Old Regime legitimization was tied to the representation of a male body. Equally important, the consistent and not just occasional—as in the brief episode whereby Hercules was adopted as a figure of popular revolution[60]—choice of a man to represent the republican nation might have revealed too much about the new regime's continued partiality. The nation's legitimacy—in contrast to that of its monarchical predecessor—rested on universal participation, not partial membership. What, then, of women, a large segment of the new regime's "excluded Others"? On this point, I agree with Marina Warner, who writes, "A symbolized female presence both gives and takes value and meaning in relation to actual women, and contains the potential for affirmation not only of women themselves but of the general good they might represent and in which as half of humanity they are deeply implicated."[61] I hope to call attention to the processes by which representation both gives and takes in relation to changing social circumstances. In any event, it is startling how in this crucial period of the formation of modern nationalism "the cultural subject found his or her social identity through *identification with a female imago*."[62]

In this context, I address the ways in which metaphors of the body of the new democratic sovereign were anchored in a gendered epistemology of difference. I ask how the visual rhetoric of liberty and equality both enabled the overcoming and obscured the maintenance of social and sexual difference within democratic, republican France—in other words, how representations worked to both give and take back the very possibilities that they appear to express. Likewise, I contrast rationally derived, morally grave neoclassical allegories to the myriad grotesque, ridiculous, and irregular caricatures that also populated revolutionary print culture. By construing these genres as not entirely autonomous but mutually imbricated, we can explore their role in conditioning and transforming the central metaphor of Old Regime political society, the body politic. As Stafford suggests,

> For the age of encyclopedism, the human body represented the ulti-mate visual compendium, the comprehensive method of methods, the organizing structure of structures. As a visible natural whole made up of invisible dissimilar parts, it was the organic paradigm or architec-tonic standard for all complex unions. Whether ideal or caricatured, perfect or monstrous, it formed the model for proper or improper man-made assemblies and artificial compositions. Impersonation gen-erated a wide range of tropes. These intersected with the biology, psy-chology, religion, and philosophy of living, historical agents. The metaphor of the body politic, for example, was embedded in the addi-tive and subtractive scatological methods of political satire. Visual and verbal constructions permitted a host of puns fragmenting an all too corporeal state. They literally incarnated features that were out of joint, ill-assorted, crippled, and otherwise malformed.[63]

Stafford speaks of broad cultural trends in the eighteenth century without accounting for the specific political transformation wrought by revolutionary change. However, in the shift from the undivided sovereignty of the absolutist monarchy to the anonymous popular sovereign of the new Republic, the metaphorical unity of the absolutist body politic was forever shattered. Nonetheless, far from being abandoned with the fall of absolutism, the metaphor of the body politic proved enormously resilient—an imaginative re-source of tremendous power in the legitimization of democratic authority and popular sovereignty.[64] In Chapters 1 and 2, I address the paradox of a female representation of Republic in the context of a heightened suspicion of visual culture, and the association of visuality with the scorned feminized behaviors of Old Regime society. Chapter 1 addresses how images signify, how they make arguments with political effects, and what role they play in the wider context of early modern print culture. I focus on two characteristic genres of revolu-tionary print culture, allegory and caricature. I am interested in these genres' relationship to aesthetic and political discussions within Old Regime and rev-olutionary society, especially those concerning the alleged feminine character of the image and visual culture in general. In Chapter 2, I look at the extent to which gendered imagery figured in the process by which the body politic was redefined and represented with the nation and its populace, not the king, at its center. I point to the irony of the system of visual representation becoming feminine just as the traditional semiotic system tied to the visible body of the father-king was being displaced by a competing symbolic order of words. However, I underscore the heterogeneous mix of text and image, as well as the continuing force of the image in emerging definitions of national identity. I propose that to better understand the role of visual imagery in modern French nationalism, it is necessary to apprehend the special power of an embodied figure to trigger strong emotions, feelings of affection and intimacy. In Chapter 4, I pursue this theme further, arguing that because the nation is figured as a body, the citizen can *imagine* its embrace. By calling on the powers of imagination, the patriot makes individual what is collective, and collective what is individual.

Republic, Liberty, and *La Patrie*—the different names under which a female representation of the French nation paraded—were not the only female representations populating the revolutionary public sphere. Indeed, many anonymous females had the privilege of becoming allegories of a host of eternal values, while real men who achieved publicity served as moral examples for the populace. In addition, representations of female grotesques in republican art made palpable the continuing threat posed by corrupt female nature and disorderly women to the virtuous republican body politic. In Chapter 3, I examine the metaphors of female virtue and vice in the context of democratic representation, on the one hand, and, on the other, against the "coercive aspects of identification" accompanying the promotion of approved forms of femininity and masculinity within the new republican culture.[65] I point to the contradictory possibilities posed by images of the female body, particularly the ever-present tension between a juridically stable body of the nation, which the female goddesses of Republic and their companions promised to secure, and the actions of live women in the public and private spaces of French society. In other words, what is at stake here is not just the embodiment of female virtue but the female embodiment of republican values. Insofar as republican virtues were represented through the body of a woman, such values were potentially risked in actions taken by republican women. No wonder, then, that women's proper roles and their behaviors were topics of great concern to republicans.

I propose that representations of the female body offered a symbolic repertoire that could be claimed by any party of warring men for contrasting motives. A representation of woman might function positively as a symbol of liberty, equality, nature, or truth. But, negatively, she might embody all of the worst features of the enemies of republican freedom for some or of the republican Terror for others. Either way, what counts are the fears incited, especially by the public activities of women. And it is noteworthy that both republican men and their enemies might experience similar gender anxieties. To pursue the argument initially advanced in Chapter 2, then, I argue that the exclusion of women from the practice of revolution and their inclusion in representation reaffirmed the masquerade of equality within the masculine republic. Indeed, the entrapment of women within a picture was central to the successful legitimization of the Republic according to the values of universality, equality, freedom, and reason. The myth of full equality facilitated, as much as it exposed, the denial to women of the full exercise of equal rights within the democratic republic.

In Chapter 4, I confront directly the persistent female iconography of modern nationalism. I take exception to the familiar argument that the sexual coding of Republic or *La Patrie* was occasioned almost entirely by the fall of (male) monarchical authority or by its grammatical gender in Latin-derived languages.[66] What seems like an accidental feature is thereby given a deterministic cast. Nor do I think that *La Patrie* is just a drag queen—or that, as Hunt proposes, "the nation as mother, *La Nation*, had no feminine qualities."[67] In fact, none of these reasons is sufficient to explain how the nation's female body operated to consolidate the heterosexual investments of modern nationalism. By examining the erotic dimension of patriotism, I explore the dynamic consolidation of a new national (hetero)sexual identity. Accordingly, I contend that the repetitive presence of a seductive (metaphorical) female body in the imaginary place of the nation may lure men to attach deep romantic longings to the state.[68] I explore the way in which the vulnerable male citizen was offered the chance to guard the allegorical body of the nation, as well as how the citizen's heterosexual position offered him the opportunity to become a father in and of the fatherland.

For those who would insist that the presence of nonerotic images leads to different conclusions, I would agree that not all female representations of the Republic in revolutionary print culture are eroticized. But my point is to establish how often this is the case, and to argue that to overlook this is to neglect the erotic dimension of modern patriotism. In that respect, my illustrations are chosen carefully to demonstrate the variety of ways (and not just the sheer volume) in which the seductive body of Republic is portrayed. Nor does my argument rest only on the presence of overtly erotic elements. I assume that the presence of a female body in the place of the nation calls on conscious and unconscious responses that have much to do with socially experienced relations of gender and intimacy. As Patrice Higonnet points out in his splendid study of Jacobinism, "The *patrie* was every Jacobin's mother. . . . 'The love of one's *patrie*,' wrote Grégoire on the occasion of the *fête* for

Simoneau, was 'almost innate.'"[69] Similarly, I do not see my argument as contradicting but as complementing the work that has been done on the homosocial dimension of French republicanism and modern nationalism. Nothing I say about the affective charge of the heterosexual formation negates the possibility that male friendship also contributes to the emotional bonds of modern nationalism. But, on the other hand, I claim that, by itself, homosociality cannot explain the way in which the nation's female body calls on a passionate response from its male subjects, one that has much to do with the sentimental attachments associated with heterosexual, romantic love.

These studies are meant to illuminate, but not to foreclose, further debate and discussion on the problem of gender and representation in this period. Whereas I seek to account for images that possessed power in the past, I also approach this task as something of a cultural archaeologist, aiming to archive critical moments in history that might shed light on our present circumstances.[70] Finally, just as I posit that representations are not static objects but ones available to be put to use in different ways, I see my own enterprise as just that—a way of putting to use the representations of the revolutionary period in order to think through once more the relationship of women to the modern public sphere.

Image as Argument in Revolutionary Political Culture

The Image in an Age of Print

IN HIS 1793 *Sketch for a Historical Picture of the Human Mind* the philosopher Antoine-Nicolas de Condorcet contrasts alphabetic writing to two earlier forms of writing, that of pictures and visual signs. In the earliest or hieroglyphic mode, "objects were signified by a more or less exact representation either of the object itself or of an analogous object"; in the second mode, "the only writing known to the Chinese even to this day," a method of writing developed "in which a separate conventional sign was attached to each idea."[1] In the infancy of language, he speculates, "nearly every word is a metaphor and every phrase an allegory. The mind grasps the figurative and the literal sense simultaneously. The word evokes the idea and at the same time the appropriate image by which the idea is expressed." However, over time, and "by a process of abstraction," the secondary and metaphorical sense comes to dominate, and the original, normal meaning is nearly effaced. This loss is further compounded by the manipulation of knowledge and exploitation of the written word by the priestly and teaching castes—those whose "aim was not to dispel ignorance but to dominate men."[2] By investing allegorical language with sacred and hidden meanings, the priestly caste promoted their secret doctrines and absurd creeds.

Picture writing and hieroglyphics are not merely a different form of expression. In Condorcet's philosophy of history, textual knowledge and graphic writing are placed on an unmistakably higher plane than visual understanding.[3] Condorcet rejoices in alphabetic writing's role in "assuring the progress of the human race for ever" and, as in ancient Greece, of giving "all men an equal right to know the truth."[4] He credits words with stripping figures and signs of their mysteries. Only with the invention of alphabetic writing does knowledge (begin to) become certain and truly historical. However, writing's full potential is only achieved in a further communications revolution. With the invention of printing, the dispassionate exercise of critical reason by solitary and silent readers of printed texts supplants the waywardness of representation. But it also facilitates communications among nonproximate readers "all over the world." Neither distance nor the accident of birth and location need hinder the communication networks that printing enables. Those communications are the basis for a "new sort of tribunal," a court of (universal) reason in contrast to the provincial, prejudicial instruments of state or church power. All of this is possible because, in Condorcet's estimation, readers are rational subjects who do not succumb to the passions associated with live assemblies, nor are they seduced into false beliefs by the rhetorical arts of persuasion that accompany the image. In a memorable passage, Condorcet celebrates the power of the print revolution. With printing, he writes, "men found themselves possessed of the means of communicating with people all over the world. *A new sort of tribunal had come into existence in which less lively but deeper impressions were communicated*; which no longer allowed the same tyrannical empire to be exercised over men's passions but ensured a more certain and more durable power over their minds; a situation in which the advantages are all on the side of truth, since what the art of communication loses in the power to seduce, it gains in the power to enlighten."[5]

Thus, Condorcet credits printing with the birth of public opinion and the spread of enlightenment, with multiplying the effects of the word and suppressing the mysteries of the image. Printing even has the potential to erase the hierarchies of class and region: "Without this art," he asks, "how would it be possible to produce in adequate numbers books suited to the different classes of men and to the different degrees of education?" Moreover, he adds, "Has not printing freed the education of the people from all political and religious shackles?"[6] Although he recognizes that the arts also benefited from the invention of printing, Condorcet explicitly links the art of printing characters to human progress, including the advancement of social and political institutions. In the following passage he implies that the old authorities (priests and kings) had much more to fear from uncontrolled words than from uncontrolled images:

To those who have not reflected much upon the progress of the human spirit in the sphere of scientific discovery or of artistic method, it might well seem amazing that such a long period of time should have elapsed between the discovery of the art of printing designs and the discovery of the art of printing characters. Doubtless some engravers had thought of such an application of their art; but the difficulties of its execution had weighed with them more than the benefits of success; and it is indeed fortunate that nobody had suspected the full extent of future success, for priests and kings would surely have united to smother at birth an enemy who was to unmask and dethrone them.[7]

If the valuation weighs in favor of words and not images, it is because Condorcet stresses the higher processes of intellection that accompany writing, on the one hand, and the false seductions and mystifications that beset images and allegorical picture writing, on the other. He suggests that despots have much to fear from the word, but that they keep surprisingly good company with images and rhetorical figures, spoken or painted. For Condorcet and other republicans, the deceptiveness associated with visuality could not be dissociated from its role in papist and absolutist oral and visual culture.[8] But he frames his view in a wider perspective. Just as human progress is associated with the growth of freedom, images and visual thinking come to be replaced by texts and rational argument.[9]

Condorcet's high regard for the print revolution is confirmed in recent scholarship. As Roger Chartier argues, "After Gutenberg, all culture in western societies can be held to be a culture of the printed word, since what moveable type and the printing press produced was not reserved (as in China and Korea) for the administrative use of the ruler but penetrated the entire web of social relations, bore thoughts and brought pleasures and lodged in people's deepest self as well as claiming its place in the public scene."[10] However, far from triumphing against images, as Condorcet believed, Chartier and other students of print culture largely agree that the printing press also augmented the opportunities for the dissemination and consumption of visual signs. As Elizabeth L. Eisenstein stresses, images became more rather than less ubiquitous after the establishment of print shops throughout Western Europe.[11] Print culture was from its inception allied with a series of new activities arising out of the production of pictures as well as writing.

Even a cursory glance will confirm the fact that images—produced by the method of woodcut or copperplate engraving—are to be found liberally distributed across the whole range of early modern printed matter. They might be

independent objects or companions to other printed matter, most notably political broadsides or printed placards designed for reading, handling, and post-
ing. They extended from the merely illustrative to complex visual metaphors
and political prescriptions. Printed objects were as various as great folios and
pocket books, books of hours, marriage charters, and hagiographic pamphlets
devoted to the life of a saint. The French monarchy, too, took advantage of the
possibilities for reaching a wider populace afforded by the many mechanisms
of print from deluxe engravings and popular broadsheets to the stamping of
medals and coins.[12] Although religious images were the most commonly circulated images of the age, over time images began to refer not solely to Scrip-
ture but to a greater variety of writings from the past and the contemporary
world. Nor did the relationship between text and image conform to a simple
division between lettered and unlettered people. As Roger Chartier observes,
"The image was joined with the text in a mobile relationship of implication,
proximity, and hierarchy." Printed images were not simply directed toward the
"ignorant" or illiterate among the populace but offered a mode of address
aimed at various audiences.[13] Printed images, like words, facilitated the fashioning of voluntarily constituted publics in early modern society, much like
the new communities of interest that have erupted on the Internet today. In
light of these developments, it is possible to ask whether such publics might be
counted as enlightened or rational. To what extent was the visual mode of
communication endowed with the same power that Condorcet conferred on
the written word?

The Vagaries and Utility of the Image

On first examination, there seemed to be at best a modest place for the
image in the rational social arts that Condorcet and other enlightened thinkers
promoted. Yet not only were images a vital and recognized component of revolutionary culture, but their place was also the cause of considerable discussion
among republicans. Like Condorcet, republicans generally distrusted the seductive qualities of the image, which they linked to the spectacular, ceremo-
nial culture of the Old Regime. In addition, they feared that the people were
easily swayed by images and given to vulgar sensations. In the extreme, although their aims were never wholly achieved, the most committed iconoclasts
and atheists of the period protested against representation itself, concerned
that any compromise with the idolatrous practices of the Old Regime would
undermine the Republic's foundation.[14] For example, throughout Year II Jean-
Baptiste Salaville, editor of *Annales patriotiques et littéraires*, denounced the

temptation to allegorize and objected to the personification of republican values on the model of Christian practice. By spectacles and ceremonies, he
wrote, the priests had seized hold of men's sensations in order to direct and
dominate their ideas. As a temporary measure, he did grant the practicality of
substituting "a sort of ephemeral cult of moral beings for the cult of the im-
maculate virgin, of the [male and female] patron saints, of the male and female
saints of the old calendar." In the long run, however, in order "to lead the people to the pure worship of Reason" and to avert the establishment of a kind of
polytheism, Salaville insisted, "the metaphysical principles of [John] Locke
and [the Abbé de] Condillac will have to become popular; the people will have
to free themselves of the old allegories, and become accustomed to seeing in a
statue only stone, and in an image only canvas and colors."[15]

Salaville's radical iconoclastic position was the exception, not the rule,
although his iconoclastic attack on the Cult of Reason was echoed by partisans
of the Cult of the Supreme Being. On the larger question of the place of the
image in revolutionary culture, however, it is now accepted that most republicans sought not to repress but to put the visual lexicon to work for good purposes.[16] The effort to achieve an entirely antispectacular form of revolutionary
festival, true to Jean-Jacques Rousseau's aspirations, was undercut by the continued use of theatrical devices, conscious staging, and even the use of live actors and actresses.[17] In devising a new calendar to replace the traditional
Christian one, the Jacobin Fabre d'Eglantine explicitly defended the need for
images: "We don't conceive anything except by images: in the most abstract
analysis, in the most metaphysical combination, our understanding only becomes aware because of images, our memory is supported by and rests on images."[18] Perhaps most famously, the Abbé Grégoire defended the need for
images for the seal of the Republic in his *Rapport sur les sceaux de la République*
of 1796:

> The ridiculous hieroglyphs of the blazon are no longer for us anything
> more than historical objects. When rebuilding a government anew,
> everything must be republicanized. The legislator who failed to recog-
> nize the importance of the language of signs would be remiss; he
> should not omit any opportunity to impress the senses, to awaken re-
> publican ideas. This way the soul is penetrated by ever reproduced ob-
> jects; and this composition, this set of principles, facts and emblems
> that ceaselessly retraces before the eyes of the citizen his rights and du-
> ties, shapes the republican mold that gives him his national character
> and the bearing of a free man.[19]

According to Grégoire, the image could serve the faculties of understanding. By impressing the senses, the visual sign could "awaken republican ideas." The image was more than a needed supplement for the imperfections of the written word. It was a rational vehicle for representing and understanding events, persons, and ideas. Grégoire was also quick to distinguish between past and present, improper and proper uses of the image. The revolutionary approach to allegorical language shared nothing with its despotic and "ridiculous" uses in former times. What had once been a mysterious icon had become pedagogical instruments—that is, nothing "more than historical objects" for regenerating the subjects of the new Republic. Grégoire's appreciation of the visual dimension of human cognition and morality went further. As he stated on another occasion, "In general, very few men act on principles; almost all of them imitate: the character of most of them is more the product of the examples that have passed in front of their eyes than it is of the maxims which we have attempted to inculcate in them."[20]

Such attention to the faculty of sight, along with the defense of the visual component of reason, suggests a positive answer to the question posed earlier about the role of images in constituting enlightened publics. Those who most enthusiastically upheld the use of symbols even gestured toward a fusion of sign and meaning that approximated something like the utopia that Condorcet had located in the infancy of language when "the mind [had grasped] the figurative and the literal sense simultaneously." This was especially evident in the de-Christianization campaign culminating in the Cult of Reason in the fall of 1793, Year II. At the festival at Notre-Dame on 10 November 1793 (20 Brumaire Year II) where the Commune and the Department of Paris assembled, a beautiful young woman (*"image fidèle de la beauté"*) clad in white, wearing a blue cloak on her shoulders and a red bonnet, and carrying a long pike in her right hand emerged from a small Greek-style temple bearing the word philosophy and set atop a symbolic mountain in the choir loft of the cathedral. Participants sang a Marie Joseph Chenier hymn to liberty, which concluded with the lines "You, holy Liberty, come to live in this temple, Be the goddess of the French!"[21] The Goddess was then carried in procession to the National Convention, whereupon her identity somehow changed from Liberty to Reason. There, the leader of the cortège Anaxagoras Chaumette announced, "Legislators! Fanaticism has ceded its place to reason. Today an immense people have been carried under these Gothic arches, which for the first time have served as an echo to the truth. There the French celebrated the only true cult, the one of liberty, the one of reason . . . there we have abandoned the inanimate idols for this animated image, a masterpiece of nature."[22] Jacques-

Antoine Brouillet, the official orator at a provincial festival of reason, 30 Frimaire Year II in the region of the Marne, was equally emphatic in addressing the beautiful young woman impersonating Reason: "Goddess of Reason! Man will always be man, in spite of his proud sophistication and stubborn, self-conceited egotism. He will always need some perceptible images [signs] to raise him to the level of imperceptible objects. You offer us such a natural representation of Reason, of which you are the emblem, that we would be tempted to confound the copy with the original. You unite in yourself the physical and moral means to make Reason lovable."[23]

But the female enactments of central republican values drew strong criticism as well as praise.[24] Salaville, the critic of personification, published a letter by a reader of the *Annales patriotiques et littéraires* from Limoges named Picard, who was astonished to learn that Reason was a woman and asked whether the figure ought to have been Liberty and not Reason: "For the senses and the philosophical imagination are both equally shocked at the idea of a woman—especially a youthful woman—representing Reason. In women, this pure faculty is identified so to speak with *weakness*, with *prejudices*, with the very *attractions* of this enchanting sex. In men, its empire is free of any error: *force*, *energy*, and *severity* are linked together in them. But above all, reason is *mature*, it is *solemn*, it is *austere*, qualities that would ill suit a young woman. I thus believe it necessary to apply the idea of *youth* to *Liberty*, whose empire is just beginning."[25] In sum, Salaville proposes that a beautiful young woman might enact French Liberty, which was still in its youth; but only a mature man could properly embody austere Reason. Worse yet, the woman who portrayed the Goddess at Notre-Dame was reported to be a popular actress from the opera.

Visual Thinking and Sexed Bodies

In these discussions, the debate over the proper role of images in revolutionary culture and pedagogy was joined to another controversy over the use of gendered symbolism for the representation of the central values of the Republic. Neither the plea for a masculine embodiment of Reason nor the desire to banish the image altogether proved to be a satisfactory solution for republican anxieties about either gender or visual culture. In fact, female imagery in republican culture was not the exception but the rule in revolutionary and postrevolutionary French republicanism. Even Salaville conceded the utility of images as well as (selective) female representations as a sort of way station on the road to a more mature and enlightened society. On the other side, admiration for the efficacy of imagery (whether "animated" or inanimate) was tempered by the fear that images might produce irrational rather than rational publics, and by the suspicion that visual culture was allied with the feminine and the vagaries of female nature.

In this context, it is useful to recall how, in his defense of print, Condorcet contrasts two sorts of impressions: those that are lively and those that are "less lively but deeper." Whereas he associates the former with the seductive impressions produced by images, the latter are tied to the power of enlightened reason to reveal truth and act as a sort of tribunal. In the writings of eighteenth-century sensationalist philosophy, such distinctions were related to arguments about the different psychological and intellectual capacities of the sexes. In his 1746 *Essay on the Origin of Human Knowledge*, the Abbé de Condillac discriminates between primitive imagination—deemed closer to instinct, a nonverbal mental operation shared by animals and humans—and combinatory imagination—involving, in its highest form, the use of language.[26] Primitive or instinctual imagination preserves the perception of some bodily sensation. Perception (or its stored reflection) results from the chance action of an external object on the body's senses. On the other hand, with memory it is possible for the mind to operate apart from sensations or perceptions, by retaining and retrieving the *signs* for perceptions. Such a process presumes the existence of society, and this in turn leads to the combinatory imagination that is the basis for forming complex ideas and artistic innovation. Notably, these two sorts of imagination are associated with the different capacities and qualities of the sexes. Despite a chapter on the embellishments the imagination gives to truth, where Condillac appears to consider combinatory imagination as feminine, in general he divides the imagination into gendered components by the function of the sign. As Mary Sheriff explains, "Condillac conceives the sign's function as dividing a newly socialized imagination (now a power only of the mind) from sensory stimulation (or the body). Resulting from this division are differently gendered powers of imagination: a feminine one that remains dependent on the body and receives impressions easily and a masculine one (higher imagination) that lines up with the sign. Closest to instinct, feminine imagination in and of itself can produce no new ideas; it can only reproduce sensations. Based on memory, combinatory imagination is the agent responsible for cultural production."[27]

Condillac outlined the dangers that could result from women's exercise of the higher powers of imagination. Whereas voluntary connections involving the use of language produce ordered knowledge, involuntary connections resulting from external impressions might arise without the subject's awareness.

Drawing on these notions, the period's medical practitioners commonly argued that "the susceptibility of woman's organs (to impressions) and the rapidity of her sensations pushed her towards a disorderly, inappropriate, and often involuntary combination of ideas."[28] In his influential *Système physique et morale de la femme* of 1775, Pierre Roussel argued that woman's active sense organs caused her to live more on the level of sensations than ideas or reasoned reflection. Likewise, in his 1805 work, *Rapports du physique et du moral de l'homme*, Pierre Cabanis disputed women's ability to acquire real knowledge. Notwithstanding their lively conception of things, they are incapable of "the lively and profound pleasures of a deep meditation."[29] In addition, women's limited mental abilities were thought to carry definite risks. According to eighteenth-century sensationalist psychology, woman's greater sensitivity—indeed, her entire organic makeup—produced in her a susceptibility to madness and other nervous diseases, as well as disorderly and inappropriate thought.

Eighteenth-century sensationalist psychology helps to explain Salaville's protest about the different consequences of reason in the sexes. In women, he identifies reason with weakness and prejudice, whereas among men, he celebrates "its empire. . . free of all error." He questions the need to build a temple to Reason, asking "Is not each man a temple to Reason?"[30] But Salaville is aware that men do not always live up to these lofty ideals. To the extent that the people succumb to superstitions, abstractions, and personifications—which he terms "the principal cause of human error"—they are behaving in a feminine manner. He worried about not only the erroneous embodiment of austere Reason in a female, but also the wrongful act of looking instead of thinking or reasoning, which in eighteenth-century sensational thought is characteristic of the instinctual, visual, and feminine attitude toward the object.

However, the contrasting response by the provincial orator Jacques-Antoine Brouillet to a woman playing the role of Liberty or Reason in a festival in the late fall of 1793 is equally revealing. Brouillet suggests that Reason, like the other abstract values of the new Republic, would be by itself much too austere to be embraced. For him, the female performance operates on both a physical and moral plane. The actress succeeds in making lovable what would otherwise be intangible and ineffable. The same point applies to inanimate images. As I argue in the next three chapters, by physically depicting incorporeal values, female imagery helped to consolidate French citizens' loyalties to their nation and to discriminate against those considered outside the body of the Republic. Fabre d'Eglantine was right to notice the way in which memory and understanding were abetted by both imagery and the sensory response that it evokes. For now, it is sufficient to note why a consistent materialist like Salaville would regard such an appeal as nothing but a subterfuge and a retreat to the practices of a discredited church. Yet how distant were Mary and a host of female saints from the elevated bodies of the Cult of Reason? In fact, Mona Ozouf reports that not only did different deities often symbolize Reason in the many festivals throughout France in her honor, but local beauty queens were chosen to play Reason and other republican deities, and Christian imagery was put to republican purposes. According to Ozouf, "The people's club of Rodez suggested keeping the colossal Virgin that crowned the bell tower (the four evangelists surrounding her could, no doubt, be turned into [Michel] Pelletier, [Jean-Paul] Marat, Chénier and. . . [Pierre] Bayle!). . . . So we should not see all these female figures as emblems of a de-Christianizing policy."[31]

Robespierre drew a different conclusion, substituting for the extreme an-tireligious impulses of the Cult of Reason a deistic and patriotic Cult of the Supreme Being. The latter was a decidedly more masculine, even virile, affair than was its predecessor. The Cult of Reason was discredited for both its athe-ism and its idolatry, and as various commentators have noted, it was tainted by the role women played in these ceremonies. According to Marie-Hélène Huet, the incarnation of Reason by women was held by the partisans of the Supreme Being to be "unstable, impure, polymorphic. It is primarily, as on the stage, a role, and a feminine one at that." Ozouf agrees, stating that it is "quite likely that the unbearable oddness of the Festival of Reason [to its critics] was partly due to the role played in it by women: by introducing an element of illusion, not to say of subversion, their presence in the festivals seemed to harbor a dan-ger." Furthermore, as Hunt remarks, "The Cult of the Supreme Being erased not only the idolatry implicit in worshipping an actual image of reason but also the association of that imagery with feminine qualities. [Jacques-Louis] David's program for the festival took up again his earlier separation of the sexes in *The Oath of the Horatii* and *Brutus*; when they arrived at the site of the cer-emony, the column of men stood on one side of the mountain, the column of women on the other."[32]

The double repudiation of idols and the feminine in the effort to create a sublime religion by backers of the Cult of the Supreme Being, according to Huet, had strong parallels in iconoclastic traditions. She draws on Jean-Joseph Goux's insight that, in Sigmund Freud's understanding of the passage from matriarchy to patriarchy, the prohibition against making an image of God implies that "sensory perception takes a back seat to the abstract idea. It con-secrates the triumph of the spirit over the senses, or more specifically a renun-ciation of instincts." Yet, according to Goux, Freud fails to state explicitly "the particularly illuminating relationship *between the Judaic prohibition against image adoration and the incest taboo with the mother.* By carving images of Gods, one is making a material image of the mother, and adoring the maternal figure through the senses. By tearing oneself away from the seduction of the senses and elevating one's thoughts towards an unrepresentable god, one turns away from desire for the mother, ascends to the sublime father and respects the law."[33] In a similar fashion, Huet finds inextricable links between the image and the maternal in the specific efforts undertaken by revolutionaries to erase the sensuous representations of Reason and Liberty in the Cult of the Supreme Being.

But this applies not only to the maternal; for the discussions surrounding the image and its representations reveal the extent to which—following the principles of sensationalist psychology—a deep connection is posited between the feminine and the senses and between women and the lower, more immediate, more instinctive forms of cognition. Certainly, David did try to contain the multiple effects of femininity by designing a festival in which women would be represented only as mothers and spouses and the family would be reaffirmed.[34] Even as the erotic was coupled to the maternal, however, it threatened to escape its familial container. Moreover, the problem of the feminine representation of national values transcended the specific turn of events between the Cult of Reason and that of the Supreme Being. Alongside live actresses and respectable *citoyennes* who performed the role of festival deity, the public spaces of the new Republic were populated with countless female allegories, suggesting that in the process of national formation, sensory perception did not routinely take a back seat to the abstract idea.

Revolutionary Print Culture

Bought, sold, posted, carried on placards, or imprinted on official documents and ephemera, revolutionary images were part of a larger world of objects, or a material culture. As Chandra Mukerji argues, once produced, objects become parts of the material world in which people function, and to that extent they can be "both a physical and symbolic constraint" on human action.[35] Moreover, representations are not static. They are available to be put to use and interpreted in different ways by groups and individuals. They can elicit a range of cognitive responses from the sensory to the analytical, from reassurance to disquietude. As we have seen, even though most republicans were ready to "make use of the sensualist medium of spectacles, images, and ceremonies," they saw that such initiatives ran the risk "of misleading the people's faculty of reason, perceived as vulnerable to overloads of meaning and errors of signification." Accordingly, Antoine de Baecque observes, republicans worried about the

> wanderings of the imagination that could divert correct interpretation toward either demagogy or error. That is why Grégoire spoke of shaping a "republican mold," and why Jacques-Louis David, in his monumental project for an allegory of the French people, insisted on inscribing word values on the body of the People. Whenever they invoked allegorical representation, the revolutionaries introduced educational discourse, the correct orientation of the gaze, the measured and reasonable limits of interpretation, as if they absolutely needed to channel the excess power of metaphorical signs. Republicans were obsessed with the over-readability of representation, with the ideal of a univocal allegorical image. They sought to classify, educate, and regiment the body and gestures of the allegorical incarnation of the Republican in order to check their fear of the power of the image.[36]

Thus, republicans sought to impose order and discipline on images, even as they feared that those for whom these images were intended would read them in "anti-disciplinary" ways. Ozouf's classic study of the revolutionary festival highlights these antithetical tendencies of public ceremonies during the Revolution: spontaneous and eruptive, on the one hand, and didactic and moralizing, on the other. She points out how festival organizers doubted people's ability to interpret images correctly.[37] Theoretically, images can consolidate and disrupt power. Whether and how such possibilities are realized is partly a result of the circumstances under which a given image or series of images is appropriated, partly a result of the audience's response, and partly a consequence of the nature of the image itself. Some images, as we will see, are more transgressive and others more integrative, but in principle any image can be read in a counterdisciplinary way.

Additionally, the images that circulated during the Revolution were commodities produced for sale under volatile circumstances: the lifting of censorship, a constantly changing political landscape in which legal and extralegal forms of harassment were exerted against political opponents, the pressure to produce timely images linked to contemporary events, lively commercial competition, and fluctuating public preferences.[38] Political identifications facilitated the sale and distribution of these objects. In addition to offering advice or political news, however, prints offered their viewers and purchasers occasions for entertainment.

The anonymous character of so many of the surviving prints speaks to the political pragmatism, risks, and the sometimes hasty means of execution undertaken by their makers, who were offering these works for commercial sale in an increasingly charged political environment.[39] The crumbling of Old Regime censorship did not mean that artists were entirely free from official or peer pressure. From the outset, both the government and the populace engaged in efforts to patrol the contents of printed materials by those who published or hawked them. Throughout the period, crowds attacked their opponent's presses. Governmental measures were taken against works judged to be indecent or immoral in character. For instance, in January 1794, on the anniversary of the king's execution, searches of publishers and merchants were conducted for materials that were deemed immoral and offensive to "the foundation of the Republic."[40]

As posted broadsides or illustrations in the revolutionary press, publicly displayed prints might be seen by a large number of people who did not or could not immediately possess them. These opportunities were made more likely by the fact that prints were produced in large quantities, in contrast to the singular painting of an academically trained artist—although public viewing in fairs or art salons and the production of engraved copies of original works meant that even before the Revolution singular objects such as paintings were visually available to a wider audience than would be constituted by a small circle of privileged owners and their company.[41] As Denis Bruckmann explains, "Prints, like texts, are printed. Prints, like texts, have editions, impressions and states, which are often organized in complex relationships. Like texts which may be offprints, journal publications, etc., each print often circulates in multiple bibliographic units—a frontispiece reproduced from one work to another, an illustration re-used in several periodicals, etc. Lastly, like texts, each print, with a very few exceptions, is produced in large numbers and circulated. From the 17th century on, it has not been unusual for a print— especially when it is an illustration in a book—to have several thousand copies."[42]

In addition, Claudette Hould reports that a print that was produced for a government commission during the Revolution would result in a minimum of 1,000–1,200 published proofs. Nearly 1,000 copies were sent to the National Assembly deputies alone, and the same number offered to subscribers to the Friends of the Arts Society. A copper plate of the revolutionary period could normally produce from 2,000 to 2,500 good proofs, although plates might be retouched to produce larger quantities. Consequently, the small prints of a popular newspaper such as Louis Prudhomme's *Révolutions de Paris* are barely

legible in certain editions. Wood-block engravings, though generally less frequently used than copper plate engraving, nevertheless allowed for the production of a practically unlimited number of copies and can be found among the
cheap popular images that also constituted part of the revolutionary output.[43]

Commercial viability for an engraver depended first and foremost on multiple sales and broad circulation. As the architect Athanase Détournelle, publisher of *Journal de la société républicaine des arts* from January through June
1794, remarked, "Engraving is a money-making art."[44] Noting such profitabil-
ity, merchants might even buy back copper plates from artists in order to produce "commercial" editions of the same print or an improved version of the
original image.[45] As for subject matter, the satirical, overtly sexual, or manifest
political contents of many revolutionary prints suggests that such ingredients
were intended to elicit humor, argument, and pleasure from their audiences—
a likely lubricant for expanded sales. Alternatively, the sobriety of allegorical
images and the dissemination of newly invented symbols of revolutionary culture—including the tricolor cockade, the Phrygian or liberty cap, also a red
bonnet, the fasces, the pike, the level, or the mountain—aimed to elicit patriotic identifications from emerging national publics. For the artist or merchant,
the proliferation of revolutionary symbols likely amounted to a safe and prof-
itable commercial investment. As was true of their British and continental
counterparts, then, French printmakers delighted in the propagandistic opportunities of their craft.[46] As Hould notices, "Engravers and politicians saw
the possibility of multiplying images, propagating facts and passing on a political message as the most immediate advantage, and clearly stated so in their
advertisements. For example, in February 1794 Petit-Coupray, painter of the
famous work representing Marat at the podium of the National Convention,
informed his customers of his intention 'to start a subscription to propagate
the image of this Martyr of Liberty through engraving.'"[47]

Certainly, the makers, publishers, and distributors of revolutionary images
may have sought to regulate spontaneous behaviors or to instruct the populace
in the forms of self-discipline required of citizens in the new Republic. To observe the stabilizing intentions of the image, however, in no way vitiates the
larger point that the reception of any cultural product is subject always to fric-
tion, resistance, and possible remaking. Symbolic and material contestation or
mediation is itself part of the wider cultural field that, as Pierre Bourdieu recognizes, is insinuated in turn within a broad field of power.[48] In the radical
struggle over power and symbolic meanings in revolutionary France, art was
invested with highly charged, politically contested (and contestable) meanings. By looking at two leading genres in revolutionary art, allegory and

caricature, we can see how image-makers deployed the female body as they aimed to create new affective solidarities and political publics, to express popular energies, or to anticipate and forestall possible dissent. I make no claim that women were the only topic of revolutionary iconography. For example, prints ridiculing the French clergy constitute perhaps the largest category of all revolutionary caricatures. Yet my interest in gendered imagery in the revolutionary tradition leads to a focus on the way in which women's bodies provided a vehicle for the expression of moral and political values in allegorical as well as caricatural images.

Allegory

During the Revolution, a great number of allegorical works were produced by the many anonymous artists who executed inexpensive, hand-colored engravings, as well as by the highly skilled neoclassical draftsmen who worked as designers, printmakers, and publishers of deluxe print editions or officially authorized allegorical and emblematic images. The use of allegories and emblems was a widely practiced form of visual and political persuasion in Europe, at least since the Renaissance. On the other hand, the allegorical tradition had suffered attacks by reformist thinkers during the decades leading up to the Revolution. Enlightened thinkers such as Denis Diderot decried its abstraction and frigidity; empiricists and materialists worried about its obscurity and obscurantism.[49] As early as 1739, in his *Histoire du ciel*, the Abbé Pluche pleaded for clarity against the mystifying practice of allegorical figuration: "Since a picture is only supposed to show me what I am not being told, it is ridiculous to have to struggle to understand it. . . . And, in any case, when I succeed in guessing the intention of these mysterious personnages, I find that the message is hardly worth the price of the envelope."[50] Paradoxically, then, revolutionary artists resorted to preexisting models of classicism in their attempt to fashion a new, more natural style and to discover a natural language unsullied by the disguises and cultural accretions of prerevolutionary French society and baroque art. The product of their efforts is termed neoclassicism, a nomenclature that aptly captures the incongruous adherence to more ancient authorities in the revolutionary arts. Similarly, revolutionary artists borrowed from an established rhetorical tradition, allied with poetry, in which personified images served as an artistic means "to give force and expression" to the subject. As the English architect George Richardson wrote in 1779 in an introduction to his English-language edition of Cesare Ripa's *Iconologia* of 1593, "Iconology . . . is derived from two Greek words which signify speaking pictures, or discourse of images."[51]

Like their predecessors, then, revolutionary artists continued to be drawn to the universalizing vocabulary of iconography because of its seeming capacity to override differences and unite tempers. Hubert François Gravelot and Charles Nicolas Cochin's 1791 edition of the *Iconologie par figures*, which guided their efforts, called for allegory to serve a "universal language of all the nations" by being "clear, expressive, eloquent." Thus, the authors were critical of Ripa's inability to penetrate the truths of allegory. They warned against obscurantism or an undiscerning reliance on the ancients, on the one hand, and, on the other, the resort to neologisms, which they referred to as the abuse of new emblems.[52] In other words, allegory's advantage, which derived from its indirection and ability to encode values in an abstract language, was also acknowledged to be its flaw. That is, the overly coded image could be illegible for the broader public it aimed to reach. Rather than expressing, it might deny the contending forces it claimed to express. Iconology, as James Olson asserts in his study of eighteenth-century American traditions, was always a contradictory project: "At the heart of rhetorical iconology are the ambiguities of appeals for agreement among people whose interest, concerns, values, feelings, and expectations may be in conflict."[53]

Two prints exemplify the impact of the elite emblematic tradition on the revolutionary graphic arts, and the latter's strong affinity for female goddesses in antique costume. Deriving from an older iconological tradition, such goddesses spoke in pictorial terms of the revolutionary embrace of a host of civic virtues and republican values: liberty, fraternity, equality, unity, reason, friendship, wisdom, force, nature, truthfulness, humanity, conjugal love, and devotion to the fatherland. These prints illustrate the simultaneous obscurantism and political effectiveness of allegorical representation and the ability of established graphic artists to meld humanistic traditions to a popular republican project. For example, in this 1792 etching and mezzotint, after a design by the noted sculptor Jean Guillaume Moitte (1746–1810), the celebrated engraver of luxurious multiple-plate color prints Jean-François Janinet (1752–1814) represented *Liberty* (Figure 1.1) as one of the period's three principal civic virtues.[54] Liberty wears a Roman laurel wreath in her hair, the sign of civic virtue. Seated on a throne and raising a Phrygian cap in one hand, Liberty holds in her other hand a club and steps on the carcass of the Hydra of despotism. The symbol of the Hydra appeared frequently in revolutionary prints, especially in images of the taking of the Bastille in which the third estate is depicted as triumphing over such a many-headed beast. Thus, by holding the club, which together with her own foot holds down the crushed, defeated Hydra, the body of this otherwise staid Liberty emanates a great deal of force. Her torso, though at

Figure 1.1. Jean-François Janinet, after Jean Guillaume Moitte, *Liberty*. 1792. Courtesy of the Bibliothèque nationale de France.

rest, has a physical energy, represented by the posture of her legs and the fold of her garment. In other words, this representation of Liberty joins classical motifs such as the Roman laurel and central symbols of the popular revolution, such as Hercules' club and the Hydra, to the well-established attributes of Liberty that long predated the Revolution. For instance, Ripa's *Iconology* contains this description of Liberty: "Liberty denotes a state of freedom, as opposed to slavery. It is allegorically expressed by the figure of a woman dressed in white robes, with a cap on her head. She holds a sceptre in the right hand and with the left she is breaking a yoke, as a mark of releasement [*sic*]. . . . The cap of Liberty on her head, is in allusion to the custom of the Romans, in setting their slaves free."[55]

Furthermore, the added device of a verbal motto attempts to anchor the sliding signification to which all female allegories were susceptible. Like the bonnet Liberty holds in her right hand, a verbal prop could be of particular utility in making legible the symbols of revolution before an expanding public. After all, for those without a classical humanistic education, was Liberty all that different in appearance from the female goddesses depicting Peace, Equality, Fraternity, Wisdom, or Truth, to name just some of her compatriots? Equally important, the woman with the Phrygian cap, as Maurice Agulhon has established, is a double allegory: "She represented both Liberty, an eternal value, and at the same time the newly constituted régime of the French Republic."[56]

The more remote the values under expression, the more likely that the artist would have had to resort to an emphatic instructional frame. Thus, the etching *Republican Calendar* (Figure 1.2), by another well-established artist, Philibert-Louis Debucourt (1755–1832), depicts a seated figure who is identified in the inscription as Philosophy, although like Liberty she wears a Phrygian cap.[57] Her marble throne is decorated with the many-breasted Diana of the Ephesians, symbol of fertility, and her feet rest on the "Gothic monuments of error and superstition"—crumpled remnants of the Gregorian calendar and a papal insignia—who are charged with an "ignorant and ridiculous division of time." From the "great book of nature," Philosophy dictates the principles of the new calendar to her attentive genius. At her side are the book of morals and the triangle of equality, the inscription of which proclaims the unity and indivisibility of the French Republic. In sum, the new calendar is intended to be at once the product of nature and reason and an espousal of republican civic virtues.[58] This print is evocative of the hopes heralding the coming of a new age in which all members of society, irrespective of their status, would come to share in the benefits of reason. Visually, however, this is a remarkably dense image, full of references to humanistic learning rather than popular traditions.

Only the figure of the genius, a winged infant, offers a more colloquial reading: Instead of a scribe, the genius might be taken as child of Republic. Yet such a parental relationship is at the same time disrupted by the Goddess's side pose—her attention focused on the book rather than the infant.

Both of these prints are examples of the application of emblematic culture by highly trained artists who continued to produce works aimed at *amateurs* or for direct service to the state; although, of the two images, *Liberty* is the more direct, more expressive of revolutionary energies. Allegorical imagery was also commonly used in the hastily produced colored broadsheets intended for sale to members of a wider populace. From the Revolution's outset, allegorical imagery served as a vocabulary for depicting the traditional and reformulated relations among the three estates of the new nation. *Liberty Triumphant,*

Figure 1.2. Philibert-Louis Debucourt, *Republican Calendar.* 1794. Courtesy of the Bibliothèque nationale de France.

Destroying Abusive Powers (Figure 1.3), a 1790 etching from Camille Desmoulins's newspaper *Révolutions de France et de Brabant*, demonstrates the way in which allegory could be exploited for more popular aims. Because the print was initially limited to journal subscribers who had the issues bound with their collections, its circulation was not as wide as that of the broadsheets. Nevertheless, this particular illustration of Liberty partakes more of popular styles than do the two former examples of highly sophisticated, coded illustrations by academically trained artists.[59]

A half-naked Liberty with long, flowing hair rises above the detritus of the Old Regime, lifted gracefully on a pillow of clouds. In her right hand she holds a pike topped by a Liberty cap. With her left hand she throws a lightening bolt at the symbols of despotism, monarchy, clerical rule, and aristocracy. On a pedestal, topped by a raised flag of liberty, a sign proclaims the abolition of seigniorial rights. To her rear is the period's most recognizable (and most frequently depicted) documentary image—a partially dismantled representation of the Bastille prison. Similar to the crushed Hydra in *Liberty*, the Bastille is meant to symbolize the people's triumph over despotic rule.[60]

A sunburst surrounds this more naively drawn Liberty, who possesses none of the hard lines or classical proportions of Debucourt's or Janinet's allegories. Like the halo encircling holy figures in Christian iconography, the sun's rays here associate her with (the upward movement of) universal enlightenment. Her pose is frontal, active, and aroused; energetic rather than composed. She reveals both breasts—in fact, she is naked to the waist. Her softly rounded breasts and fleshy body add to the figure's allure. Likewise, her posture—which could seem awkward or ethereal—is nevertheless beckoning. The clouds lift her not only upward but also forward—toward the spectator.

In contrast to the force that is merely suggested in *Liberty*'s body—and signaled there by the powerful connotations of her external accouterments—*Liberty Triumphant*'s body is animated from within. Even her robe swirls above her to mark her bodily movement. She exemplifies the widespread appeal of the female allegory from the outset of the Revolution. She indicates how allegory could be deployed in exhortative as well as static postures, depicted in a naive as well as a formal neoclassical style. But all of these images are affirmative. The female representations are vehicles for political values, not illustrations of specific women or types of women. Despite their differences, these images all register the optimistic hope that the constitution of the new regime would result in a unified will among the populace, without the divisions that marked the former society.

LALIBERTÉ TRIOMPHE ET DÉTRUIT LES ABUS

Figure 1.3. *Liberty Triumphant, Destroying Abusive Powers.* From *Révolutions de France et de Brabant,* vol. 6, no. 51, 1790. Courtesy of the Musée Carnavalet. Copyright Photothèque des Musées de la ville de Paris.

Caricature

Caricature, on the other hand, by its nature admits of division. It allows the artist to comment on current events and political perspectives. Like allegory, the genre of caricature predated the Revolution. Important precedents for eighteenth-century political graphics can be found in the caricatural art of Italy and the rich tradition of prints produced in Northern Europe (Germany, the Netherlands, and Britain) during the early modern period. Italian *caricatura* (a charged likeness) was at the outset an art of the aristocracy, for the aristocracy. It presumed an intimate knowledge of the physiognomy and personality of an individual whose features were then comically deformed by the artist. On the other hand, the first political prints produced during the height of the Protestant Reformation constituted a broader form of caricature, aimed at satirizing power and its institutions as well as the occupants of powerful offices.[61]

Caricaturists delighted in the transgressive possibilities of humor, often drawing on the traditions of popular revelry in early modern Europe, in which the commoners had opportunities to parody their everyday existence. The strategy of inverting categories of high and low or proper and improper was ideally suited to literary, visual, and festive commentary on the appropriate positions for men and women in both family and society. In caricature, the female body also carried particular resonance. Fears about women's unruliness were registered in characterizations of the female body—particularly the lower parts that were associated with childbirth and bleeding—which was held to be disorderly by nature. Similarly, the playful notion of "the world turned upside down" echoed popular anxieties about women, even as it offered a way of spoofing the regulative patterns of behavior. As Natalie Zemon Davis has urged, whether by dressing or masking oneself as a member of the opposite sex, or by simply playing a role characteristic of one's opposite, sexual inversion or the possibility of switching sex roles was "a multivalent image that could operate, first, to widen behavioral options for women within and even outside marriage, and, second, to sanction riot and political disobedience for both men and women in a society that allowed the lower orders few formal means of protest. Play with the unruly woman is partly a chance for temporary release from the traditional and stable hierarchy; but it is also part of the conflict over efforts to change the distribution of power within society. The woman-on-top might even facilitate innovation in historical theory and political behavior.".[62]

The anonymous print *Well, Well, J . . . F . . , Do You Still Say Long Live Nobility?* (Figure 1.4), a commentary on the women's march to Versailles in October 1789, links the symbolism of gender inversion directly to the dramatic

eh bien, J...F..., dira-tu encore vive la Noblesse?

Figure 1.4. *Well, Well, J . . . F . .., Do You Still Say Long Live Nobility?*
Frontispiece of *Act of Contrition of Monsieurs the Body Guards of His
Majesty Louis XVI or the Cards Face Down.* London, 1789. Courtesy Rare
and Manuscript Division, Cornell University Library.

political and social changes starting to unfold in France.[63] A woman of the
third estate is depicted riding astride the back of a member of the king's
bodyguard who is forced on all fours in the posture of a mule. Pinching his
ear—painfully registering the force of the third estate on his body—the
woman taunts this soldier to answer whether or not he still sings the praises of
the nobility. The massive female presence of the marchers is condensed brilliantly into the single body of one woman who is "on top" both literally and

figuratively. Apart from the reversal of (class and gender) roles, the woman herself is sympathetically drawn. In contrast, as I discuss in Chapter 2, numerous depictions of the October Days present the female marchers in a more menacing light. The (in/famous) market women are shown with grotesque gestures and faces, carrying decapitated heads on pikes, armed and riding astride cannons, the barrels of which protrude forward from between their legs or from the rear under their buttocks; they are even depicted as prostitutes parading as respectable *citoyennes*.

Not only did the female revolutionaries risk losing their femininity, but men were accused of impersonating women. Such a charge was made by the monarchical right against Armand Désiré de Vignerot du Plessis-Richelieu, duc d'Aiguillon, noble representative to the Estates-General and future émigré, one of the most ardent early supporters of the Revolution among the nobility, who renounced his noble privileges on the night of 4 August 1789. As in the anti-Orleanist pamphlets deriding the nobility's revolutionary enthusiasms, this satirical portrait, [*Portrait of a Fishwife*]/*The Monstrosity in the Flesh* (*Le Gros ad vivum*) (Figure 1.5), mockingly accuses d'Aiguillon of having participated in the events of 5–6 October 1789 disguised as a woman, a *poissarde*—with all the ambivalent associations attached to such women's public, revolutionary actions.[64] Thus, in the hands of skillful caricaturists, the trope of gender reversal could be joined to that of an upset of the established hierarchy between humans and animals, as in the gentle spoof *Well, Well J. . . F. . .*, wherein an honorable soldier is forced by his inferior, a common woman, to act the part of an animal. These satirical possibilities were further accentuated in various overtly zoomorphic scenes that, especially after the king's capture at Varennes in June 1791, featured the royal couple along with other members of the royal family as the lowest sort of animal.[65]

Caricaturists gleefully played with the eruptive and scatological meanings attached to the new subject of the Revolution by imagining a partner for the sansculotte in the *sans-jupon*. The anonymous etching *Aristocratic Woman* (Figure 1.6) mocks the loose morals of female aristocrats and derides their debased understanding of both republican freedom and equality. A female aristocrat is pictured in a relaxed pose of disrobing: Except for her plumed headdress marking her status, she wears casual clothes, possibly undergarments, revealing one breast and lifting her skirt. Joyously, she greets the Revolution with these words: "Thanks to the Constitution, we will soon go without our skirts". Accused of mistaking freedom for sexual license, she is the easy victim of the new patriot mentality wherein aristocracy and whoredom were often equated.

In a series of prints bearing the title *Patriotic Discipline or Fanaticism Castigated*, aristocrats and members of the secular and religious orders are

Figure 1.5. [*Portrait of a Fishwife*]/ *The Monstrosity in the Flesh*.1789. Courtesy of the Bibliothèque nationale de France.

made to suffer humiliation and public exposure. Numerous caricatures dating from July 1789, featuring these scenes of flagellation, echo the satirical pamphlets of the period and cast doubt on the morality of the individuals being whipped. For example, one such incident led to the whipping at the Palais Royal of a nobleman and his wife for spitting on a portrait of Jacques Necker. A second wave of images depicting "patriotic whippings" were published in April 1791, this time directed against suspected refractory priests and nuns who resisted the Civil Constitution of the Clergy. In Figure 1.7, *Patriotic Discipline or Fanaticism Corrected: The Period begun during the Week of the Passion* 1791 *by*

Figure 1.6. *Aristocratic Woman*. ca. 1790. Courtesy of the Bibliothèque nationale de France.

*the Women of the Market. According to an Exact Count, there were 621 Buttocks
Whipped; 310 and one-Half Butts, since the Treasurer of the Miramion(s) has Only
One [Cheek]*, a nun is whipped at center stage by two women as a third eggs
them on, while other nuns are seen desperately fleeing from their patriotic
tormentors.[66] The spanking by market women of other women—whether religious women, political adversaries, or unpopular neighbors—or, as in complementary images, whippings by men against male clergy or aristocrats, was a
socially sanctioned form of patriotic discipline or rough justice. The humor of
exposed buttocks in this print is compounded by the preposterous count,
which is cited in the print's title, producing an odd number of buttocks! Yet
satire could also give way to sober circumstances. In a famous incident in May
1793, Théroigne de Méricourt—heroine of the October Days and Girondin

sympathizer—was seized by Jacobin women outside the Convention and accused of being a Brissotin and a moderate. Her skirts were lifted and her bare
flesh whipped, but she was saved from further harm by Marat, who, arriving
on the scene, shielded her from the women.[67]

Figure 1.8, *A Nose Thumbed, or the Aristocracy Crushed* (*Le Pied de nez ou
L'Aristocratie écrasée*) is a splendid example of how revolutionary artists exploited both caricature and allegory in the spirit of Voltaire's famous battle cry
against bigotry and superstition, *Écrasez l'infâme!*[68] In the revolutionary context of 1790—following the abolition of feudal privileges, the nationalization
of Church properties, and the passage of the Civil Constitution of the Clergy
requiring the clergy to take an oath of loyalty to the French nation—the print
calls for the crushing of the holders of all privileges. Clergymen, nuns, and aristocrats are shown growing exaggerated, long noses, connoting both their men-

Figure 1.7. *Patriotic Discipline or Fanaticism Corrected: The Period begun during the Week of the
Passion 1791 by the Women of the Market. According to an Exact Count, there were 621 Buttocks
Whipped; 310 and one-Half Butts, since the Treasurer of the Miramion(s) has Only One [Cheek].* 1791.
Courtsy of the Bibliothèque nationale de France.

LE PIED DE NEZ
ou
l'Aristocratie écrasée.

Figure 1.8. *A Nose Thumbed, or the Aristocracy Crushed*. 1790. Courtesy Rare and Manuscript Division, Cornell University Library.

dacity and their sexual depravity. These bodies are what the literary critic Mikhail Bakhtin termed grotesque—that is, bodies "in the act of becoming."[69] The grotesque body is a mobile, split, and disproportionate body, the very opposite of the beautifully proportioned classical body. These figures seem helpless to control the growth of their own protuberances, ears as well as noses. Once beautiful, they are now ugly and, by innuendo, sexualized, for the symbolism of the nose is linked to the phallus in both carnival imagery and literary sources, as Bakhtin has observed.[70] Thus, hideous and impure aristocrats are lowered from the ethereal sphere of their pretended nobility and spirituality to the base order of the body and its most elemental needs. They are debased literally and figuratively.

A kind of catechesis in both the print's title and its central imagery joins feet to noses. In the left foreground a scantily robed, crowned masculine figure (a symbol of the monarchy) is splayed out, gripping a serpent (another symbol of distrust and sexuality) that originates in his mouth as the hooked end of his nose and comes out of his anus. Contorted by his effort to grip his own serpent tail, he has fallen backward, feet in the air. His allies are of no help. The head of a demonlike figure is glimpsed in the right foreground, bowed low by the effort of tugging on his own growing nose. Standing triumphantly above these ruined, hapless creatures is an allegory of the nation, her raised sword gesturing triumph over the forces of despotism. A winged Fame trumpets victory and holds a garland crown over France's head. Both figures' wings bear the tricolor stripes. The female allegory of France here assumes the position of the classical body and, although the print predates the creation of the Republic in 1792, it is noteworthy that the national body is represented by a female figure. She is erect, monumental, and orderly. The world—a globe on which she stands—has become her pedestal, upsetting monarchy in the process. While the print exploits the possibilities of grotesque humor, it also invites the spectator to gaze up toward this statuesque, universal figure. She alone seems outside the corrupt order of time. Together her justice and her force—symbolized by the sword—have vanquished the decaying remnants of Old Regime France.

Or perhaps the Old Regime was crushed by the people's derision, which has humiliated the privileged orders and deformed their bodies. The print's title exploits both a visual and a verbal pun. A *pied de nez*—literally a nose a foot long; figuratively to thumb one's nose at someone—is a gesture of derision that consists of extending the hand, fingers spread out, by putting one's thumb on the nose. Moreover, *écrasé* carries with it the multiple meanings of being flattened, trampled, and squashed. By the power of exaggeration, these bodies have been disfigured and reduced.

This image is complex and draws on the classical and elite motifs of the allegorical tradition as well as on the popular rhythms and folk humor of carnival and everyday life. It operates in both a verbal and visual register. The print's central pun calls on the viewer's own gestural response. Although outside the print's borders, the people are the cause of the aristocracy's humiliation. In this regard, the print's mode of address is "performative" in the sense applied by James Rubin in his study of revolutionary painting. The viewer is invited to perform an act of violation, a *pied de nez*, to make happen the very debasement that is the subject of the print. The spectator is given license to participate in a carnivalesque process of inversion, this time in the political and social arena. On the other hand, a powerful allegorical figure occupies center stage. She seems to arrest all further action. On the level of allegory, the print is "constative": her presence interpolates the viewer as the subject of a new order. Rubin remarks about revolutionary art in general: "Yet that is the process of Revolution: stripping individuals of connections with one social order to create a new solidarity based solely on ideas—deconstitution/reconstitution."[71] Indeed, the print *A Nose Thumbed* seems to embrace the possibilities of what Michel de Certeau terms an "anti-discipline" and Richard Terdiman a "counter-discourse." At the same time, the possibility is instantiated of a new disciplinary power through which the spectator may once again be suspended, his or her actions deferred.[72]

The popular prints of the Revolution are, then, hardly naive, transparent objects. In Barbara Stafford's estimation, "caricature, or the 'low life' of art, is where the performative, the comic, the experimental, and the journalistic meet."[73] The masterful studies of revolutionary caricature by Antoine de Baecque and counterrevolutionary caricature by Claude Langlois are a definitive answer to what has been until now a rather sterile academic debate over the elite or popular character of this art. As Michel Vovelle affirms, "If caricature borrows from popular culture a part of its figures (carnivalesque inversion, the emphasis on the body and its natural functions), and if besides it aims more toward a popular public than a circle of initiates, it nevertheless remains that it is the work of artists who are anything but naive, of an organized apparatus of production, and that it is supported by a sometimes elaborate discourse."[74]

Caricature cannot be reduced to a manipulative instrument; nor can it be said to reflect public opinion passively. While responding to public opinion, both caricature and allegory contributed powerfully to the creation of what de Baecque alternately terms "a popular imagination" or a "political imaginary." But it did so in the context of an organized apparatus of commercial production. Printmakers produced these images for sale on the market. In contrast to the makers of deluxe engravings, purchased by a wealthier clientele, the artists who made inexpensive hand-colored etchings and engravings responded hastily to rapidly changing events and politics. They were inventing a universe of symbols and figures, articulating a graphic language, and in the process, according to Vovelle, they were "giving to the arm of laughter or derision a redoubtable violence synonymous with its efficacy. Satire leaves the salons in order to invest itself in a political scene open to all viewpoints."[75] In a similar way, allegory burst out of its previous provenance in elite culture to produce an art intending to speak to the broader populace.

Politics and the Image

The majority of men, women, and children in France at the time of the Revolution were not able to read or write, although regional variations such as the higher literacy rates in Paris and the north of France are important considerations.[76] Political prints were one of many means—and these included songs and speeches—by which writings could be communicated to an oral or semiliterate populace.[77] Produced in vast quantities, illustrated broadsides were sold, posted, and distributed; they were thereby made available for commentary by a large public audience, who were then able to approve, reject, or revise their contents.[78] As Rolf Reichardt argues, broadsides performed more than a supplementary function: "They not only rendered the revolutionary message accessible but also drew ordinary people into the communication and opinion-making process of a widening public sphere, with its tendency toward democratization. These prints were at once a means of political education and testimony to popular ideas."[79] Thus, images can be said to have played a central role in the formation of revolutionary publics and in the articulation of political arguments, to an extent that is not encompassed by Condorcet's less generous attitudes toward visual signs in his *Sketch*.

From a gratifying number of different disciplines and radically independent intellectual traditions, students of the image have come to appreciate that seeing is a complex, conceptual process. It is widely acknowledged that the process of constructing an image is complex, mediated, and multilayered.[80] The relationship of image to thought is not, then, one in which only thought is symbolic and opaque, vision presymbolic and immediate. Seeing and visualizing involve representation—not simply because representation is a cultural variable that can be added, taken away, or transcended in some more perfect mental universe or social structure. They are cognitive processes of great complexity, evolutionary acquisitions of the human species.

With respect to the role of images in eighteenth-century culture, some caveats are in order. The technologies of mechanical reproduction associated with printing encouraged the development of a new and highly differentiated visual culture, within which different types of visuality coexisted. Books, maps, medals, playing cards, broadsides, and printed fabrics were all mechanically reproducible, but they were also differentiated from the outset. Each object established its own rules and protocols for the reading or viewing of its contents. Each type of printed object addressed an audience, highly specialized or wideranging: astronomers and the scientific community; adventurers and colonists; aristocrats, the bourgeoisie, and the popular masses; the avant-garde; the literate middle classes; female readers; Bible-reading artisans: and members of consuming publics.[81] We are speaking, then, of different modalities and diverse publics for the differential products of the printing press. However, while to this extent independent, artifacts nowhere function strictly as monads. Rather, the evidence suggests a rich pattern by which objects intercommunicate. By attending to their encapsulation effects, it is possible to appreciate the ways in which communication processes are unleashed within a given culture.[82]

There is one final, vexing issue involving the relations between image and text. I refer to W. J. T. Mitchell's observation that the relationship between word and image is rarely innocent or equivalent, as words are apt to "police" images.[83] One can legitimately query whether this pattern holds in some universal sense, while simultaneously acknowledging the strong efforts taken during the Revolution to anchor images to words and to stabilize meanings—stylistically through the deployment of increasingly abstract images, often of an allegorical type. Lynn Hunt and James Leith write of the revolutionary government's deliberate attempts to imbue public authority with new symbols, especially after the abolition of monarchy and the establishment of the Republic on 21 September 1792. Mona Ozouf directs attention to the proliferation of speeches and banners (with texts), commentaries on the proper interpretation of images, and extensive written directions to participants and organizers of revolutionary festivals. She writes of a transfer of sacrality from the old religion and state to such objects as the Declaration of the Rights of Man and Citizen, the Constitution, patriotic anthems, civic sermons, and constitutional oaths. Ozouf proposes that the entire spectacular realm of the festival was an area of concern for the pedagogically minded festival organizers, not least because of their fear of the emotional charge of images. De Baecque concedes that revolutionary caricature was surprisingly short-lived. It began to recede in importance after the establishment of the Republic, the outbreak of war, and the institutionalization of radical leadership.[84] Borrowing a term from the anthropologist Victor Turner, Vivian Cameron describes this same course of events as the end of the Revolution's "liminal" stage.[85]

I am certainly not suggesting a sudden rupture away from one mode of representation toward another. Allegories had strong precedents in the elite

emblematic tradition. As we have seen, allegorical representations also served
the popular arts from 1789 onward. In his study of revolutionary visual codes,
Klaus Herding provides striking examples of engravings in which abstract
codes, supported by writing, compete with mythological, allegorical, or realistic codes. He also observes that "this intermixing was a complicated, at times
confusing structure." Most decisively, Herding concludes that a process of additional coding marked revolutionary graphic art. This was not a move in the
direction of didactic explicitness and greater simplification. Nor was it a break
away from the iconographic secret languages of the past. In other words, these
changes cannot be accounted for within a simple model of revolutionary art as
propaganda.[86]

The allegorical prints we have considered from the graphic arts of the Revolution do suggest that texts and textual traditions may dominate images.
However, the examples provided from revolutionary caricature and popular
allegory also demonstrate an ongoing, dynamic relationship between, to paraphrase Mitchell, revolutionary iconoclasm and revolutionary iconophilia.
Moreover, as Herding observes, the paradigm change that accompanied the
Revolution was accomplished in good measure by means of visual imagery—
not merely at its expense. He writes, "Whereas during the ancien régime,
especially in the eighteenth century, art was valued as mere *art*, the Revolution
reintroduced an appreciation for art that demanded not only respect for the
form but also veneration for the contents. However . . . if the image embodies
the truth, then false conceptions had to be wiped out in the end by the image.
The veneration of the image and the destruction of the image are very closely
connected."[87]

In Chapter 2, I explore the role played by visual imagery in the revolutionary processes of iconoclasm and iconophilia. Specifically, I consider the
ways in which imagery contributed to the construction of a new imaginative
universe for the nation—a universe in which the female goddess Liberty came
to substitute for the sacred body of the king. Simultaneously, I ponder the importance of the feminization of the visual order of political representation in
the new Republic.

Representing the Body Politic

EVEN UNDER optimal circumstances, the trial and execution of a king as occurred in France in 1793 would not be a trivial matter. To the king's supporters, the revolutionaries were guilty of the most awful form of parricide and a capital crime against the whole community. The Convention's action was predicated on a striking inversion: The king's once sacred body had to become first a criminal body—one condemned according to a new, higher morality of crimes against the public's liberty and the state's security.[1] Any judgment implies both a judge and the law. Indeed, in this unusual proceeding, a new (popular) sovereign, its representatives, and its legal code were in evidence. In this sovereign's name the regicides acted. Standing behind, empowering, authorizing, and legitimating the decisive vote of the Convention was a sovereign power whose claim to authority was no less absolute than that of either God or king, the twin pillars of Old Regime France: In the name of the people and its liberty, the nation and its security, justice was being done. In the words of Jean-Jacques Rousseau, the most uncompromising eighteenth-century theorist of popular sovereignty, "Sovereignty is inalienable, it is indivisible." Indeed, like its predecessor, this new sovereign power is "entirely absolute, entirely sacred, and entirely inviolable."[2]

According to the doctrine of kingship by which Louis XVI and his ancestors ruled France, the king possessed two bodies: a material body subject to corruption and decay, and a spiritual body symbolic of the life of the community.[3] It was natural and expected that a king should die. But the trial and execution of this king exceeded nature and ancient law. It struck at the heart of the central metaphor of Old Regime France. By decapitating the sacred, corporate body of the ancien régime, necessarily its "head," the revolutionaries risked the continued life of the body politic.[4] Yet in the political imaginary of the new nation, in the language of the social contract from which the new Republic derived its legitimacy, the central trope of the body politic lived on. As Article 3 of the Declaration of the Rights of Man and Citizen posited, "The source of all sovereignty resides essentially in the nation. No body, no individual can exercise authority that does not explicitly proceed from it."[5] Even earlier, Rousseau had refused to cede the old metaphor to his political opponents. In *On the Social Contract*, for example, he writes, "Just as nature gives each man absolute power over all his members, the social compact gives the body politic absolute power over all its members."[6] Rousseau's sovereign is nevertheless extremely abstract. His body politic exists symbolically in the law. His effort to anchor political representation in the concept of the general will bequeathed a troubling legacy to his followers.

The project of redefining and representing the body politic with the nation and its populace, not the king, at the now vacant, sacred center proved vexing from a visual as well as a political standpoint. Political and religious idolatry was a frequent target of eighteenth-century republicans. As Thomas Paine protested, "The old idea was that man must be governed by effigy and show, and that a superstitious reverence was necessary to establish authority. . . . The putting of any individual as a figure for a nation is improper." Perhaps more striking is John Quincy Adams's formulation: "Democracy has no monuments. It strikes no medals. It bears the head of no man on a coin. Its very essence is iconoclastic."[7] In France, Rousseau's influential formulation of the general will led some to resist the very notion of representation. This challenge concerned the Revolution's symbolic repertoire, as Quincy Adams and Paine recommend, as well as its political practices.[8] As Rousseau stated, "The instant a people chooses representatives, it is no longer free; it no longer exists."[9] However, as discussed in Chapter 1, despite their strong iconoclastic leanings, French republicans ultimately conceded the need for images and sought ways in which to channel their power toward approved ends. Similarly, at the political level, the sheer impracticability of governing a nation as populous and diverse as France according to antique principles of direct democracy resulted in departures from Rousseau's theory of the general will. Here, however, we have nearly the reverse of the compromise made on the symbolic level. Neither Rousseau's ideas of the general will nor his hostility to representative bodies was laid to rest. Keith Baker has argued convincingly that the Abbé Sieyes theorized what amounted to a "modern" practice of democracy, but he concedes that Sieyes nevertheless "failed, in the constitutional debates of 1789, to secure its institutionalization as the controlling discourse of the Revolution. In the years to come, the language of the general will was constantly to subvert the language of representation."[10]

In this chapter, I investigate further the interaction between visual and political argumentation during the Revolution. No more compelling site exists for what I would like to term a "graphic politics" than that of the representation of the body politic. In France, moreover, we are confronted by the often noticed but still perplexing substitution of the goddess Liberty for the body of the king.[11] A closer investigation of body imagery in revolutionary popular prints in light of the political thought and practice may help to identify a series of paradoxes within the territory of iconic and symbolic practice. One way to frame the discussion that follows, then, would be to ask how Rousseau's vision of an absolute, sacred, and inviolable new sovereign power fares once it is embodied in the allegorical figure of a woman.

We need to observe initially something of the improbable origins of the democratic body politic as articulated by Rousseau and his revolutionary admirers. Over a century before the French Revolution, Thomas Hobbes had devastated the naturalistic and organic underpinnings of medieval, corporate rule, only to save the body politic for other uses. Through the metaphor of the social contract, Hobbes linked the issue of political authority to that of personification and representation. His Leviathan, a living god, amounts to a grand artifice, an artificial person, created through a contract by which commonwealth's members are made complicit in the sovereign's absolute power and authority. As individuals, according to Hobbes, are nothing more than impersonators, actors, bearers of masks, it is entirely consistent that the "feigned person" of the sovereign be an extension of each individual subject's will.[12] By contracting together, they have represented, authorized, authored, and engendered the sovereign. A multitude has "made *One* Person. . . . For it is the *Unity* of the Representer, not the *Unity* of the Represented, that maketh the Person *One*."[13] Hobbes's subjects are not born into natural submission as hapless creatures in the old order of social station; they have the privilege of *willing* their own domination.

The frontispiece of the 1651 edition of *Leviathan,* and in whose creation Hobbes is said to have had a direct hand, says it best: The authorizing members of the (artificial) body politic are seen from the back, their bodies literally compose the sovereign's armor. All leveled, none more equal than any other, the members of the body politic are figured as awed spectators of this terrifyingly absolute sovereign whose justification to rule is depicted in the pastoral image of a peaceful, prosperous, and protected countryside. He exists for their "common benefit." Surely, it is of some import for students of gender and politics that only decades after the end of Elizabeth's reign and the more immediate experience of civil war, the person of Hobbes's imposing sovereign is decidedly male.[14]

Rousseau is equally anxious about the effects of political and social division, although unlike Hobbes, he sought a democratic, not an authoritarian, solution to these problems. His myth of the social contract takes Hobbes's argument one step further. If Hobbes's metaphor requires a metamorphosis, Rousseau asks for nothing less than transubstantiation. By willing the good and the general, each member of the political body is at one with the whole. Mysteriously, the members not only authorize and legitimate the sovereign, but they become the sovereign as well: "Each of us puts his person and all his power in common under the supreme direction of the general will; and in a body we receive each member as an indivisible part of the whole."[15] The end result of all of this willing, then, is not a person but the popular sovereign, the evanescent body of the people and their laws. Rather than follow Hobbes in the direction of a theatrical theory of representation, Rousseau refuses the assistance of all masks and representations. He evokes instead a transparent, natural basis of power, forgetting, as the revolutionaries themselves ruefully discovered, that "the theatrical is the political."[16] Despite radical challenges to the legitimacy of all representations, the revolutionaries were never able to impose a strict Rousseauian program in either politics or culture.[17] The need to achieve a new representation of the altered body politic remained a pressing concern of the leadership and the revolutionary publics.

The dynamic process by which France broke with past symbols and images and struggled to create new ones can be examined from three distinct but constantly overlapping perspectives. First the manner in which a body politic was refigured; second, dismembered; and third, re-membered. As the movement from the masculine visage of the monarch to the goddess Liberty underscores, the logic of representation in the Revolution is also gender coded. In the earliest years of the Revolution, a plethora of prints were produced that referred, typically in allegorical terms, to the reorganization of the old corporate body of France, the Estates-General, into a modern parliamentary body, the National Assembly, under a constitutional monarchy. The people are triple—not yet subsumed under a single, abstract personification. Figure 2.1, *Farewell Bastille*, couples a description of the changed social and constitutional circumstances to a much less optimistic rendering of the course to be taken by the new body politic. A member of the third estate stands playing a bagpipe.

This representative of the new nation causes two marionettes dressed as a nobleman and a clergyman to dance to his tune. In the background, patriots with pickaxes dismantle the Bastille, the hated symbol of the despotic Old Regime. The presence of the Bastille, the print's one realistic element, reinforces the dominant message of this allegory: As the Abbé Sieyes proclaimed, the third estate is everything—"nobody outside the Third Estate can be considered as part of the nation." The popular allegory of a world turned upside down is joined to the theatrical space of the fairs and little theaters. The people, represented as a great puppeteer, now control political space and their own destiny. As for the monarchy, its despotism is tamed. Not the third estate—whom Sieyes described as being "like a strong robust man with one arm still in chains"[18]—but the monarchy (symbolized by a lion) lies in chains at the feet of the people's representative. *Farewell Bastille* presents the monarchy as tamed, even domesticated, to fit its place in a reformulated state in which monarchy shares power with (is leashed to) a new legislative body, the National Assembly.

In contrast to monarchy, which had a vital place in the reformulated state,

ADIEU BASTILLE.

Figure 2.1. *Farewell Bastille*. 1789. Courtesy Rare and Manuscript Division, Cornell University Library.

the aristocracy was a suspect category in patriot imagery from the Revolution's outbreak. On the eve of the Revolution, leaders of the first and second estates had equated despotism with abuses in the monarchy. However, there soon emerged a more radical discourse of liberty and despotism, as in the Abbé Sieyes's influential pamphlet *What Is the Third Estate?* Similarly, Nicolas Bonneville's journal, *Le Tribun du peuple*, equated despotism with "exclusive and hereditary privileges" and warned the nobility against obstructing the desires of the third estate: "The Third Estate, which really is the whole nation in its entirety and the sole legislative authority, creates or deposes officials and kings as it pleases."[19] Visual images from the period admonish obstructionists and celebrate popular victories. The allegory of the armed citizenry decapitating the many-headed Hydra of despotism or aristocracy in the many popular renderings of the taking of the Bastille enhances the demand for a complete reform of political institutions.[20] Likewise, the presence of severed heads of victims of popular violence—such as Bernard René Jourdan, marquis de Launay, governor of the Bastille prison; Jacques de Flesselles, prévôt de marchandes, the chief of the royal municipal administration of Paris; the intendant of Paris, Louis Bénigne François de Bertier de Sauvigny; and Bertier's father-in-law, the royal minister Joseph François Foulon, all in July 1789—is a sinister motif in many early revolutionary prints, emphasizing the dire consequences of inaction or obstruction by the privileged classes.

In numerous depictions of the October Days, such as Figure 2.2, *Triumph of the Parisian Army Reunited with the People upon Its Return from Versailles 6 October* 1789, the crowd's potential for violence is emphasized by the parading of severed heads. In this celebration of the people's return from Versailles, the aristocracy and clergy are completely offstage, replaced by women from the popular classes, national guardsmen, and soldiers. The women are far from passive. This is an affirmative image of emancipation—the women and soldiers carry liberty trees—not a representation of Edmund Burke's vile furies.[21] Still, the women show disturbing signs of possessing strong sexual and martial appetites, underscoring their Amazonian nature.

In fact, in the rhetoric of the period the market women are regularly referred to as "heroines," "Amazons," "new Amazons," and "modern Amazons." In a description of the October events appearing in the *Courier national, politique et litteraire* market women are described as being "united in a 'corps'" and as "new Amazons, dragging canons with them, set[ting] off for Versailles." The text of another print depicts them as returning on horseback and with cannons, accompanied by the National Guard.[22] In the image under review, there are especially menacing allusions. The women (in effect, soldiers of "the

Parisian army") carry bread and heads on pikes. One woman straddles a cannon, whose barrel comes between her legs; another woman is caught in a compromising posture with a soldier whose intentions are evident.

The issue of gender is encoded forcefully in a series of royalist caricatures on the birth of the constitution of 1791. Figure 2.3, *Monsieur Target Giving Birth* is a rather explicit image of the *engendering* of the new body politic. The lawyer Target, deputy of the third estate from Paris and member of the committee charged with drafting the new constitution, is seen sitting with his legs spread apart, having just delivered a baby (the new constitution). The female revolutionary Théroigne de Méricourt witnesses the baby's baptism, accompanied by three males allegorizing the three estates: The nobility is represented by the Duc d'Aiguillon, whom we have seen in Chapter 1 was the but of counterrevolutionary humor. Here he is no doubt remembered for his speech on the night of 4 August 1789, which earned him the special enmity of the monarchical right; in this speech he renounced his noble privileges, setting off the great flood of renunciations and attacks on feudal rights and privileges.[23] Lynn Hunt presents this etching as an almost unbelievable confirmation of Carole Pateman's argument that "the story of the original contract tells a modern story of masculine political birth. . . . [It is] an example of the appropriation by men

Figure 2.2. *Triumph of the Parisian Army Reunited with the People upon Its Return from Versailles 6 October 1789.* 1789. Courtesy of the Library of Congress.

of the awesome gift that nature has denied them and its transmutation into masculine political creativity." For Pateman, modern contract theory represents a particular version of the masculine genesis of political life, "a specifically modern tale, told over the dead political body of the father."[24] Hunt observes that the mother of *la nation* has no threatening feminizing qualities.[25] Rather, Méricourt is reduced to an assisting role.

On the other hand, as Claude Langlois stresses, the royalists habitually allied Méricourt with the populace both symbolically (for her support of the Constituent Assembly) and because of her alleged loose morals (she was a courtesan before 1789). Behind this casual joke, then, there resides an obsession with the theme of the world turned upside down. According to Langlois, "The Revolution not only perverted the political order, but even more profoundly it turns that of nature upside down."[26] Surely, then, Méricourt's appearance functions as a satirical accent with respect to the forces that have

Figure 2.3. *Monsieur Target Giving Birth.* 1791. Courtesy of the Bibliothèque nationale de France.

engendered this new political body. In the traditional order, fishwives (*poissardes*) witnessed the birth of royalty. In the post-1789 France, the position of attendant to the birth of constitutional arrangements is given to a woman of notorious sexual and political reputation who attends the birth of constitutional arrangements. There is certainly something laughable also about a man caught in the compromising and unnatural scene of birth.

There is little doubt about the satirical intent of the royalist lampoon in Figure 2.4, *The Great Rout of the Anti-Constitutional Army* (*Grand Débandement de l'armée anti-constitutionelle*) (1792).[27] Again Méricourt makes an appearance, now in a company of notorious women of the aristocracy who openly supported revolutionary ideas.[28] In the manner of counterrevolutionary caricature, the targets of the attack are not anonymous but identifiable. Méricourt, "la demoiselle Teroig" as she is called here, shows up as a general leading her troops of aristocratic women. Méricourt frightens the emperor's troops by revealing her "république," a pun on *res publica* (Latin for "republic" but also a public or sexual thing). The print equates Méricourt's sexual parts with her republican sympathies and continues the slander by making reference to the revolutionary sympathizer Marquis de Villette. In the pamphlet literature (of both the Right and the Left), Villette, a notorious sodomite, was claimed to always prefer anal intercourse, even on those occasions when he had sex with women.[29] By raising their skirts and baring their buttocks, the women each present a "villette."

The print bitterly mocks the cowardice of the counterrevolutionary armies arrayed against a poorly outfitted contingent of women with their few sansculotte and jacobin supporters who are carrying nothing so terrible as pikes topped with hams and sausages; what the catalog *French Caricature* terms "the phallic spoils of war."[30] The real power of the revolutionary forces as portrayed here lies in their "sex." This provocative image achieves a humorous but deeply disturbing condensation of political and sexual anxieties. On behalf of the royalist cause, the *Journal de la Cour et de la ville* caricature cleverly borrows from anti-absolutist appeals to aspiring, virile male citizens against the emasculating and illicit influence of upper-class women. Instead of courtly women's nocturnal manipulations, it appeals to the populace's dread of the openly sexualized appetites of women that the Revolution is shown to have unleashed.

Sharing the transgressive strategies of revolutionary caricature, and notwithstanding their antithetical intent, these counterrevolutionary images also contributed to the body politic's dismemberment that was well under way in patriot discourse and imagery. For example, in *The Great Rout of the Anti-*

GRAND DÉBANDEMENT DE L'ARMÉE ANTICONSTITUTIONELLE.

Figure 2.4. Chez Webert, *The Great Rout of the Anti-Constitutional Army*. From *Journal de la Cour and de la Ville*, 2/19/1792. Courtesy of the Bibliothèque nationale de France.

Constitutional Army, loyalty to the king's cause itself is pushed to the limits, reduced to a fear of sexually emasculating women. The virility and military prowess of his soldiers are called into question by their impotence in the face of troops led by a woman of questionable honor.

What is being dismembered is the carefully articulated sacred body politic of Old Regime France, which culminated directly in removal of its head.[31] The basic theory of kingship had its roots in the Middle Ages, wherein intermediate groups stood in a kind of graduated order between the supreme unit and the individual; a political and individual body that necessarily repelled any hint of monstrosity:[32] "On the analogy of the physical body, to avoid monstrosity, finger must be joined directly, not to head but to hand; then hand to arm, arm to shoulder, shoulder to neck, neck to head. . . . '[T]he [medieval] constituencies are organic and corporatively constructed limbs of an articulated People.'"[33]

Moreover, under royal absolutism, the spectacular figuration of power was tied ineluctably to the masculine subject of the monarch. All circuits of desire pointed in the direction of the king's body, and the king's claims to rule were buttressed through visual representations, court rituals, and public discourse.[34] Classicizing artists found their ideal subject matter in history painting and royal portraiture. Engravings after painted portraits of the royal family circulated widely. They ran the gamut from those produced at a relatively low cost and made available to a wide public for display in their homes to gilded and polychromed works aimed at an elite clientele. But following conventions that congealed in the metaphor of the well-articulated and sacred body politic, representations of royalty—indeed, all expressions of official high culture—took the form of a classical body. Radiant and transcendent, the classical body is what Mikhail Bakhtin terms a finished and completed body.[35]

The dismemberment of the classical political body involved the transgressive symbolic practices of grotesque realism. In the process, the king's body was made to appear gargantuan in its physical appetites, cuckolded by a sexually avaricious and disloyal queen who also appeared as a harpy or a panther, parodied as a low form of barnyard or wild animal, and at the extremes, where material reality and satire literally converged, disembodied.[36] In his medusan image of the king's severed head dripping blood, raised up by a disarticulated hand, *Matter for Thought for Crowned Jugglers/May Our Fields Run with an Impure Blood* (1793) (Figure 2.5), the revolutionary artist Villeneuve[37] captured with horrible effect the grotesque reversal of the king's classical body, which in reality occurred at the guillotine.[38]

Dismemberment of the royal body was a long, involved process. Jean-Pierre Guicciardi, for instance, locates its origin in what might be referred to as the "sexual reign" of Louis XV, proposing that "the king's sex, that fabulous phallus, was one of the major instruments of *political subversion* in France toward the end of the ancien régime."[39] Certainly, the extensive political and sexual pornography in printed and visual matter directed at the aristocracy, the clergy, and above all the royal family in the last years of the Old Regime and the early years of the Revolution was a major factor in the symbolic process of political dismemberment.[40] Louis XVI's impotence was a topic of general discussion, and it was made worse by rumors of the queen's infidelities and perverse sexuality.[41] Indeed, Antoine de Baecque has made a persuasive case for

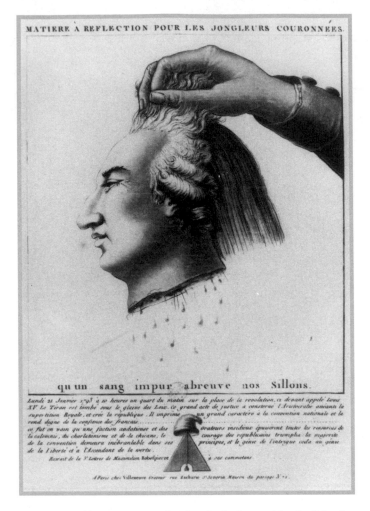

Figure 2.5. Villeneuve, *Matter for Thought for Crowned Jugglers/May Our Fields Run with an Impure Blood.* 1793. Courtesy of the Bibliothèque nationale de France.

the extent to which Louis XVI's defeat, culminating in the physical loss of his body, began some twenty years earlier in the scandalous tales of his bodily impotence.[42]

A series of prints from the period of the royal family's flight and capture at Varennes in June 1791 are especially revealing. In a bizarre representation of a paralyzed, two-headed monster, *The Two Are but One* (Figure 2.6), the king

wears the horns of a cuckold and has the body of a ram, while the queen is car-
icatured as a hyena wearing a medusan headdress, snakes flying forth, punctu-
ated by ostrich feathers, a pun on her Austrian heritage. Other etchings depict
the royal family as pigs en route to market, or to slaughter, as was true as well
of the radical discourse of the period. Thus, in his heated description of the
king's flight, the radical journalist Camille Desmoulins refers to the king as a
"proud beast," an "animal-king" whose "nature" is that of an "eater of men" (*un
mangeur d'hommes*), a "crowned Sancho-Panza," a "pig," but also a "tiger and
a hyena, with the eyes of a mole."[43] These words and images more than fulfill
Edmund Burke's haunting prophecy of 1790 that once "the decent drapery of
life" is torn off, "a king is but a man; a queen is but a woman; a woman is but
an animal; and an animal not of the highest order."[44]

The bestial is closely joined to the theme of sexuality, as in Figure 2.7, *The
Stride of the Holy Family from the Tuilleries to Montmédy*. A grotesquely disproportionate queen, in a low-cut dress and ostrich plumes, uses her body to form
a bridge from the Tuilleries Palace to Montmédy on the northeastern frontier.
Looking particularly ridiculous and effete, the (diminished) king rides on the

Figure 2.6. *The Two Are but One*. ca. 1791. Courtesy of the Library of Congress.

back of the queen, whose infidelities and counterrevolutionary intentions are reinforced by the presence in the print of several notorious émigrés and personalities from the infamous Diamond Necklace Affair. Two of the central figures in this affair, Mme de la Motte and Cardinal Rohan, as well as one of the queen's alleged lovers, the Duc de Coigny, all stand below the queen's open legs, directly staring up as La Motte raises the infamous necklace. As in the pamphlet literature surrounding the affair itself, monarchy's demise is satirically attributed to the queen's enormous appetites, sexual and otherwise.[45] In Figure 2.8, *Bombardment of All the Thrones of Europe and the Fall of Tyrants for the Good of the Universe* the king's mouth and anus serve as the grotesque openings for a marvelous scatological caricature. Three tiers of bare-bottomed deputies (literally sansculottes) to the Legislative Assembly are shown defecating "liberty" and the notorious revolutionary song, "Ça ira," on the crowned heads of Europe. Liberty stands on top of the deputies, igniting a cannon that fires into the posterior of Louis XVI, forcing him to vomit vetoes that rain on the crowned heads, the pope, and William Pitt, England's prime minister. A

Figure 2.7. *The Stride of the Holy Family from the Tuilleries to Montmédy.* ca. 1791. Courtesy of the Library of Congress.

monstrous, bare-breasted Empress Catherine II rises above her fellow monarchs, trying to humiliate them into attacking France.

In contrast, what first appears to be a more benign representation of the king in 1792, *Louis XVI, King of the French: Cap of Liberty* (Figure 2.9), partakes as well of the transgressive dynamic of dismemberment, whereby the categories of high and low are exchanged. By placing a red cap of liberty on a familiar image of the king based on a painted portrait of the period by the artist Joseph Boze just prior to July 1789, the print recasts the king's classical body. He appears as simply another citizen of the French Republic. After all, the king had first to be symbolically leveled before he could be beheaded.[46] This print also conveys the fact that by this point in the Revolution the king has been made a captive of the people. Other representations of the king in a liberty cap show him toasting the nation—no longer even in control of his own speech—as he had been made to do by the Parisian crowd when they invaded the Tuileries Palace on 20 June 1792 to protest the king's veto of measures aimed at strengthening the war effort. By representing the king in republican costume, this anonymous artist violates all of the iconographic conventions of royal portraiture.

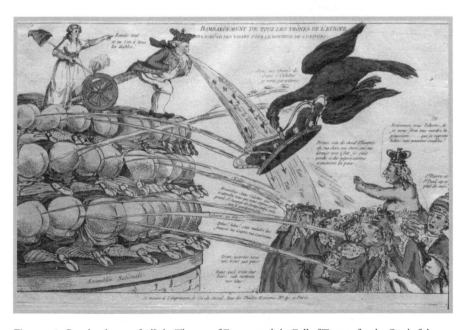

Figure 2.8. *Bombardment of All the Thrones of Europe and the Fall of Tyrants for the Good of the Universe.* ca. 1792. Courtesy of the Library of Congress.

And, in the gap opened up between representations of the once-sacred father-king and the people's friend, there lies the possibility for further caricature and ridicule.

The king's political body is a corporate body whose upper limbs are composed of the clergy and the aristocracy. Numerous scatological and pornographic prints of the period caricature the members of the two privileged orders as feeding on the nation, in dire need of an emetic; as sexually promiscuous; as being in league with the devil. Animal-like noses bring the aristocracy and the clergy down from the ethereal, spiritual realm to the material order of the lower body. Reiterating grotesque themes already observed in anti-

Figure 2.9. Anon., after painting by Joseph Boze, *Louis XVI, King of the French: Cap of Liberty*. 1792. Courtesy of The Metropolitan Museum of Art, The Elisha Whittelsey Collection, The Elisha Fund, 1962, (62.520.333).

royalist imagery, the pornographic cartooning directed toward the privileged orders further weakened the crown's sexual and political potency. Under these circumstances, the king could no longer be the "erect member" of the body politic of France.[47] Not surprisingly, the literature of the opposition under the late Old Regime and during the Revolution was rife with gender-laden metaphors. Not only did powerless men feel themselves to be "unmanned" by the absolutist power of the monarchy, but Louis XVI himself was said to be impotent and cuckolded. Moreover, the entire Old Regime was excoriated by its republican critics for encouraging women in their exercise of sexual and political power.[48]

A series of images show the sexualized body of the aristocracy as a female body. Figure 2.10, *The Aristocratic Body with the Face of a Woman Dying in the Arms of the Nobility* drives home the extent to which the revolutionaries were intent on excising the excessively feminized and feminizing dimension of the old body politic.[49] Admittedly, no direct reference is made in this image to the monarch. However, the representation of the corporate body—traditionally, a sanctified male body—as a dying feminine body contributes to the interment of the monarchy's patriarchal and sacred claims to absolute rule by undermining its physical and symbolic support within the aristocracy. This print also exploits one of the great themes of the Revolution's ribald literature, that of health. As de Baecque points out, "Its purpose is to contrast the healthy patriotic body and the diseased aristocratic body. It gave rise to an explanation and justification of the 'political and moral rebirth' of the Revolution—a rebirth that would purify the sexual act and bring it under the purview of the new government."[50]

Finally, there is the topic of re-membering. In Figure 2.11, *Liberty, Patron Saint of the French* an allegory of the Republic appears as the patron saint of the French people. This is merely one of myriad images of Liberty, who became an important republican and national symbol during the nineteenth century and has remained so to the present day.[51] Attached to her tricolor sash, she wears a lion-headed sword, attesting symbolically to her triumph over superstition, despotism, and the monarchy. Syncretically combining Christian and republican symbols, this virginal figure wears the Phrygian cap, yet she is surrounded by an aureole. She is figured as young, innocent, and pure. Happily, the sinful female body, the corrupt aristocratic or royal whore, is made over into a virtuous (and virginal) republican body. As opposed to the sexually threatening images of the female aristocratic body, this particular feminine representation of the reinvented body politic seems almost to call out for the protection of virile republican men.

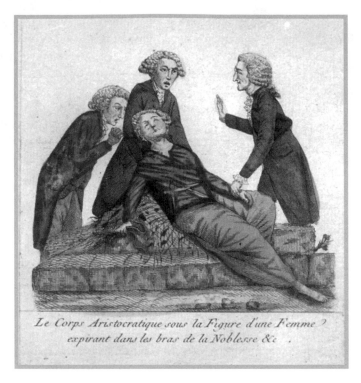

Le Corps Aristocratique sous la Figure d'une Femme
expirant dans les bras de la Noblesse &c.

Figure 2.10. *The Aristocratic Body with the Face of a Woman Dying in the Arms of the Nobility.* ca. 1790. Courtesy of the Library of Congress.

There is, however, something odd about a female figuration of the body politic in the context of a Revolution that enfranchised men but not women.[52] As Marina Warner cautions, however, "Liberty is not represented as a woman . . . because women were or are free."[53] Hunt concurs, stating, "The proliferation of the female allegory was made possible, in fact, by the exclusion of women from public affairs. Women could be representative of abstract qualities and collective dreams because women were not about to vote or govern."[54]

Indeed, Liberty seems to satisfy the foremost requirement of the new symbolic system: to achieve an abstract, impersonal representation that carried none of the connotations of monarchical rule. In the old body politic, any and all representations of an individual king operated as a metonym for the corporate populace of the realm: Part stood for whole, precisely because a recognizable individual who occupied society's premier role was in turn endowed with mystical qualities that allowed his person to substitute for the entire body

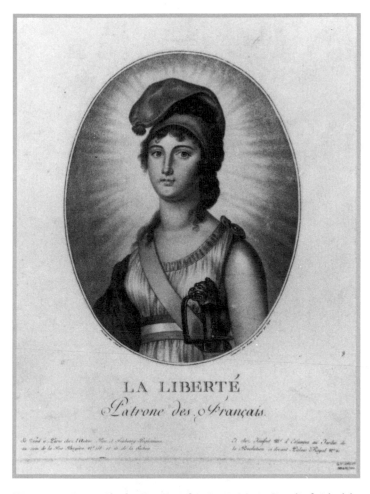

Figure 2.11. Louis Charles Ruotte, after Louis-Marie Sicardi, finished by Jacques-Louis Copia, *Liberty, Patron Saint of the French*, after Louis-Simon Boizot. ca. 1795. Courtesy of the Avery Collection, Miriam and Ira D. Wallach Division of Art, Prints and Photographs, The New York Public Library, Astor, Lennox and Tilden Foundations.

politic. In contrast, the female representation of the nation works best because it effaces the identifiable features of any known female person. Because of her generality, Liberty stands as a metaphor—not a metonym—for the whole social community, free from any and all divisions.[55] Even before the Revolution artists and writers depicted France—as well as justice, liberty, force, truth, and science—as female allegories, but their aim was to personify abstract principles or virtues, not to depict real, living subjects.[56]

Ironically, the men of the late eighteenth-century body politic, like the kings before them, were expected to be absolutely sovereign—in absolute control of their bodies—in a physical and a political sense. Dorinda Outram argues that a kind of redistribution of the divine body took place, leading to an intensification of the interaction between public men and their audiences. The virtuous heroic man, *homo clausus*, exhibited remorseless control over his body and his emotions. But if male virtue required a certain stoical, public self-exhibition, women's virtue was tied to chastity and fidelity within marriage: "Virtue, far from being the linchpin of a monolithic 'discourse of the Revolution,' in fact bisected the apparently universalistic discourse of the general will into distinct destinies, one male and the other female. Both were part of *le souvereign,* but somehow one half of *le souvereign* could function only at the price of the sexual containment of the other."[57] In this light, we might want to view Liberty as a symbol of an entire public culture, but one that hides the extent to which the values of rationality, universality, autonomy, and emancipation were predicated on a gendered division between public and private, male and female domains.

Moreover, the re-membered body is an internally contradictory thing, pointing forward and backward at the same time. Even as the revolutionaries sought an absolute rupture with the past, they suffered from what Mona Ozouf tellingly calls a "horror vacuii."[58] Their iconoclastic passion to purge all memories of the past, to empty out the sacred contents of everyday life, was accompanied by efforts to resacralize the present by way of a primitive model of Roman and Greek antiquity. Like all the female goddesses who graced the new Republic, Liberty appears in antique dress.[59] She is an emblem of the revolutionaries' desire to bypass their own national history, to institute an ideal, nondespotic Republic wherein personal liberty and communal togetherness would be reconciled joyously. Like her sister goddesses, she is a tutelary figure. Her virtue is meant to serve as an example to all who would banish selfish private desire in order to serve the whole. For women, her discipline involves their socialization into a virtuous domestic routine. For men, Liberty teaches the virtue of civic action and universal sociability.

But it does so on whose behalf? Even though there was a strong taboo against erecting any symbol that would revalue the patriarchal polity, it may be that Liberty's innocence and purity functioned to her benefit as a talisman: not against masculine politics in itself but against the historically tainted form of the old body politic. For, ultimately, the re-membered body is another fatherland. Strikingly, Ozouf confirms just this point in her discussion of festivals: "Never shown, the invisible fatherland was nonetheless the focal point of the whole festival: the altar was the altar of the fatherland; the defenders were the defenders of the fatherland; the battalion of children was the hope of the fatherland; the duty of every citizen, as every speech hammered home, was to be worthy of the fatherland; and the injunction on all the banners was to live and die for the fatherland."[60]

The body of the nation, the re-membered body politic, is a deeply gendered construction; like its predecessor, it privileges the masculine. It is an invisible construction, says Ozouf. It is an absolute sovereign who possesses no human face, according to Rousseau. This sovereign hides behind universal law, universal reason, and the nation. But if Ozouf is right, and I believe she is, how are we to account for the paradoxical fact that the new body politic appears in the guise of a female goddess? The Republic even acquired a female name, Marianne.

Ozouf directs attention to the proliferation of speeches and banners (with texts), commentaries on the proper interpretation of images, and extensive written directions to festival participants and organizers. She writes of a transfer of sacrality from the old religion and state to such objects as the Declaration of the Rights of Man and Citizen, the Constitution, patriotic anthems, civic sermons, and constitutional oaths. Above all, she proposes that visual allegories—and, indeed, the entire spectacular realm of the festival—were areas of concern for the pedagogically minded festival organizers. Ozouf points out, for example, a contradiction between the (masculine) forms that symbolized the festivals and the fact that they were populated by female figures. She cites one protester's anguished observation: "'Women everywhere, when what we need is a vigorous, severe regeneration!'" Ozouf also notices the organizers' suspicion of the public: They doubted the people's ability to properly decode images, and they feared the emotional charge of images. Accordingly, she states, "The Revolutionary festival was certainly verbose. . . . [It] said more than it showed." The horror of exhibition was balanced by an utterly unqualified fascination with words: "The Revolutionary sensibility expected words to have an immediate contagious effect."[61] Visual images by themselves were deemed suspect; they were becoming textualized, made increasingly responsive to legal forms of public discourse.

I have sought to establish the logic by which France's old iconic order was disestablished and reconstructed. In the process, the masculine iconography of the absolutist body politic gave way to a female representation of Republic. But the feminization of the visual order of (political) representation occurred just as the traditional semiotic system tied to the visible body of the father-king was being displaced by a competing symbolic order of written and spoken words. One way to reconcile the dilemma posed by these contradictory developments is to conclude that the place of woman is preserved only in the visual realm. By this reasoning, Marianne amounts to nothing but a picture. She neither reflects nor authorizes women's actions. At a higher level of abstraction in the newly dominant symbolic order of representation, the invisible fatherland need not be and ought not be pictured. It is spoken and written. The nation's body is a discursive body.

Intellectually, Hobbes and Rousseau prepared the way for this change in the order of political representation. The relationship between a nation and its citizens exists on a higher level of abstraction than that between the monarch and his subjects. Even though Hobbes authorized an anthropomorphic image for the frontispiece of his book, he gave a rational, not a mystical, version of the body politic—a version in which subjects are cells, not functional members of an organic body. His Leviathan is not a person but a symbolic construct: the residual outcome of a series of verbal contracts entered into by each of the nation's subjects. Rousseau confirmed Hobbes's break with sensuous representations. His sovereign bears no human face. The law is not pictured but written.

There is a problem, however, with a wholly discursive theory of rational, legal sovereignty that ignores the extent to which this sovereign—and France is not alone among modern nation-states—was pictured in a female form.[62] In the revolutionary break with the old absolutist order, the system of visual representation was not abandoned; nor was it entirely powerless and irrelevant. Furthermore, the re-membered body politic is not a simple, one-dimensional construction. There continued to be a dynamic interplay between the linguistic and visual definitions of national solidarity and identity, and visual representations themselves reflect the heterogeneous mix of text and image.[63] But we need to take account of the continued force of visual culture in the context of a revolution that so emphasized the power of words. Neither the Hobbesian nor the Rousseauian argument grasps the emotive power of sensuous representations, especially in the public realm. Of course, for some republicans, as I discussed in Chapter 1, recourse to images was nothing more than a simple archaism. The populace, deemed hopelessly credulous or atavistic in their instincts, would need to be instructed, monitored, and (in the parlance of the day) "regenerated." But as a policy, strict iconoclasm never succeeded. Owing to the palpable impressions created by visual culture, and also for strategic reasons, the promotion of images continued apace. Like the women at festivals bemoaned by Ozouf's source, they were everywhere!

As for female icons of the nation, Liberty, like her sister allegories, is not the only emblem of modern France. Among France's best-known signifiers down to the present-day, we count the tricolor, the bonnet rouge, the coq, the pré-carré or four-square map of France, and also the Marseillaise and the principles of universal human rights.[64] But while abstract signifiers may certainly trigger strong emotions, the embodied female figure stands apart in its power to evoke feelings of affection and intimacy. In her study of Tamil nationalism, Sumathi Ramaswamy provides an important clue to the way in which female allegories of the nation serve to anchor what she wisely terms the "somatics of nationalism." Allegorical images, she writes, "carry with them the profundity and power of concrete immediacy, and provide highly visible and visual reminders of intangible abstractions such as 'language,' the 'nation' or the community.' Most crucially, constituted as they are as the very embodiments of compassion and selfless love, they require, indeed demand, the reciprocal 'filial' attachment of the communities that are imagined around them, even to the point of sacrificing life and limb in their cause."[65] Because the nation is figured as a body, the citizen can *imagine* its embrace. By calling on the powers of imagination, so underscored in sensationalist psychology, the patriot makes individual what is collective and collective what is individual. By an act of the political imagination—both simple and collective, instinctual and rational, to borrow the Abbé de Condillac's categories discussed in Chapter 1—the embodied nation crosses the boundaries between what is material and ideal, conscious and unconscious, voluntary and involuntary.

But the female embodiment of the nation is a profoundly ironic symbol, a public representation of a polity that sanctioned different roles for men and women.[66] Mother, sister, lover: she also exists in a wider field of representations, not only those that elicit women's participation in the new polity but also those that repudiate female sexual and political behavior. Even Republic was not always the chaste goddess she officially represented. Common, coarse, whore: It is said that the name Marianne, given affectionately to her over time, was originally pejorative; it was the derogatory nickname preferred by her enemies. As late as 1848, speculates Maurice Agulhon, a woman who had once been a goddess during the Revolution could still be regarded by her compatriots with a kind of awe "mingled with terror or deference (depending upon one's point of view)."[67] In Chapter 3 I pursue the dilemmas posed by the multiple embodiments of femininity in revolutionary iconography before I explore further in Chapter 4 the erotic dimension of modern nationalism. Thus, the question I posed at this chapter's outset—How does Rousseau's vision of an absolute, sacred, and inviolable new sovereign power fare once it is embodied in the allegorical figure of a woman?—leads to a more expanded discussion of the convergence of the patriotic and the erotic within the ideology of nationalism. At the very least, we can surmise that the female personification of Republic stimulated the imagination of France's citizens in a way that Rousseau did not anticipate in arguing for the power of political abstractions. Is this to conclude that the French were less modern than they presumed? Or was it that they (like other moderns who invented symbols and allegories of their own nation-states) discovered what Agulhon calls "one great truth," made all the more urgent once the state becomes collective and anonymous? That is, "the State, even the Nation or the Motherland, are entities too abstract to appeal to the imagination or to inspire passionate feeling."[68]

3

Embodiments of Female Virtue

I N REGARD to revolutionary culture, it is useful to remember Edmund
Burke's observation that "abstract liberty, like other mere abstractions, is
not to be found. Liberty inheres in some sensible object."[1] As I have argued earlier, however, the female goddess Liberty, who anchored the new nation's legitimacy, operated as a metaphor. She transferred legitimacy not to
women, ostensibly Liberty's "sensible objects," but rather by analogy to the
people: in reality, the men who contracted together to form the new republican body politic. Speaking of "the people" as a metaphor for the social referent
itself, however, Linda Orr observes that "the people" still exists: "Everything in
which it circulates, contradictory and warring, gives it back the effect of a most
physical shape, something thick and consistent, with adamant desires and a
will."[2] Similarly, by publicly expressing their own "warring," conflicting, and
particular desires, women threatened to give back to Liberty a physical shape
or "social referent" wholly at odds with the nation's juridical body.

In this chapter, I examine the metaphors of female virtue in the Revolution's print culture in the context of revolutionary political culture and in relation to the paradoxical nature of democratic representation.[3] I reconsider
how the impulse to give shape, substance, and will to an abstraction called "the
people" resulted in the contradictory circulation of metaphorical shapes but
potentially real female bodies possessing willful, warring desires. Certainly, the
figuration of the nation as a female muse was paradoxical in the sense of making present an absence (the actual members of the political community who
were being represented), which is at the core of all forms of representation. In

addition, however, Liberty as a political metaphor obscured the stunning masquerade by which the masculine republic represented itself as the unified body of the people.[4]

Liberty and her alter ego, Republic, were not isolated cases. Accompanying them was a party of female goddesses who reflected the virtue and political rectitude expected of republican women. In this manner, anonymous females had the privilege of becoming allegories of a host of eternal values and of purging the old body politic of its tainted feminine matter. In contrast, female grotesques materialized the perceived threat of corrupt and disorderly women to the reformed political order, as well as personal life. The mute, chaste, classically proportioned allegories of virtue that stood in the place of the despised women of the Old Regime signaled that public and private excesses were incompatible with maternal duty and republican female morality. In addition, women's lofty place in the order of representation offered women compensation for their real social and political inequality; while the female face worn by republican and democratic values of liberty, equality, universality, and reason was a critical device for ensuring the continued legitimacy of the Republic.

Allegory, Narrative, and Action

It is useful to distinguish, as Philippe Bordes suggests, between emblematic and narrative allegory. The latter was of long-standing importance, and as recently as the reign of Louis XV and Louis XVI, painters applied narrative allegories to raise contemporary themes to a more exalted historical dimension. During the Revolution, too, such allegories remained the most efficacious means of translating into images new ideas and situations. Often allegorical figures simply appeared as a minor element of a historical scene, or they could play a major role alongside real people. Ordinarily expressing the sense of history, allegory might serve equally to deprive events of their much too present historicity, thereby raising the overly specific from the mundane sphere of contested politics to a more general plane of universal significance.[5] Still, it is significant that reference to the universal was embodied in a female allegory.

The anonymous colored engraving *The French Nation Assisted by Monsieur de Lafayette Stamps Out Despotism and the Abuses of Feudalism Which Had Crushed the French People* (Figure 3.1) depicts Lafayette at the peak of his popularity during the Festival of the Federation in July 1790, when he swore an oath to the nation on behalf of all the national guard units of France. The print is an excellent illustration of how a recorded event and an illustrious person might be raised to historical stature by the addition of allegory. The French nation appears in the shape of a female figure. She is garbed in a fleur-de-lis–patterned cloak, registering France's still monarchical constitution. Wearing Minerva's helmet and carrying bolts of lightening in her hand, she is shown stomping out despotism and the abuses of feudalism. One vanquished figure of Despotism, entwined with a serpent, may be masculine, though his crouched posture conceals his visage and his gender. The second figure of abuse, who is being stomped on by France, is unmistakably a winged figure of Discord and coded female within revolutionary iconography, as it was traditionally. Discord possesses the traits of a female fury—the drooping breasts of an old hag, medusan hair, serpents flying, fingers in a clawed posture, and a muscular upper body.[6] The figure's androgyny—especially the powerful musculature—only makes "her" femininity that much more terrifying. It is of some importance that Despotism/Discord is being crushed by her virtuous opposite, the French nation: as in the whole repertoire of revolutionary iconography, figures of female good and evil are juxtaposed here.[7] Nevertheless, the central gender contrast in this image revolves around the live person(ality) of the man Lafayette and the female allegory of France. The national guardsmen under his command appear in the rear and echo Lafayette. As is often the case, the combined efforts of such a real/ideal couple work to defeat the nation's enemies and to inaugurate the reign of liberty.

Certainly, allegory was not the only vehicle for presenting women in revolutionary prints. Copious illustrations of elite and popular provenance serve to document the actual presence of women in the new public sphere created by the events of 1789. As one example, the topic of aristocratic women's participation in the Festival of the Federation is registered in many prints celebrating the events marking the first anniversary of the fall of the Bastille.[8] Similarly, numerous prints record Lafayette's involvement alongside Parisian women in the celebrated events of October 1789. In comparison, the engraving *The French Nation Assisted by Monsieur de Lafayette* operates to effect a substitution. Not only does the great man Lafayette supplant historical individuals of both sexes who also participated in these events, but tellingly, insofar as women are represented, it is only as "Woman"—in an ideal, abstract, and suprahuman form. "Woman"—that is, the Nation—underscores the meaning of these events; she abets and secures for posterity the efforts of this great man.

The documentary engraving by Louis Le Coeur after Jacques-François Swebach-Desfontaines commemorating the Civic Oath of 1790, *View of the Altar of the Fatherland [La Patrie] and of a Part of the Champs-de-Mars at the Moment when Monsieur de Lafayette, in the Name of All the National Guards of*

La Nation Française assistée de M.ͬ De la Fayette terraße le Despotisme et les
Abus du Regne Feodel qui terraßaient le Peuple.

Figure 3.1. *The French Nation Assisted by Monsieur de Lafayette Stamps Out Despotism and the Abuses of Feudalism Which Had Crushed the French People.* 1790. Courtesy Rare and Manuscript Division, Cornell University Library.

France, Swore an Oath to Be Ever Faithful to the Nation, the Law and the King (Figure 3.2), offers another valuable corrective to the allegorical viewpoint of Figure 3.1. By foregrounding the people of both sexes and all three estates, adults and children, it places Lafayette himself and the altar in the far distance. The print's accompanying text states that the artistic perspective was intended to capture the patriotic scene in its full magnitude. As a result, Lafayette, to whom the print is dedicated, is barely visible, registering the fact that he would not have been seen by some three-fourths of the crowd who gathered that day on the Champ-de-Mars.[9]

The text operates, to some extent, to recuperate what is lost, for the principal males appear in the print's dedication and within its textual explication. In that sense, the text interprets the wider scene, including the presence of a broader populace, for the more literate audience for whom this print was most likely intended. On the other hand, the print stands in marked contrast to various other commemorative engravings of this occasion. In these other panoramas, the crowd is presented from the rear, and the assembled nation of guardsmen and citizens, men and women, are presented facing forward with their full attention directed toward the altar, often with their arms raised in the act of oath-taking.[10] In *View of the Alter*, however, only the uniformed guardsmen and soldiers in the print's distant and middle planes are depicted from the back, with their complete attention focused on the altar and their arms raised in unison. In the foreground, we see a relaxed, mixed crowd of bourgeoisie, clergymen, aristocrats, respectable mothers and their children—a good many of whom are not even attending to the events on the stage but chatting or minding distracted children. A woman of the popular classes twists backward toward two adjacent couples, while her arm directs the attention of these more casual participants toward the altar and the day's solemn events. Nevertheless, the print lacks the didactic intent of many others produced for this occasion, and it even hints at a less than patriotic face of the crowd. Some people might have attended the event because of festive, not political, motives.

Still, the issue remains of how female allegories were deployed within the larger print culture. In marked contrast to female abstractions, real men who achieved publicity could serve as moral examples. They were revered as friends of humanity (Benjamin Franklin, Gabriel Bonnot de Mably), heroic defenders of liberty (Brutus, William Tell), incorruptible leaders during their lifetimes (Robespierre), martyrs after their deaths (Louis-Michel Lepeletier, Jean-Paul Marat), and hallowed *philosophes* (Voltaire, Rousseau). The early public acclamations on behalf of Jacques Necker in the late 1780s; the decision on his death in April 1791 to bury Honoré Gabriel Riqueti, comte de Mirabeau in the newly

Figure 3.2. Louis Le Coeur after Jacques-François Swebach-Desfontaines, *View of the Alter of the Fatherland and of a Part of the Champs-de-Mars at the Moment when Monsieur de Lafayette, in the Name of All the National Guards of France, Swore an Oath to Be Ever Faithful to the Nation, the Law and the King.* 1790. Courtesy of the Uppsala University Library.

created Panthéon or Temple of Immortality; the subsequent transferral of the remains of Voltaire (in July 1791), Marat (in September 1794), and (after Thermidor) Rousseau to the Panthéon in imitation of classical apotheoses[11]; the proliferation of busts of esteemed men in public squares, societies, and assemblies; and the wax cabinet of Philippe Curtius (founder of the Paris waxworks and uncle of Madame Tussaud)[12] were all manifestations of the revolutionary public's impulse to throw up heroes and the revolutionary leadership's desire to instruct citizens in lessons drawn from the lives and deeds of illustrious men.[13]

Even prints of a more caricatural or scatological cast managed to deploy female allegories to glorify the immortalizing accomplishments of an illustrious man. In the radical print *June 21* [*The Triumph of Voltaire* 11 *July* 1791] (Figure 3.3), the philosopher is exalted while the king and the institution of monarchy are desecrated. A cortège with Voltaire's ashes moves toward the Panthéon, created on the site of the former church of Saint-Geneviève in Paris. An irreverent, bare-bottomed Fame trumpets the accomplishments of Voltaire, whose crowned bust appears on a pedestal, as it did on the occasion of the first performance of his play *Brutus* in Paris shortly before his death.[14] Its inscription reminds the audience that *la patrie* recognizes great men.[15] From Fame's rear, another trumpet rings out, its banner reading "*Journée du 21 Juin,*" registering the treasonous flight and ignominious capture of the king at Varennes. The transfer of Voltaire's ashes took place on 11 July 1791—decreed the anniversary of Voltaire's death by the Constituent Assembly on 30 May 1791—just days after the return from Varennes. Thus the two dates of the print highlight the difference between the king and the philosopher. Fame's other banner reads "*Un Roi n'est plus qu'un homme avec un titre auguste. Premier sujet des loix est forcé d'être juste*" ("A king is nothing but a man with an august title. The first subject of the law is forced to be just"). As the events of the king's trial and execution would subsequently affirm, the king had been made to submit to justice like any ordinary citizen.[16] Fame kicks the king's bust from the other pedestal, which reads "*le faux pas*" (the "misstep")—reducing the centuries-long monarchy to a mistake made by the people. The print's inscription reiterates these themes even more caustically, addressing the enemies of the Republic: "*Ce Monstre votre idole horreur du genre humain, Que votre orgueil trompé veut retablir en vain. Tous les vrais Citoyens ont enfin rappellé la liberté publique. Nous ne redoubtons plus le pouvoir tirannique*" ("This monster, your idol, horror of human kind, that your mistaken pride wants in vain to restore. All true citizens have finally restored public liberty. We no longer fear tyrannical power").

Thus, it could be said that great men, in conjunction with female allegories,

Figure 3.3. *June 21* [*The Triumph of Voltaire,* 11 *July* 1791]. Courtesy of the Musée Carnavalet. Copyright Photothèque des musées de la ville de Paris.

helped to fill the void left by the destruction of the sacred body of the king, but with an important difference. To divinity, heretofore the privileged realm of kings and saints, the lay cult of great men counterposed a human and implicitly democratic dimension. By venerating and glorifying mere mortals, the cult promised the rehabilitation of all humans. Freed from their submission to the divine, each individual was confirmed to participate in "the excellence of human nature." Men of letters and legislators, and later heroes and martyrs in military operations, were deemed to be forging the image of a new France and contributing to the foundations of the Republic.[17] As the Marquis de Sade (signing himself "*le citoyen Sade de la section des Piques*") eloquently proclaimed following the deaths of Marat and Lepeletier, "The dearest duty of truly republican hearts is the recognition granted to great men. From the outpouring of this sacred act comes all the virtues necessary to the maintenance and glory of the state."[18] The somber engraving from the 19–26 January 1793 edition of

Figure 3.4. *Honors Rendered to the Memory of Lepeletier.* From *Révolutions de Paris*, no. 185, 19–26 January 1793. Courtesy of the Maclure Collection, Annenberg Rare Book and Manuscript Library, University of Pennsylvania.

the journal *Révolutions de Paris, Honors Rendered to the Memory of Lepeletier* (Figure 3.4), documents the grave ceremony that occurred at the bier of Michel Lepeletier, as men filed past ("*le corps du martyr de la Liberté*") to pay homage to one of the nation's fallen martyrs. In effect, greatness came to reside in the stature achieved by men who could then serve as dignified representatives of the nation.

By their accomplishments, not their birth, men achieved honors.[19] However, these men were not slated to be substitute fathers. As is well recognized, the French arrived at a different resolution to the problem posed by the political and symbolic transferal of power from a monarchical to a republican form of government than did the Americans who conceived of their first president as a new father figure and developed a myth of the nation's "founding fathers."[20] In contrast, French republicans stressed fraternity and equality.[21] In any event, the vagaries of political change, intense political factionalization, and the striking rapidity with which personal reputations rose and fell made any pretensions to real or assumed kingship difficult to achieve in practice.

From our perspective, it is significant that patriotism and the fashioning of a new nation allowed men spaces for the making of a public reputation and afforded them opportunities for public actions in the very arenas in which women's presence was generally becoming less accepted and, in some instances, proscribed—the literary public sphere, the state or political public sphere, and the militias and the army.[22] Because men had the opportunity to act in public and aspire to excellence through their deeds, unlike women they were able to achieve the kind of greatness that public memory celebrates.[23] The Panthéon, created by the new legislators of France to celebrate human (implicitly, masculine) immortality, was intended as a "sanctuary of collective memory, a sanctuary to the nation (*la Patrie*),"[24] and appropriately it was populated by deceased men whose actions and words had won them their place of honor. In sharp contrast, women who acted in public risked achieving not greatness but personal notoriety (Méricourt, Gouges, Roland, du Barry). They came to exemplify the dangers unleashed once women entered the public realm.[25] As for the posthumous heroines of counterrevolutionary myths (Charlotte Corday and Marie-Antoinette), to republicans they symbolized the most appalling consequences of women's participation in the political realm. The paradox was reflected on the level of imagery itself. Just as virtue had its counterpart in corruption within republican thought, the iconography of the female body within revolutionary imagery vacillated between goddesses and grotesques.[26]

Instilling Virtue

> The word *virtue* comes from *strength*. Strength is the foundation of all virtue. Virtue belongs only to a being that is weak by nature and strong by will. . . . Who, then, is the virtuous man? It is he who knows how to conquer his affections; for then he follows his reason and his conscience; he does his duty; he keeps himself in order, and nothing can make him deviate from it.[27]

Etymologically, from its Latin root *vir*, meaning "man," the word *virtue* literally denotes manliness and is associated with valor, worth, strength, force, and energy, as well as, according to Rousseau, self-control and duty. For females, virtue also requires duty and self-control, but it hardly results in the kind of independence, valor, or strength that is masculine by definition. Indeed, the manlike woman or virago from the Latin means both a female warrior and, pejoratively, a noisy, scolding, or domineering woman. As for the virtuous man, he is not expected to be entirely self-sufficient. For republicans, male public virtue required the participation and support not of viragos but of chaste, virtuous women, whose duty was circumscribed by their roles in the private sphere of the household. It is worth recalling that for women and men, virtue meant very different things: chastity, sexual purity, and physical intactness, not moral excellence, goodness, and manly courage. Neither the role of republican mother nor the imagery of female goddess was meant to elicit the kind of public action, including visible displays of physicality, available to men.[28]

Nevertheless, woman's role during the Revolution did not lack public significance, for republican mothers were entrusted with the critical duty of preparing citizens for their part within a virtuous Republic.[29] According to Elke and Hans-Christian Harten, "The natural role of mother widened and made of woman a mother of society" within specially assigned domains of activity: the education of small children, the instruction of daughters, and the organization of charitable activities.[30] The good mother who loved and nourished others became a symbol of the natural order of liberty, equality, and fraternity. Her powers derived from her place in the republican community; her citizenship was anchored in her familial role, and she was offered a central position in the national project of social regeneration. In this respect, family life and public life were very much intertwined.

Moreover, women were afforded the opportunities to play a role on the civic stage of revolutionary public culture. From the earliest days of the Revolution, mothers and wives were celebrated for their contributions to the nation, as when the wives and daughters of artists came forward to contribute their jewels at the bar of the National Assembly ("*l'autel de la patrie*"). The *Revolutions de Paris* engraving *The Beginning of Patriotic Donations, Given to the Nation* (Figure 3.5) documents this event and goes on to praise the women's action for emulating the virtues of ancient Greece and Rome.[31] The popular artists the brothers Lesueur present the theme of women's donation in *Patriotic Club of Women* (Figure 3.6). One woman reads from the *Moniteur*, while another contributes to the patriotic cause. Although the setting is political—a public space in which news is shared and discussed—propriety is the distinguishing mark of these patriotic clubwomen. The artists carefully render these women in a manner that distinguishes them from those Amazonian females who would take to the streets in acts of popular disturbance or perhaps dare to render independent judgments on political affairs.

Although they remained terms of approbation especially among activist women, *female Amazon* and *Amazonianism* were already being widely used during the first year of the Revolution. Like the word virago, Amazon in word and deed carried a double charge. In its issue of 10–17 October 1789, just after the celebrated march on Versailles by market women, the heroic "female Amazons," Louis Prudhomme's *Revolutions de Paris* nonetheless chastised the female journalist and printer Louise de Keralio for Amazonianism.[32] The context was a dispute over free speech, or the right of a journalist to slander public officials, and was dubbed by *Revolutions de Paris* "*l'affaire de M. Marat*" (referring to the public order against Marat for slandering Jacques Necker). Disagreeing with the presentation of the dispute offered by Keralio in her journal of public affairs and charging her with misunderstanding public opinion, *Revolutions de Paris* calls her a "political Amazon" ("*l'amazone politique*") and a "faulty reasoner." Women are said to lack the capacity for abstract thought, especially of a political sort: "The Marat affair has given us the opportunity to know a true political phenomenon: a political journal written by a woman. Until now it was said that women understood no other metaphysics than that of love; but Mme de Keralio has proved by the title of her journal that the most

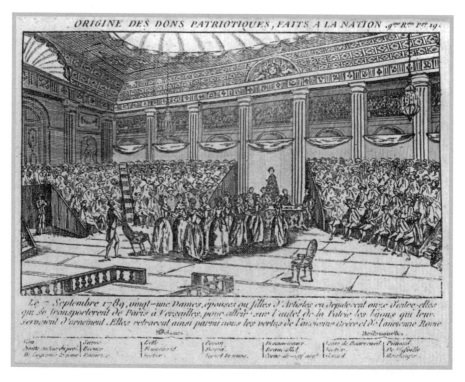

Figure 3.5. *The Beginning of Patriotic Donations, Given to the Nation.* 1789. Paris: Imprimerie des Révolutions de Paris, no. 9. Courtesy of the Uppsala University Library.

difficult abstractions do not frighten her. Her title is of that sort of metaphysics that borders on obscurity: it is *le journal d'état et du citoyen* [The Journal of the State and the Citizen]."[33]

In the context of a heightening anxiety about women's political involvement, the two prints under discussion present a tame and judicious image of early female citizenship. They accentuate the virtues of female self-restraint and sacrifice for the national cause. Yet another print, *Patriotic Donations by the Ladies* (Figure 3.7), is even more direct in defining women's patriotic duties, stating, "Oh, bravo, Mesdames, it's now your turn." The man and old woman to the left seem intent on seeing that these women of good birth also carry out their responsibilities to the nation. Even if the benefits of citizenship were not evenly distributed, women were never intended to be exempt from its duties.

Figure 3.6. Lesueur brothers, *Patriotic Club of Women*. ca. 1791. Courtesy of the Musée Carnavalet. Copyright Photothèque des musées de la ville de Paris.

As this print underscores, women were expected to sacrifice for the national cause.[34] Certainly, donation reiterates the familiar Catholic custom of good works, whether contributing to the collection plate or giving alms on behalf of the poor. In contrast to involvement in the universal Church or within the local community, however, patriotic donation was predicated on participation in the highly esteemed work of national regeneration.[35] Donation as a practice of female citizenship—a private act (generosity) endowed with public significance—accorded well with the institution of republican motherhood. Nothing about donation, or so it appeared, threatened to disturb women's primary responsibilities as mothers and wives.

Yet women did interpret the call to act on the public's behalf in broader, sometimes even violent ways, and the figure of the heroic Amazon threatened to upset men's efforts to restrain women's conduct. As Dominique Godineau affirms, "Women wanted to be female citizens: the word *citoyenne* recurs constantly in pamphlets by women. In these revolutionary times, the word was not

Figure 3.7. *Patriotic Donations by the Ladies.* ca. 1791. Courtesy of the Musée Carnavalet. Copyright Photothèque des musées de la ville de Paris.

restricted to the neutral meaning of the inhabitant of a country. Under women's pens, it resounded with civic sentiments, sometimes as the demand for rights, but more often, it was primarily when stating the duties of citizens that women, timid and prudent, tried to insert in the political space opened by the Revolution that strange individual, a female citizen without citizenship."[36] Between 1789 and the repression against women that occurred in the fall of 1793, women sought on many occasions to enact a broader definition of civic virtue and to expand the meaning of female citizenship.[37] In a series of proposals to the Confédération des Amis de la Vérité, Etta Palm d'Aelders advocated for women's rights (the elimination of primogeniture, protection against wife beating, the passage of a comprehensive divorce bill, and political equality for women); a system of clubs to care for and educate children, especially the offspring of destitute women; and free clinics and work for indigent women. Palm d'Aelders used the rhetoric of bourgeois propriety, including fears of moral disorder, on behalf of women's enlarged civic involvement, especially in welfare work.[38]

Even more destabilizing were women's proposals to arm themselves. In July 1791, according to *Revolutions de France et de Brabant*, "at Bordeaux, four thousand *citoyennes*, mothers of families, having at their head a Madame Courpon, wife of a major in the national guard, met on the champ-de-Mars; and there, reunited with *la patrie*, they vowed to die for the defense of the nation and the law."[39] In Paris and elsewhere in the nation, women's demands escalated in the period of growing political radicalization between autumn of 1791 and the overthrow of monarchy on 10 August 1792.[40] On 6 March 1792, the activist Pauline Léon proposed organizing a women's militia for defense of their homes against aristocrats, and presented a petition to the Legislative Assembly with more than three hundred signatures to that effect.[41] A report by the *Journal de Perlet* about a request by *citoyennes* to carry arms with pikes and perform exercises on the Champ de la Fédération suggests that the women had a clear and gendered notion of domestic and external space: "While external enemies meet their death under the fire of their husbands, they will save the interior of the empire from the blows that are delivered, with much skill, by instigators of troubles who throw mistrust and disorder into the midst of the citizens that such a cause has reunited."[42] Théroigne de Méricourt followed up these demands with a call to female citizens to organize themselves in army corps, and four months later eighty female citizens of the Hôtel de Ville section again demanded that the Legislative Assembly decree that "true female citizens" be armed.[43] In April, a group of female petitioners demanded for their sex the full enjoyment of natural rights, denied by long oppression, and asked that women be admitted to civic employment and the military and requested the granting of the right to divorce, in compensation for their long and amiable suffering under conjugal tyranny.[44] In festivals held during the spring 1792, pike-bearing *citoyennes*, often also carrying children, marched alongside men as patriotic mothers, daughters, and wives.

Moreover, in the critical juncture of revolution and national mobilization for war through the spring and summer of 1792, women were active participants in popular uprisings, including the journées of 20 June and 10 August, which culminated in the fall of the monarchy. In the spring of 1793, Pauline Léon and Claire Lacombe founded the Society for Revolutionary Republican Women, a political club for women, with the aim of forming an armed body of women. The society took an active role in the insurrection of 31 May to 2 June that led to the ousting of the Girondins from the National Convention. Although women's active involvement in political affairs was suppressed in the fall of 1793, they were present in dramatic crises over food shortages and political turmoil at least as late as the uprisings of Germinal and Prairial Year III. The engraving *French Women [Who] Have Become Free* (Figure 3.8) captures the attitude of these politically assertive women. The woman's cap bears the tricolor cockade, and she carries a pike inscribed with the motto "Liberty or Death." A medal on her tricolor waistband is inscribed with the motto "Libertas Hastata Victrix! 14 Juillet" ("Liberty [when she is] armed with her pike [is] victorious! 14 July"). As Darline Gay Levy and Harriet B. Applewhite speculate, regarding another version of this image, "Contemporaries may have associated this figure either with Pauline Léon who had publicly expressed her determination to fight, pike in hand, during the *journée* of August 10, or with her equally militant friend, Claire Lacombe, whom the fédérés decorated with a tricolor sash for her role during this *journée*."[45]

There is also evidence that among militant women, a woman's political actions could earn her public acclaim. At a session of the Society of Revolutionary Republican Women, a male observer reports that "femme Monic" spoke of biblical, ancient, and contemporary examples of women in arms. They included "the colony of Amazons whose existence has been cast into doubt because of people's jealousy of women" and the "*citoyennes* of Lille who, at this moment, are braving the rage of assailants, and while laughing, are defusing the bombs being cast into the city." Monic applauded women's involvement in the storming of the Bastille, the October Days, and the second revolution of 10 August, stating,

FRANCAISES DEVENUES LIBRES.

.... Et nous aussi, nous savons combattre et vaincre.
Nous savons manier d'autres armes que l'aiguille et le fuseau. O Bellone !
compagne de Mars, a ton exemple, toutes les femmes ne devroient-elles pas
marcher de front et d'un pas égal avec les hommes ? Déesse de la force et
du courage ! du moins tu n'auras point à rougir des *FRANCAISES*.

Extrait d'une Priere des Amazones à Bellone

De la Collection Générale des Caricatures sur la Révolution Française de 1789.

Paris chez Villeneuve *Graveur,* rue Zacharie, *St. Severin Maison de Passage* No. 21.

Figure 3.8. *French Women [Who] Have Become Free.* 1792. Courtesy of the Musée
Carnavalet. Copyright Photothèque des musées de la ville de Paris.

In 1788, during the siege of the Palais, women exposed themselves to the brutality of soldiers hired by the court, in order to hail stones down upon them. At the storming of the Bastille, women familiar only with fireworks exposed themselves to cannon and musket fire on the ramparts to bring ammunition to the assailants. It was a battalion of women, commanded by the brave Reine Audu, who went to seek the despot at Versailles and led him triumphantly back to Paris, after having battled the arms of the *gardes-du-corps* and made them put them down. In spite of the modesty of our president [Claire Lacombe, the day's presiding officer], she marched valiantly against the château, at the head of a corps of Fédérés; she still bears the marks of that day.[46]

Yet the male observers attending this session do not so much dispute the women's heroism as ridicule it. Pierre Alexis Roussel reports that he and his companion, the English Lord Bedford, found the proceedings, as well as the women's demands to be full political subjects, to be both grotesque and hilarious. He speaks of having to suppress his laughter. As Roussel's response displays, ridicule was one of the most important tactics that revolutionary authorities used to defuse and finally repress women's claims to political power and citizenship.

Ultimately, it was not the figure of the armed woman but rather a more modest domestic role that won the day in republican circles. In 1791, the women citizens of Clermont-Ferrand wrote to the French National Assembly, "We see to it that our children drink an incorruptible milk and we clarify it for that purpose with the natural and agreeable spirit of liberty."[47] The maternal role was featured in revolutionary festivals. Thus, in the Festival of the Supreme Being designed by Jacques-Louis David, participating women were presented as chaste mothers. In Year II a law regarding national festivals was proposed to the Convention; in this proposal, nursing mothers would occupy first place behind the officials. When they had enough children, they would be awarded a medal bearing the inscription "I have nurtured them for the fatherland—the fatherland gives thanks to fertile mothers".[48] The Convention took seriously the need to legislate on the issue of maternal duty, decreeing on 28 June 1793 that if a mother did not nurse her child, she and the child would not be eligible for the state support offered to indigent families. As for unmarried mothers, it was decided that "every girl who declares that she wants to nurse the child she is carrying, and who has need of the help of the nation, will have the right to claim it."[49] Carrying on the theme, in his 1793 utopia *La Constitution de la lune. Rêve politique et moral*, the author Louis Abel Beffroy de Reigny imagined a "register of honor" for women who had nursed their own babies; after four children, they could receive a "certificate of honor." Similarly, in the utopia of a "natural" republic imagined by Guillaume René Le Fébure, women obtained, for each child that they had breastfed themselves, an insignia in the form of a pineapple (but without a leaf if the child, despite everything, had not survived to its first year).[50] As Marilyn Yalom states, "Nursing was no longer a private matter with ramifications only for the infant and its family. It had become, as Rousseau had hopefully envisioned, a collective manifestation of civic duty."[51]

The theme of motherhood is also presented iconographically as a politically salient symbol of reformed manners and family life in the new political order. Numerous instances of mothers are to be found in revolutionary prints, either in small domestic tableaux—most typically, nursing small babies, but also minding children—or incorporated into crowd scenes, especially the celebrations of various festivals. The colored etching *Festival Celebrated in Honor of the Supreme Being, 20 Prairial Year 2 of the Republic: The True Priest of the Supreme Being Is Nature* (Figure 3.9) is an allegory of the people in relation to the values of the Republic. The people are represented not by one figure—as in the early revolutionary imagery where, as we saw in Chapter 2, a sansculotte might embody the third estate or the people—but by a family group (man, woman, and three children) depicted paying homage to the figures of Nature and Republic. Under the auspices of the Supreme Being in the shape of the level of equality surrounding an all-seeing eye, the beneficent goddesses bestow their favor on present and future generations of the French citizenry.[52] Both women and men are shown in relation to their duty to the family, but only women were expected to devote themselves entirely to the latter. While her husband gazes at Nature and Republic, his wife attends to her children.

Revolutionaries dreamed of a republican mother, capable of banishing her own vanity, passions, and self-interests in the name of her children and the nation. However, the very doctrine of republican motherhood, which celebrated female goodness, cannot be understood apart from republicans' suspicions of women and female nature and their anxiety about female independence in both the public and private spheres, including the possibility that the latter would result in women's sacrifice of family interest. These attitudes owe much to Jean-Jacques Rousseau's vision of a reformed society. In Rousseau's estimation, the "good" man acts spontaneously, not through strength or self-control. However, he opined that only outside society were goodness, sincerity, and spontaneity truly possible; civilization corrupted man's natural goodness and undermined the possibility for solidarity.[53] As a substitute for natural goodness,

FÊTE CÉLÉBRÉE EN L'HONNEUR DE L'ÊTRE SUPRÊME.
Le 20 Prairiale l'an 2.me de la Rep.

Le véritable Prêtre de l'Être suprême, c'est la Nature, son temple l'Univers, son Culte la Vérité, ses fêtes la joye d'un grand Peuple rassemblé pour resserer les doux noeuds de la Fraternité, et Jurer la mort des Tirans.

Figure 3.9. *Festival Celebrated in Honor of the Supreme Being, 20 Prairial Year 2 of the Republic: The True Priest of the Supreme Being Is Nature.* 1794. Courtesy of the Bibliothèque nationale de France.

he advocated for the rule of law, justice, and morality. Yet even inside civilization, Rousseau held out considerably more hope for the goodness of common folk, isolated men, savages, and free peasants; he placed women, along with aristocrats and city dwellers, among the worst examples that corrupt, civilized existence had to offer.[54]

As Rousseau taught his followers, without women's participation and support, the prospect for a democratic, virtuous community was dim indeed; at the same time, however, he doubted woman's loyalty and morality. Of the two sexes, Rousseau deemed women to be the more desiring, men the more passionate. Only in men does reason operate as the true governor of the passions. The case of women is considerably more complex, perhaps even contradictory. On the one hand, Rousseau proposed that in women modesty and shame rather than reason operate to brake unlimited desires.[55] On the other hand, he deemed women's sexuality to be a rudimentary source of rational control and judgment. In his estimation, "Women's judgment is formed earlier than men's. Since almost from infancy women are on the defensive and entrusted with a treasure that is difficult to protect, good and evil are necessarily known to them sooner."[56]

Alluding to women's empire in the family, Rousseau attributed to nature the role of arming the weak with modesty and shame "in order to enslave the strong." Dictating that men "ought to be active and strong," women "passive and weak," he nonetheless feared that women would fall easily into dissipation, frivolity, inconstancy, and all manner of corruption.[57] The unfaithful woman is more than a weak member of the social community; she threatens its continued existence. According to Rousseau, "She dissolves the family and breaks all the bonds of nature. In giving the man children which are not his, she betrays both. She joins perfidy to infidelity."[58] Therefore, Rousseau proposed a different, more severe course for women's education from men's. He advocated subjecting girls early on to strict discipline and constraint, because they (unlike men) would have to learn to live for reputation and opinion. He prescribed rules of decorum and propriety for everything from appearance to conduct. Woman's duty is to be tied to the family, her purpose to the tasks of reproducing and nurturing children.

Accordingly, Rousseau believed that a girl must be taught vigilance and industry in the service of passivity and malleability. He surmised that "from this habitual constraint comes a docility which women need all their lives, since they never cease to be subjected either to a man or to the judgments of men."[59] Through discipline—above all, a kind of bodily discipline dictating her appearance as well as her behavior toward others, premised on her confinement to certain appropriate social spaces—woman's (purportedly) ideal "nature" is socially constructed. Starting from the premises of sexual difference, women's greater desires and hence their sexual dependency, Rousseau aimed to lay the groundwork for women's social dependence and their sexual captivity in the family. By this avenue, women would come to achieve their highest virtues— decency and chastity.

Virtue Embodied

In revolutionary iconography, the traits of proper, chaste, natural woman-hood are transposed onto a larger canvas that is populated by a series of antique goddesses representing woman's natural goodness rather than her social virtue through motherhood. As a result, motherhood is magnified and glorified— stripped of its mundane, ultimately conventional character—by its association with the antique past and a future, regenerated Republic. Classical female bod-ies bore the names of Liberty, Republic, Victory, Philosophy, Reason, Nature, and Truth. They functioned to instruct all of the public on the cardinal virtues of republican France: unity, fraternity, equality, and brotherly love. Occasion-ally, however, they attested to the special virtues of women: modesty and chastity.

The print *Equality* (Figure 3.10) fuses several independent iconographical symbols and syncretically joins concrete references to French political liberty with universal motifs. A seated allegory of Equality holds her own emblem, a carpenter's level, here suspended from a tricolored ribbon, the symbol of the new French nation. She echoes Renaissance representations of Justice holding the scales. Equality is represented wearing a Phrygian cap embroidered with a cockade, another emphatic reference to Liberty and Republic. She embraces a tablet of the laws, engraved with the articles of the Declaration of the Rights of Man and Citizen. A small figurine accompanies Equality, a multibreasted, crowned Diana, whose pedestal is wrapped in oak leaves, grapes, and gourds— evoking associations to fertility, the harvest, and social regeneration.[60]

In the print *Fraternity* (Figure 3.11), the goddess Fraternity is represented as the protector of two small children or cupids—one white, the other black— whose mutual affection is sealed with a kiss. Fraternity is dressed in antique robes with a tricolor sash; one breast is revealed, as in classical sculpture but also as a reminder of the emphasis that revolutionaries following Rousseau placed on the breast as an organ of maternal care, not female vanity.[61] Around her head she wears a garland of oak leaves, the mark of rebirth and social virtue, and holds a double heart in her hand, a borrowed reference to Christian love

L'ÉGALITÉ.

Figure 3.10. Chez Deny, *Equality*. Courtesy of the Musée Carnavalet.
Copyright Photothèque des musées de la ville de Paris.

and charity. The embracing, naked children step on a multiheaded serpent, a
reminder of the old despotic order, which they will supplant through their natural innocence and brotherly love.

   The goddess in *Nature* (Figure 3.12) nurses an infant on each breast. These
two children of separate races represent the harmonious future of a republic in
peaceful union with the principles of nature, a republic wherein all subjects
will be equal. Nature wears a garland headdress of laurel leaves, flowers, and

Figure 3.11. Antoine Carré, after Claude-Louis Desrais, *Fraternity*. ca. 1794.
Courtesy of the Musée Carnavalet. Copyright Photothèque des musées de
la ville de Paris.

vegetables. She is surrounded by other symbols of the harvest—fruits and vegetables abound. To her rear, a grapevine grows and a mountain rises—symbol
of the Montagnard faction in the Convention. Despite her repose, she is an
emblem of the radical revolution and its regenerative ambitions. In the context
of the struggle against slavery in French colonies, the incorporation of a black

Figure 3.12. Chez Basset, *Nature*. ca. 1794. Courtesy of the Musée Carnavalet. Copyright Photothèque des musées de la ville de Paris.

child in Figures 3.10 and 3.11 symbolizes the Republic's claims to nurse all her children, black and white, and to stand for universal freedom.

Modesty (Figure 3.13) addresses directly the women subjects of the new regime and evinces the revolutionaries' high regard for female chastity and propriety. She sits in a reserved pose, demurely defending her honor. She is veiled and fully garbed; her dress rises to the collarbone (no peeking breasts here!). She holds up a branch of lilies, a further reference to her purity and her spiritual transcendence, while stepping on a turtle, sign of material existence and

Figure 3.13. Chez Basset, *Modesty*. ca. 1794. Courtesy of the Musée Carnavalet. Copyright Photothèque des musées de la ville de Paris.

possibly also female sexuality.[62] Both her costume and her lily—an emblem of purity and an attribute of the Virgin Mary in medieval Christian iconography—attest to this anonymous artist's redeployment of Christian attitudes toward female sexuality within a republican vocabulary.

Philosophy Uncovering Truth (Figure 3.14) exploits an allegorical trope that is well established in eighteenth-century iconography. For example, an image of the unveiling of truth by Reason with the help of Philosophy, all feminine allegories, also appeared on the frontispiece to Denis Diderot and Jean Le Rond d'Alembert's *Encyclopédie,* designed by the artist Charles Nicolas Cochin (coauthor, with Hubert François Gravelot, of the *Iconologie* that was so influential in the 1790s).[63] Here Philosophy stands not just for a human attribute or the cognitive process by which appearances are pierced but in particular for the greatness of one man's, Rousseau's, unique contribution to the unveiling of truth. Philosophy holds a torch and lifts the veil from Truth, who is depicted naked to the waist. Truth stomps on a satyr's head, signifying the end to an era of superstition and lies. She holds a mirror with her left hand, a reference to the study of appearances, which leads to the knowledge of essences. Also, she looks straight ahead, in a posture of pure transparency, refusing to look at her own image in the glass, as would those vain women against whom Rousseau railed. In her right hand, Truth supports a tablet engraved with the title of Rousseau's major work of political philosophy, Du *contrat social.* Other explicit references to Rousseau appear throughout the print. A bust of the esteemed philosopher appears on the wall, and two books lie in the foreground, one open to the title page of the *Emile.* Finally, on the floor is a multibreasted Diana of the Ephesians—a reference to nature's bounty and beneficence and to the generative power of republican virtue.

The print *Victory, to the Shades of Lepeletier and Marat* (Figure 3.15) celebrates the immortal spirits of two martyred republican heroes, Louis-Michel Lepeletier and Jean-Paul Marat—the former assassinated on the day after he voted for the king's death, the latter the victim of the female assassin Charlotte Corday in July 1793. Both men's bodies were placed in the Panthéon, the site of those the Republic deemed worthy of immortality, although given the quickly changing politics of the period, it was not easy to guarantee permanent mortality for the Revolution's heroes. Lepeletier only resided there until the overthrow of Robespierre and his allies on 9 Thermidor Year II (July 27, 1794), and Marat did not receive these honors until after the collapse of the Jacobin dictatorship. At his death, Marat's corpse was wrapped in a wet sheet and exposed before burial at the Cordelier courtyard, and his heart was interred at the Luxembourg Gardens. As planner of these events, Jacques-Louis David insisted that "his burial would have the simplicity appropriate for an incorruptible republican."[64] This print is one of numerous republican images of "manes"—a Roman term for the shades or spirits of dead ancestors and godlike men—in which the realistically rendered portrait-heads of the new immortals are placed in a cameo medallion, accompanied by revolutionary

Figure 3.14. Jean-Baptiste Gautier, after Boiseau, *Philosophy Uncovering Truth*. ca. 1794. Courtesy of the Musée Carnavalet. Copyright Photothèque des musées de la ville de Paris.

symbols and larger-than-life goddesses. Winged Victory alludes to their spiritual worth. She carries her two attributes of fulfillment and exaltation, the palm and a crown. The laurel leafed crown also signifies the dead martyrs' rebirth and social virtue. Victory's palm grows out of a representation of the mountain, the symbol of the Jacobin movement, which is further decorated with laurel leaves and on which the medallion is perched.

The presence of the goddess Victory in this image affirms the revolutionaries' faith in their cause despite the abhorrent deeds of the Republic's enemies. The eye in Victory's necklace, an Egyptian-derived Masonic symbol, testifies to her role in watching over these divine souls and guarding against the Republic's enemies. Ironically, the assassinations of Marat and Lepeletier signified their purity and innate goodness and further raised their stature among revolutionary publics. Moreover, in the logic of war and the Terror, their deaths attested to the presence of evil within the Republic, confirmed the need to purge

Figure 3.15. Chez Basset, *Victory, to the Shades of Lepeletier and Marat.* ca. 1793. Courtesy of the Musée Carnavalet. Copyright Photothèque des musées de la ville de Paris.

the republican body politic, and impressed on the people the necessity of re-maining forever vigilant.[65] Revolutionaries distinguished the people, who were closer to nature and less depraved, from their enemies. As Robespierre postu-lated, "I tell you that I have understood this great moral and political truth an-nounced by Jean-Jacques, that men never sincerely love anyone who does not love them, that *le peuple* alone is good, just, and magnanimous and that cor-ruption and tyranny are the exclusive appanage of those who disdain *le peuple*."[66]

Victory, like her sister goddesses, is of course an abstraction. In contrast, the immortals are dignified, committed, and honorable men, martyrs of lib-erty. She is female; they are male. She is anonymous; they possess personalities. She is eternal; they have earned their right to an apotheosis. Because of their heroic and virtuous actions, their words and their deeds, Lepeletier and Marat have been elevated to the (republican) heavens populated not by formerly liv-ing women but by deities. The embodiments of virtue in republican visual im-agery, like the public and private life to which republicans aspired, were strongly differentiated on the basis of sex. Men achieved the public celebrity and personal honors accorded to a person who had lived a just life.[67] Even a male child of thirteen could be celebrated as a martyr-hero of the Republic and, as shown in *Bara Crowned by Liberty* (Figure 3.16), be crowned by a fe-male deity.[68] Women, too, were expected to be virtuous, but their virtue was linked to their idealized role within the family, and the display of virtuous womanhood required a posture of modesty, propriety, and respectable silence in both the public and private domain. Consequently, the attention that a woman drew to herself could be taken to be a sign of her immorality or im-modesty, and a symptom of the menace posed to social order by the presence of women acting (out) in public.

The presence of allegorical females in images praising real men raises yet another issue concerning women's power to judge—and thereby affirm or cast aspersions on—male honor. These goddesses all appear to be watching male actions. In this regard, the allegorical female operates as a substitute or positive reversal for women's gossip.[69] They are mute, but they signify, unlike the lo-quacious Parisian women condemned by Rousseau for their "inexhaustible gossiping."[70] Both the goddess and the gossip judge honor, but the force of one is positive, the other negative. Moreover, the gossip is one who has free rein in the community. Her words spread calumny. Her actions presume an ability to violate the boundaries of respectability, to pass easily between—and pass judg-ment on—public and private matters. Her knowledge is enhanced by an abil-ity to see what is best not seen, to speak about what is best not spoken—especially, if the reputations of men are to be preserved. Unlike the goddess,

Figure 3.16. André Boissier, *Bara Crowned by Liberty*. ca. 1794. Courtesy of the Uppsala University Library.

she is no guardian of manners: She lives to find out and disseminate the hypocrisy of those who violate the codes they pronounce upon.

Manners, in effect, meant everything for the ongoing republican struggle against corruption, and women's manners—their behavior and their appearance—were a certain sign of either their pure or fallen (because "public" and open) character. For this reason, no doubt, Rousseau had insisted, "It is important, then, not only that a woman be faithful, but that she be judged to be faithful by her husband, by those near her, by everyone. It is important that she be modest, attentive, reserved, and that she give evidence of her virtue to the eyes of others as well as to her own conscience. If it is important that a father love his children, it is important that he esteem their mother. These are the reasons which put even appearances among the duties of women, and make honor and reputation not less indispensable to them than chastity."[71]

In the aftermath of the crisis provoked by Marat's assassination in July 1793, women suffered a definite setback in their efforts to become full citizens of the Republic. In the summer and autumn months, Parisians witnessed the public executions of Charlotte Corday, Olympe de Gouges, Marie-Antoinette, Madame Roland, and Madame du Barry; women's clubs and societies were banned; and thereafter women were barred from fully participating in the revolutionary public sphere. Whereas women might continue to receive honors in republican festivals as mothers of the nation en masse, their representation as abstract beings within republican imagery affirmed the more indirect, passive role to which they were increasingly being assigned in the public sphere of the democratic Republic. Paradoxically, the preferred private and confined role for women was predicated on a new political definition of private life and on disciplinary efforts devoted to making women virtuous. Not surprisingly, doubts were raised about whether and how successfully women could be made to conform to their ideal status. In the upheaval of revolutionary politics, therefore, grotesque characterizations of women spoke to a deep-seated anxiety about women's public role. They also expressed republicans' Manichaean desires to expel all evil, to view their enemies as engaged in plots and conspiracies aimed at overturning the good Republic and its virtuous citizens. In marked contrast to *Patriotic Club of Women* (Figure 3.6), Chérieux's [*Club of Women Patriots in a Church*] (Figure 3.17) captures the repulsion felt by solemn men when faced with the independent political action of women.[72] The artist portrays the women as overly excited, excessive in their postures, and doubtful in their morality. Bearing shrewish faces and gestures, their breasts lewdly exposed, these political women are shown immodestly stretching their hands (even their bodies) to be recognized as speakers or to register their agreement and disagreement with other speakers. They are reading, writing, and speaking (in public), and one could even be a man dressed as a woman. In contrast to the women's state of frenzied exposure, a series of men line the borders of the church: All are well-robed and composed in their demeanor. The contrast is obvious—women lose all their femininity, perhaps even their sex, while men retain their gravity and disinterested posture in the political arena.

Virtue's Enemies

Never has a people perished from an excess of wine; all perish from the disorder of women.[73]

Womankind—the everlasting irony [in the life] of the community—changes by intrigue the universal end of government into a private end.[74]

Alongside the pure and chaste allegories of virtue, grotesque caricatures abounded in the Revolution's satirical print culture and were certainly directed as much, if not more often, against male as female enemies. Still, the female grotesque or monster loomed large in the patriot imagination, compounded by the links that were made between aristocracy, monstrosity, and femininity. Monstrosity by definition blurred the lines between male and female, human and animal. According to its bizarre logic, the excessive traits of the female grotesque could be applied to any object of scorn and derision. In any event, by focusing on female grotesques we may better understand how the polarization of female virtue and vice worked within the visual rhetoric of the period, and how artists exploited the charged association between female sexuality and the public display of femininity.

Female grotesques belonged to those groups that patriots deemed to be the most likely enemies of the French Republic: aristocrats, members of the royal family, the clergy, émigrés and their foreign protectors. Yet women of the lower classes were also liable to be depicted as grotesques, and not only by counter-revolutionary artists and polemicists.[75] The Lesueur brothers' image of *The Jacobin Knitters* (*Les Tricoteuses jacobines*) (Figure 3.18) captures the growing disease occasioned by revolutionary women's actions. Seen from the good patriot's vantage point, the *tricoteuse* is a dissembler. These women are only pretending to be involved in their proper domestic tasks. Tellingly, their eyes are cast outside the frame—according to the emerging stereotype, toward the violent spectacle of the guillotine. One woman (the most off-putting of the

Figure 3.17. Chérieux, [*Club of Women Patriots in a Church*]. ca. 1793. Courtesy of the Bibliothèque nationale de France.

group) has abandoned her knitting altogether, and glares off into the distance. Like the Old Regime theatrical spectators, so distrusted by Rousseau, these shrews only appear to be good. Their "interest-ed" looks tell another story that the truly virtuous citizen can read. Indeed, patriotic men (like their enemies) looked on with horror when women violently cast themselves "outside their sex" and defied the gendered boundaries separating public from private life.[76] In that instance, lower-class women recapitulated many of the crimes associated with aristocratic femininity.[77]

As we have seen, popular artists of the revolutionary era drew upon the classical repertoire of female allegories. The latter possessed well-proportioned bodies and incorporated long-established ideals of female beauty. These goddesses pointed to the spiritual, transcendent, and permanent aspects of human existence. In contrast, grotesques embodied women's base, material, and changeable attributes.[78] Rather than using the female form to represent more universal, nonsexual values, those who created images of the female grotesque called attention to women's most immediate, physical characteristics. Hence, the grotesque body was likely to be open and protruding (available for sexual pleasure; focused on the mouth, nose, stomach, or sexual organs), debased (monstrous and animal-like), subject to change (aged, pregnant, too large or too thin), and transgressive (of heterosexual object choices and behaviors). The female grotesque drew attention to the long-standing iconographic tradition of representing all evil—including discord, enmity, license, vengeance, and

Figure 3.18. Lesueur brothers, *The Jacobin Knitters*. Courtesy of the Musée Carnavalet. Copyright Photothèque des Musées de la ville de Paris.

anarchy—in the figure of a hideous female body. An early revolutionary print is illustrative of these multiple associations. *The King with His Minister Breaking the Chains of the Third Estate. Discord Takes Flight* (Figure 3.19) shows the king and Jacques Necker lifting the burdens of the third estate, who curtsies in gratitude, while Discord takes to flight. Accordingly, three men—two extraordinary, one ordinary and emblematic, as the anonymous commoner is meant to stand for all his countrymen whose freedom is being granted by his benefactors—are this image's visual focus. In contrast, the one female (an allegory) is portrayed with medusan locks, a dagger in hand, wings, and pendulous breasts. The image is characteristic of the way in which visual representations of female grotesques exploited the strong ambivalence toward public women, which was a persistent theme in republicanism. Such depictions disclosed at the level of the body the very disorder and intrigue that sexually avaricious and politically ambitious women of the Old Regime had been accused of promoting.

Trials and executions aside, no member of the royal family was subjected to the same level of excoriating criticism as Marie Antoinette. The queen was an early target of court satires circulated first among the nobility. Already by the mid-1780s, she began to appear in text and image as a female harpy, and the scandalous pamphlet literature leading up to the Revolution circulated rumors about her voracious sexual appetites, including her taste for women. Rather than subsiding, attacks on the queen escalated dramatically in the first years of the Revolution, as patriot journalists and engravers found new cause for complaint—a cause well beyond the charges leveled against the queen by noble critics of the royal family or pornographic satirists.[79] A print from 1789 attributed to Villeneuve, *M.me *** Laspict* (Figure 3.20), places the queen's head on the body of a monstrous female harpy.[80] A description from the *Petit journal du Palais Royal* from the summer of 1789 demonstrates, according to Antoine de Baecque, how the various parts of the queen's body came to be monstrously assembled to recompose the aristocratic statue in its morphologic entirety: "A magnificent bronze statue excites the liveliest admiration because of its singular composition. It has the head of a woman, the body of a harpy, the pudenda of a cat, the talons of an eagle, and the tail of a pig; it has been noted that the facial features are very similar to those of Marie-Antoinette, Queen of France."[81] Additionally, in the same year, Marie-Antoinette began to be cast as a "female monster" of Austrian origin named Iscariot (an anagram for aristocrat and a reference to the biblical figure Judas Iscariot). Iscariot's serpent hair and red locks were meant to elicit a public protest against the "Antoinette-Méduse" or the "Rousse Royale."[82]

Figure 3.19. Antoine Sergent, *The King with His Minister Breaking the Chains of the Third Estate. Discord Takes Flight.* ca. 1789. Courtesy of the Bibliothèque nationale de France.

The use of animal metaphors and monstrous imagery in the pamphlet literature directed against Marie-Antoinette reached a feverish pitch in the republican campaign unleashed by the royal family's unsuccessful flight and capture at Varennes in June 1791.[83] As noted in Chapter 2, she was now portrayed as a panther or hell-cat, a pig or a hyena, most often identified by her two visual trademarks: snaky medusan hair and ostrich feathers to mark her Austrian heritage.[84] *The Austrian She-Panther, in Her Most Distant Posterity, Sworn to Contempt and Abomination for the French Nation* (Figure 3.21), and its accompanying text, says it best. The queen appears as a mixture of all of the basest accusations in one hyperbolic fantasy of degradation and impurity bordering on nineteenth-century racist doctrine: "this dreadful Messalina, fruit of one of the most licentious and illicit couplings (concubinage), composed of heterogeneous matter, fabricated from several races, part Lorraine, German, Austrian, Bohemian." Her fiery tresses are also related to those of Judas, her nose and cheek is said to be bloated and made purple by corrupt blood and her mouth fetid and infected. From being a foreigner, suspected of betraying the nation, she has become a foreign body—an impure mix of races, the fruit of one of the century's most licentious and immoral unions. She is reduced to a sordid composition of heterogeneous material. Her royal stock is entirely discredited; she is allied with base materiality. As the *Moniteur universel* (the Revolution's most important journal of record) stated following her execution, in a less hyperbolic but no less blunt fashion, "Marie-Antoinette . . . was a bad mother, a debauched wife, and she died under the curses of those she wanted to destroy."[85]

Figure 3.20. Attributed to Villeneuve, *M.me *** Laspict.* ca. 1789. Courtesy of the Bibliothèque nationale de France.

The attacks on the queen are striking examples of the vigorous assaults leveled by republicans against all female aristocrats. Because in republican discourse hers was a corrupted, degenerate, and bestial female body, it is not surprising that representations of aristocracy easily appropriated attributes of monstrous femininity, and, of course, the queen herself was not the only female target of the prerevolutionary libels. As Robert Darnton has established,

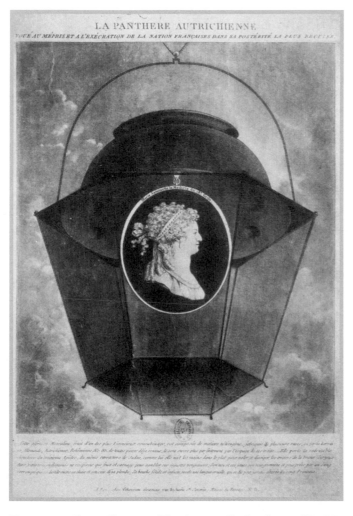

Figure 3.21. Chez Villeneuve, *The Austrian She-Panther, in Her Most Distant Posterity, Sworn to Contempt and Abomination for the French Nation.* ca. 1792. Courtesy of the Uppsala University Library.

Anecdotes sur Mme la Comtesse du Barry (1775) was one of the "supreme best-sellers" of the prerevolutionary era—and it is of no small consequence that its subject, Louis XV's mistress, was a woman who, like Marie Antoinette after her, had intimate access to the body of the king.[86] Low instead of high-born, however, du Barry was tarred with having slept her way from the brothel to the throne, and in the process she contributed heartily (or, should we say, "bodily") to the desacralization of the monarchy. The author of *Les Fastes de Louis XV* (1782), another scandalous pamphlet of Louis XV's monarchy, credits Madame de Pompadour with reigning over "an abyss for innocence and simplicity which swallowed up throngs of victims and then spat them back into society, in which they carried corruption and the taste for debauchery and vices that necessarily infected them in such a place." Under the influence of Madame du Barry, writes Sarah Maza, "the king's sceptre, a plaything in turn for love, ambition, and avarice became in the hands of the countess the rattle wielded by folly."[87]

Republican artists gleefully played upon the association between political freedom and sexual liberty, between dress and undress in their attacks on the aristocracy. *Aristocratic Woman* (Figure 1.6), depicting an old woman in a state of disrobing ("thanks to the Constitution, we will soon go without our skirts [*sans-jupon*]"), is an example of this visual and political wordplay. She lifts her skirt, in grotesque mimicry of a sansculotte, but this debauchery makes an artificial, bewigged old woman even more ridiculous. The step was not far from sexual to political vice. In one of many versions of *Aristocratic Lady Cursing the Revolution* (Figure 3.22), the privileged class of Old Regime France is figured in the shape of a fury, a familiar trope derived from classical allegory. But this startling direct image of a female grotesque does not require of its viewers any special knowledge of the classics. The old woman's sagging, shapeless breasts are mimicked in the drooping plumed headdress she wears. In place of the youthful, natural, and nurturing beauty that was so favored in republican representations of female goddesses, this anonymous artist depicts a choleric old hag with lined neck and bosom. Her ferocious stare, clenched hand, and drawn dagger embody the aristocracy's vile opposition to revolutionary change.

These images reveal that for republicans, aristocracy and femininity were intimately related. This charge is wonderfully dramatized in a contribution to the 22 November 1790 issue of *Journal de Perlet,* "Why Are Women More Aristocratic than Men?" The contributor advances an empirical observation, "especially in the capital. . . the Revolution has more detractors among women than among men." He calls on readers to judge, not flatter or blame women.

Dame Aristocrate maudissant la Révolution.

Figure 3.22. *Aristocratic Lady Cursing the Revolution.* ca. 1789. Courtesy of the Musée Carnavalet. Copyright Photothèque des musées de la ville de Paris.

In a reprise of well-known enlightened arguments excusing women's back-wardness because of their inferior education and their more limited experience with principles of government and political economy, he judges their minds to have been less prepared for the Revolution than were men's. Exempting "women of the people from these charges," because he deems them closer to nature and more patriotic, he speaks of the repugnance toward the Revolution exhibited by a great number of women, especially those of the court and aris-tocrats in general:

> They saw that in a state where political liberty is total, there would be a revolution in manners that would inevitably change the private lives of women; that they might very well be obliged to substitute their noisy and frivolous lack of occupation, and their scandalous inde-pendence, for other duties of wife, mother, and citizen. The honor of one day becoming Spartans did not at all console them for the loss of the pleasures of Athens; and the apprehension of seeing divorce intro-duced showed them in a detestable manner a revolution which would impose on them the odious yoke of compliance and virtue, of moral-ity and fidelity.[88]

In fact, this particular contribution did not go uncontested. This itself is an important indication of the extent to which the dramatically changed cir-cumstances inevitably raised the question of women's liberty. Indeed, the mat-ter was far from being settled during the earliest stages of the Revolution. On 3 December, 1790, *Journal de Perlet* published a letter to the editor titled "On the Aristocratic Spirit with which Women Are Reproached."[89] Rather than jus-tifying the denial of equal liberties to women on the basis of their greater edu-cational and political inferiority, this author turns the Enlightenment trope around. According to him, the denial of liberty to women is an outrage in an enlightened century. He also defends women's suffrage, but interestingly he is far less approving than was the initial contributor of the popular classes. The first praised the bold actions of women in such events as the storming of the Bastille, the march on Versailles, the Festival of the Federation, and virtually every threat against "*la chose publique.*" He called on all Frenchwomen in the future to become like women of the people: "How many times has the monarch received from these same women the testimony of love more flattering and more true than the vain fawning of his courtesans, and, especially, more sincere and instructive in their lessons. Let us hope that in the future all our wo-men will honor themselves in becoming, in this sense, women of the people."[90]

In contrast, the second writer is worried about the popular "fanaticism" that is mistaken for patriotism, and more concerned to defend the women of higher rank against unjust charges by patriots. This early exchange anticipates a contrast that would later became more pronounced, as between popular masculine (Jacobin) radicalism and bourgeois or moderate (Girondin) feminism, played out in late spring 1793 by the defeat of the Girondins by the Jacobins. In the context of the charge of women's inclination toward aristocracy, however, it is revealing to notice how the more "feminist-inclined" (if we can fairly use such labels) second author is more sympathetic to the educated women of higher rank. In contrast, the more "populist" first author is profoundly suspicious of such women. He posits a deep and disturbing connection between aristocracy and femininity, one that was reprised often in both the rhetoric and imagery of the revolutionary era.

Such is the case in *The Nightmare of the Aristocracy* (Figure 3.23), where a writhing, disproportionately large female body is depicted twisting toward the viewer in the throes of a bad dream of equality and liberty, symbolized by the carpenter's level topped by a Phrygian bonnet. Aristocracy's open eyes and clenched hands—one tearing at her hair, the other at her toga—underscore that this is a waking dream. A new dreaded reality has swept away the litter of the old order, which lies strewn across the floor in the shape of swords, crowns, tiaras, and scepters. Her physicality and availability makes her less, not more, appealing as a sexual object. As Madelyn Gutwirth observes, "The mood of imminent rape is underscored by the figure of the satyr functioning as handle of the ewer on the left, whose lip points between her legs."[91] Against this resolutely anticlassical nude, the printmaker exhibits the rational symbols of equality and liberty derived from Roman antiquity and Freemasonry. Where aristocracy is aggressively feminine, it appears to be even more effective to symbolize liberty not as another woman but through the gender-neutral icon of the Phrygian cap and equality as a triangular level.

The charge of aristocracy by patriots reduced a world of constantly shifting complexities to a remarkably simple dichotomy, and this tendency bore a marked resemblance to other dichotomies of modern bourgeois life, such as that between men and women. Patrice Higonnet explains how this logic of accusatory language during the Revolution affected gender distinctions: "From physicalization of aristocracy, the distance was short to its feminization as well: women, imagined by the Enlightenment to be particularly susceptible to disease and "vapors," were thought fated to *aristocratie*, which iconographically was often feminized." Other associations, like that to witchcraft, demonstrated the special affinity of aristocracy for femininity: "Concealment and hypocrisy

LE CAUCHEMAR DE L'ARISTOCRATIE

A Paris chez Desmarest, Rue J.J. Rousseau, Nᵒ de Ballon

Figure 3.23. Sébastian Desmarest, *The Nightmare of the Aristocracy*. ca. 1793. Courtesy of the Print Collection, Miriam and Ira D. Wallach Division of Art, Prints and Photographs, The New York Public Library, Astor, Lenox and Tilden Foundations.

likened the aristocrat to the witches of former times: like these demonic women, 'la tourbe impure de l'aristocratie' preferred to work in the 'ténèbres.' Aristocracy wears a mask. It was 'dissimulée,' and often concocted 'un plan atroce et habilement combine.'" [92]

However, as Figures 3.17 and 3.18 demonstrate, it would be wrong to insist that only aristocracy bore the taint of femininity. Rather, the gender/woman trope's ability to register a simplistic opposition between good and evil or approbation and discrimination derived in good measure from its mobility—its capacity, according to Rico Franses, "to fly off at a moment's notice, to take up residence in whatever situation needs radical simplification, and clear messages of good and evil." [93] Opponents of the Revolution applied these lessons in their critiques, figuring the Revolution as a grotesque woman, typically of the lower classes; but even revolutionaries put these tropes to good use. Some examples will illustrate this point. *The Contrast* (Figure 3.24), the 1792 colored etching by the British artist Thomas Rowlandson after Lord George Murray, shows two images in medallion form and represents the British public's shift away from its initially positive view of the Revolution.[94] On one side, under the heading "British Liberty," Rowlandson depicts a youthful Britannia holding the scales of justice, a lion resting at her feet as she watches a galleon sail off into the distance. On the other side, under the heading "French Liberty," is a frightening old crone with snaky hair, a scantily clad body, bare feet, and muscular arms; she carries a sword in one hand and a trident in the other. On the trident is a gruesomely impaled head, and to Liberty's rear the body of a well-attired man swings from a lamppost. The text drives home the message: French liberty amounts to "atheism . . . rebellion . . . anarchy, murder . . . madness, cruelty, injustice . . . idleness," "misery," and, above all, "equality"!

In a similar inversion, the *Moniteur universel* linked the execution of the revolutionary supporter Madame Roland to the executions of the queen and

Figure 3.24. Thomas Rowlandson, after a design by Lord George Murray, *The Contrast 1792/Which Is Best*. Published on behalf of the Association for the Preservation of Liberty and Property against Republicans and Levellers, 1792. Courtesy of the Print Collection, Lewis Walpole Library, Yale University.

the feminist agitator Olympe de Gouges: "The Roland woman, a fine mind for great plans, a philosopher on note paper, the queen of the moment . . . was a monster however you look at her. . . . Even though she was a mother, she had sacrificed nature by trying to raise herself above it; the desire to be learned led her to forget the virtues of her sex."[95] The judgment of the *Moniteur universel* is especially harsh given how hard Madame Roland had fought to fashion herself as a modest, chaste, and dutiful wife. Unlike the *salonnières* of earlier decades, she foreswore any participation in the regular meetings of the Girondins, which took place in her home between 1791 and 1793. She sat apart, preoccupied with sewing or writing letters but nonetheless alert to all that was said. By remaining silent, she offered these men a forum in which to speak without the intrusions of a female voice. She also refused the label of writer, despite the fact that she became known for her writings.[96] Even before the events leading to her arrest and execution, however, she had become the special object of abuse by members of the increasingly influential Montagnard faction. "The court of Roland and his wife" were likened to that of the king and Marie-Antoinette.[97] In his *L'Ami du Peuple* Jean-Paul Marat compared her to Lucrezia Borgia, the female poisoners Brinvilliers and Voisin, and the hated Marie-Antoinette herself.[98]

Other examples of the reversibility of the gender trope come to mind. French royalists and post-Thermidorean artists were equally adept at mobilizing grotesque figures of discord and revolutionary terror. An anonymous Thermidorean image, *The Triumph of Marat in Hell* (Figure 3.25), shows Marat greeted by Death, while a bevy of female harridans dance round in glee.[99] This portrait depicts the Terror as the corridors of hell, and with the exception of Marat and the ungendered Death, hell is populated almost entirely by monstrous women, all of whom possess familiar attributes—serpentine, medusan hair; postnurturing breasts; frozen, murderous glares; swords and daggers. On the far left, a particularly hideous woman holds the amputated leg of a small child as her mask is pulled away by another—revealing that behind the face of (what appeared to be) a man rests another monstrous female.

Thus, the female body offered a symbolic repertoire that could be claimed by any party of warring men for different causes. It might function as a generalized symbol not only of a positive sense of liberty but also, negatively, as a symbol of the enemy: the ancien régime as old crone, the democratic Republic as frightful figure of discord. Indeed, the political circumstances that followed from women's imposed banishment from public life at the height of the radical Revolution, along with subsequent legislative efforts to contain women's civic and political rights, may have helped to grant artists greater license to use

Figure 3.25. *The Triumph of Marat in Hell.* ca. 1795. Courtesy of the Bibliothèque nationale de France.

the female body as a metaphor for a whole series of constantly contested political meanings. That is, the more women were deprived of an individual presence in the public arena, the more likely those faceless women could stand in for a range of political values or positions. At the same time, the visual presence of women—that is, female figures—in these images served to remind men of the horrors associated with women's too active involvement in public life.

In this context, the decidedly unflattering portrait in the anonymous print *Citizens Born Free* (Figure 3.26) is an example of how the republican discourse on freedom might be leveled against female propriety as well as female nature. The visual pun derives from the portrayal of a "female" citizen caught in the solitary act of an (unlikely) birth. The printmaker bitterly mocks the opening line of the Declaration of the Rights of Man and Citizen, "Men are born and remain free and equal in rights," by inscribing these words in the print's title.[100] The baby is captured standing, about to walk or run from beneath its mother's skirts, in little need of maternal succor. The baby's freedom is exaggerated, more suited to the animal than the human world. Taken to its limits, freedom is shown to be less natural than unnatural, capable even of destroying the most fundamental bonds between mother and child. The mean, grimacing mother is anything but a sentimental portrait of female nurturance. Her lifted skirt also points the viewer's attention to her sexuality. Even the baby is unattractive. In jest, the printmaker seems to be asking whether this is the true offspring of the Revolution—neither chaste nor uplifting but common and gross? Here the female citizen is less an icon of liberty than a caution against freedom's frightful consequences.

The Republic and Its Subjects

In short, the imagined implications of women's public activities were disturbing. It was precisely when women acted on the possibilities of republican citizenship that they were accused most vehemently of bringing disorder to the Republic. Nor was it easy to predict which group of male politicians might turn against women at any given moment. Thus, although Girondins were generally friendly to women and their cause, the Girondin deputy and journalist A.-J. Gorsas spoke of armed militant women as "furies. . . armed with pistols and daggers; they make public declarations and rush to all the public places of the city, bearing before them the standard of license. . . . These drunken bacchanalians. . . . What do they want? What do they demand? They want to 'put an end to it'; they want to purge the Convention, to make heads roll, and to get themselves drunk with blood."[101] The context for Gorsas's remarks are understandable—the insurrection of 31 May to 2 June 1793, leading to the ouster of the Girondin moderates from the National Convention, which the Society of Revolutionary Republican Women had helped to bring about.[102] But the violence of his rhetoric is notable, and the particular associations Gorsas makes between political women and monstrosity or cannibalism recurred in the words of men of differing political persuasions. With some rare omissions, even the most forward-looking men of the first French Republic objected to the participation of women in the democratic public sphere.[103]

An especially startling case is that of Sylvan Maréchal, a man of the Left, revolutionary playwright, editor of Babeuf's *Manifesto of Equals*, anticipator of

Figure 3.26. *Citizens Born Free*. Courtesy of the Musée Carnavalet.
Copyright Photothèque des musées de la ville de Paris.

the revolutionary calendar, and author of the 1801 brochure *Project for a Law against Teaching Women to Read*.[104] Maréchal justified his arguments on the basis of nature and reason. In Article 3 of his *Project*, he declared, "Reason wants each sex to be in its place and to stay there." In Article 26, he revealed his real purpose, stating, "How contagious reading is: as soon as a woman opens a book, she thinks she's good enough to produce one." In Article 4, he insisted, "Reason doesn't want, any more than the French language, that a woman be an author."[105]

Despite Maréchal's assertion of the guarantees of reason and nature in keeping each sex in its proper place, he is clearly anxious that women have not and will not always abide by nature's dictates. Like *salonnières,* they might undertake a program of reading, writing, and the forming of opinion. Like market women, members of the revolutionary crowds, spectators at the assemblies, and participants in mixed and single-sex societies, they might occupy public space. It is of some importance that at the height of the Terror, Peter Brooks observes, "political women, scribbling women, debauched women" (referring, respectively, to Olympe de Gouges, Mme Roland, and Marie Antoinette) were drawn together "as examples of 'the sex' out of control, needing the ultimate correction in order to conform to what [Louis Antoine de] Saint-Just called the 'mâle énergie' of the Republic."[106]

Marchéchal's proposals, like Rousseau's writings on women, reveal the extent to which the so-called dictates of nature and reason required buttressing through a disciplinary program. Republican men were especially alert to the potential for women's errancy, their dangerous capacity to undermine the collective spirit. If women's reading and writing were deemed to be troublesome, visual spectacles offered an ideal didactic vehicle for the remaking of corrupt and corruptible female nature. However, this required that bodies be made to carry simple, unadulterated meanings of good and evil. In addition, a case could be made that women were particularly well suited to receive instruction in visual messages. As Rousseau proposed in *Emile,* "Almost all little girls learn to read and write with repugnance."[107]

In this context, the representation of women as goddesses symbolized the regeneration of the tainted female body associated with the repudiated old order. Conversely, female grotesques made palpable the continuing threat posed by corrupt female nature and disorderly public women to the virtuous body politic. Both characterizations of the female body worked to construct a new female subject. In the terms established by a sensationalist psychology, the case for a female goddess satisfied the power of signs to impress upon the senses the new knowledge required by a regenerated citizenry. Antique goddesses were emblematic of the revolutionaries' desire to bypass their own national history by instituting an ideal, nondespotic Republic. They instructed the populace—and especially women, who were deemed most susceptible to selfishness and vanity—on how to banish selfish private desire in order to serve the whole. They had the added advantage of transmogrifying the despised women of Old Regime society. Instead of chatty hostesses or sensual seducers, women reemerged as mute, chaste allegories for an indefinite present and a future world, as signs of the politically passive but still politically charged subjectivity entailed by republican motherhood.

On the other hand, the grotesque belonged to the world of revolutionary caricature, a universe populated by abusive, ridiculous, and highly partisan images. They were the pure expression of a logic of political Manichaeanism by which people were first stylized and then distributed according to two essential types favored by revolutionary political minds: aristocrat or patriot. Moreover, the grotesque participated in a sacrilegious movement that helped to fashion the secular society of modern France.[108] She derived her force from her ability to give a body to the Revolution's political enemies. By portraying the aristocracy or the clergy as a grotesque—and not least a female grotesque (animalistic, degenerate, too thin, too large, or too old)—the revolutionaries made their political opposition more palpable, more real. Furthermore, because the figure of the grotesque associated bodily monstrosity with political deviance, it promised to deny the opposition a place in the reformed, regenerated body politic.

The polarization of female goddesses and grotesques in revolutionary popular imagery typifies the melodramatic structure of revolutionary moralism. As Peter Brooks explains, melodrama is "a hyberbolic mode, of course, and preeminently the mode of the excluded middle, which one finds in Saint-Just's speeches and in all Jacobin rhetoric: those who are not with us are against us, there is no compromise possible between polarized moral positions, the world is defined by a vast Manichaean struggle of light and darkness."[109] Whether in rhetoric, drama, or imagery, melodrama relied on an aesthetics of embodiment and the special power of gesturing speech. Gesture permitted "the creation of visual messages, pure signs that cannot lie, the most undissimulated speech, that of the body."[110] Thus, what looks to us as gross simplifications or ridiculous exaggerations in the postures and grimaces of grotesques are best viewed as expressions of the performative urge to imbue the body with meaning. This urge was made all the more imperative in the undecided space of the democratic sovereign, as a consequence of the evacuation of sacred meaning from the traditional center of the absolutist body politic. With the collapse of a "system of assigned meanings," individuals faced an intense requirement to be accountable for their bodies, to convey and achieve meaning with their (otherwise sense-less) bodies.[111]

Whereas during the Revolution male virtue required a certain stoical, public self-exhibition, the normalized, virtuous female body possessed its own forms of self-control. For women as for men, the discipline of the body was self-discipline.[112] Paradoxically, a comportment of unassuming modesty, privacy, prudence, and silence demanded of women a strongly willed self-composure, as was ideally represented in the enclosed body of the classical goddess and betrayed by the open and exaggerated bodily form of the grotesque. As Rousseau intuited, women's shame and modesty—not their reason—guaranteed their chastity. Like the goddess, then, the female grotesque was not just outside the self or the community; she was potentially inside as well. She served as a warning to women of the urgency for safeguarding their carefully constructed political/moral identities as virtuous, republican mothers.

Finally, there remains the question of the masquerade of equality within the masculine Republic. By incorporating the very symbol of the Revolution as a female figure, compensation was made for the exclusion of women from the Revolution's political practice. Stated otherwise, women were included, but only in representation. To say that, however, is not to concede that their presence is meaningless. As I have indicated, no representation can escape its own multiple readings; and the evidence suggests that, under certain conditions, politically active women did appropriate the gendered symbols of Liberty, Republic, or the female Amazon for their own cause. Still, the power of the feminine symbols of liberty, equality, or fraternity, even for women, rests in their ability to encompass the whole populace, not just one of its parts. Paradoxically, the myth of full equality may have helped make the denial of full rights to women more palatable for the vast majority of men and women. For the discontented minority, it took the additional threat of force to expel such women from public affairs. Legal and political mechanisms, as well as police power, would continue to be required during the next century and a half in order to maintain the fiction of universal sovereignty and equality in the face of demands by women and others for equal rights.

Still, the symbolic universe that republicanism achieved cannot be discounted. Although Liberty and her sister goddesses may have resembled the goddesses who adorned the visual landscape of the ancien régime, after the Revolution they no longer signified the partiality and privileges of Old Regime authority. Indeed, the representation of liberty as a woman was instrumental in the constitution of the myth of universal equality that marked the shift to a new social order. Had liberty been represented as a man—and not just occasionally, as was sometimes the case, but insistently—it might have revealed too much about the foundation of the new regime's political ideology and thereby threatened the universalizing claims on which the new regime's legitimacy was based.

The Revolution unleashed a flood of male anxiety, not least because of all of the repeated references to freedom and equality in republican discourse and imagery. While the concepts of freedom were constrained, we have also seen how, from the outset, gender interfered with liberty. I agree wholeheartedly, then, with those critics who insist that representation both takes and gives simultaneously. Real, troublesome, meddlesome women could be banished to the home, but the representation of Liberty (and her party) undid or disturbed some of that banishing, took some of it back. Real women were never fully obliterated from the public map; nor were their roles in the private sphere ever entirely out of public view. However, their presence was registered within the public sphere in a manageable way—trapped within a picture. Women themselves were hardly free of the discipline of the image—every woman (including those who would be counted as good and virtuous) risked "making a spectacle of herself" by appearing in public. The double image *The Female Aristocrat: Cursed Revolution, The Female Democrat* (Figure 3.27), attributed to the radical republican artist Villeneuve, calls attention to the dramatic way in which opposition to public women of all stripes easily congealed. A version of the image discussed previously, *Aristocratic Woman Cursing the Revolution*, is here coupled with a scatological image, usually subtitled "*Oh the Good Decree*," which was also published separately in several versions. *The Female Democrat* grasps in one hand a rolled parchment scroll inscribed with the words "declaration of the right [*sic*] of man." The most sanctified political object of the Revolution makes its appearance here as a (displaced) male organ in the hand of a ferocious woman of the popular classes. The joke is vicious, on men's behalf but also at their expense: At least in this artist's conception, man's virility and man's political rights are one, and both are placed at risk by women's power. Moreover, the joining of these two women from seemingly opposite ends of the political spectrum says a great deal about the fear and contempt men felt for public women.

By making a public display of even the most modest kind, a woman risked losing her honor, and feminine honor was not an easily repurchasable commodity. Just as female virtue was internalized, goodness was domesticated within the private sphere. Good women were appointed to be their own guardians. They needed to control their gestures, to scrutinize their own bodies for telltale marks of impropriety, lest any man should see something untoward. Women's plight, their self-policed image-making, was the consequence of the necessary force that Rousseau posited as being at the root of virtue. Men were not immune from the force of virtue. However, reason offered them a

Figure 3.27. Attributed to Villeneuve, *The Female Aristocrat: Cursed Revolution. The Female Democrat.* ca. 1789. Courtesy of the Bibliothèque nationale de France.

route to freedom in the public sphere that was denied to women. And, in good measure, man's relationship to woman was guided in the first instance by the sense of sight; by "reading" woman's bodily signs, he could discern in what category of womanhood she belonged.

In Chapter 4, I return to the female image of the nation presented in Chapter 2 as the consequence of the legitimization and representation of the anonymous popular sovereign of the new Republic. And I examine the consequence of the nation's figuration as a female in the context of the erotic dimension of modern patriotism.

4

Possessing *La Patrie*

Nationalism and Sexuality in Revolutionary Culture

I N T H E decades leading up to the Revolution, a new notion of the father-land (*la patrie*) as a community of free citizens began to displace the sacred conception of monarchy that had served to legitimize power in the Old Regime. A king-centered view of patriotism gradually gave way to an empha-sis on the French nation, which was associated with the needs and interests of the people rather than those of the crown. For growing numbers of French subjects, monarchy was now associated with despotism and ruled out of *la pa-trie*.[1] The declaration of the Republic in 1792 was the culmination of a com-plex process by which the French people had come to belong, in Benedict Anderson's memorable phrase, to an "imagined political community"—no longer associated with the king's body and his interests.[2] The new Republic ful-filled the *philosophe* vision of *la patrie* as amounting to a great deal more than one's birthplace. As the Chevalier de Jaucourt advised in his *Encyclopédie* entry, *la patrie* embraces the "*family, society, free state*, in which we are members, and of which the laws assure us our liberties and our happiness. There is no *patrie* under despotism."[3] This reformed notion of patriotism was reaffirmed in Hegel's postrevolutionary work on the philosophy of the state. Just as em-phatically as Jaucourt and the revolutionary generation of the 1790s, Hegel yoked together public and private life and deemed individual liberty to be a component of modern national self-identity. Notwithstanding his antipathy for the radical Revolution, Hegel agreed wholeheartedly with French republicans that political freedom, within a free state, requires a strong moral foundation in both the family and the sphere of civil society.

Nationalism, a prominent feature of French revolutionary culture, developed during the eighteenth century in the context of a much wider set of changes in personal morality and family life. As George Mosse maintains, the intense interest of modern society in respectability—"decent and correct" manners and morals, along with a proper attitude toward sexuality—accompanied the emergence of nationalism.[4] The family came to be associated with the values of intimacy and sentimentality, and private morality was seen as a necessary condition for a healthy state and society.[5] Female virtue was absolutely pivotal to this new conception of public and private life, and women as a whole were divided between those who did and those who did not contribute to the nation's moral well-being. According to the *Encyclopédie* article "Femme (Morale)," a "reserved and dignified character" earns respect and happiness for the "good, natural woman." Such a woman knows her place in the domestic sphere. By contrast, the "natural" desire to please is distorted into the "continual lie called coquetry" among "women of the world."[6] Jean-Jacques Rousseau went even further, making women the very axis on which a reformed public and private morality would rest. "If women would only deign to nurse their children," he protested in *Emile*, "morals would reform of themselves, sentiments of nature would awaken in every heart, the State would become populated again; this point, this point alone subsumes all the others. The attraction of domestic life is the best antidote to bad morals."[7]

Revolutionaries elaborated on the links between the constitution of a free state, the sexual division of labor, and civic virtue. In his 1791 *Discours sur l'education nationale,* Honoré Gabriel Riqueti, comte de Mirabeau volunteered that "men, destined for worldly business, must be raised in public. Women, on the contrary, destined for the interior life, should be able to leave their paternal homes only on rare occasions." He extolled Rousseau for comprehending the "truth so familiar to ancient peoples," that "man and woman, playing entirely different roles in nature, cannot play the same role in the social state, and that the eternal order of things makes them work toward a common goal, but assigns to them distinct places." In Mirabeau's formulation, men are external, active beings, suited for the outside world. They enjoy social, economic, and *political* freedom and are fitted with a robust constitution that conforms to the character of their work—all those affairs that take place outside the family: "all that which demands considerable force, traveling great distances, courage, steadfastness, opinionated discussions, regards him exclusively. It is he who should labor, negotiate, travel, fight, plead his rights and those of his brothers, other humans, in the public assemblies."[8]

By contrast, women do not need the civil and political freedoms that men enjoy. Endowed with a distinctive nature, woman, according to Mirabeau, is ideally suited to a retired, domestic life: "The delicate constitution of women, perfectly appropriate for their main destination, making children, tending with solicitude the perilous early years of life, and in that object so precious to the author of our existence, binding together all the forces of man by the irresistible power of weakness; this constitution, I say, takes them through the timid work of the home, to the sedentary tastes required by this work, and permits them to find true happiness, and to spread around them all that they can become dispensers of, but only in the peaceful employment of a retired life."[9]

Mirabeau was expressing the attitudes of a great number of his countrymen who did not view matters of love, domesticity, and sexuality to be merely intimate encounters; nor did they regard nationalism as just a public affair.[10] Through legislative and legal efforts, reformers affirmed the political meaning of private behavior, just as they imbued public life with a deep, personal gravity.[11] Granted, this much is well understood, but I am stressing that far from being worlds apart, as is suggested by the terminology of separate spheres, the emerging conceptions of public and private were powerfully reinforcing and deeply entangled.

I do not mean to suggest that public and private amounted to the same thing, or that the situations of men and women were analogous. Membership in *la patrie* was differentially constituted, determined by the sexes' reciprocal but dissimilar (and unequal) positions and supported by a newly fashioned architecture of public and private space.[12] Anderson calls attention to this fact when he writes, "in the modern world, everyone can, should, will 'have' a nationality, as he or she 'has' a gender."[13] From this basic claim, Anderson and others have drawn the insight that national identity is a relational, not an intrinsic, property, "a function of what it (presumably) is not."[14] Analogously, man's relationship to the nation (and to his fellow men) is determined by what he is not—that is, a woman.[15] In this regard, woman's "other-ness" helps to consolidate man's identity as a national subject. One of the privileges of nationhood for every man is the promise of possessing a female, whom he pledges in turn to protect and honor, under the aegis of the nation.[16] Mirabeau makes a similar point, demonstrating the distinctiveness and interdependence of male and female citizens. Man, we recall, is not housebound but a subject endowed with rights: He is, according to Mirabeau, a laborer, negotiator, traveler, fighter, plaintiff in the courts of law and at the bar of human liberty, and participant in the public assemblies. Yet he is also joined to a woman—a person who is not similarly free but affirms his identity as a free subject. The honor, love, and protection that a woman wins from her husband (as his wife and the mother of his children) compensate for her confinement in the home: "Without doubt the woman should reign in the interior of her home, but she must reign only there: anywhere else it is as if she were displaced. The only way it is permissible for her to make herself noticed [remarked on] is by a deportment which reminds one that she is the mother of a family, or which characterizes everything that renders her worthy of becoming one. The jurisdiction of a respectable woman is not less expansive for all that. On the contrary her husband *honors her* as much as he *cherishes her*. He consults her on the most difficult occasions. Her children have for her the most tender and religious submission."[17]

Mirabeau's sentiments denote the paradoxical wish of French republicans to elevate women's status beyond what had been their lot in former times, while at the same time refusing to grant them the same liberties as men. This divided impulse—simultaneously to free and to confine women—fit uncomfortably with the doctrine of universal freedom affirmed in the constitution of the new French nation. Indeed, this was the objection raised (unsuccessfully) by those men and women who insisted on the enfranchisement of female citizens and the equality of the sexes. For this and related reasons, eighteenth-century French reformers were among the first in modern times to confront directly the strict limitations placed on citizenship and universal rights because of racial, religious, and gender distinctions. As Anne McClintock stresses, however, "no nationalism in the world has ever granted women and men the same privileged access to the resources of the nation-state." Women have been "subsumed only symbolically into the national body politic," representing in this process "the limits of national difference between men."[18]

Numerous scholars have noticed this feature of modern nationalism. For Anderson, the nation is always conceived as a deep, horizontal community: "Ultimately, it is this fraternity that makes it possible, over the past two centuries, for so many millions of people, not so much to kill, as willingly to die for such limited imaginings." Mosse argues that "nationalism had a special affinity for male society and together with the concept of respectability legitimized the dominance of men over women." The editors of *Nationalisms and Sexualities* link such "virile fraternity," the "distinctly homosocial form of male bonding" that nationalism favors, to the idealization of motherhood and the corresponding "exclusion of all nonreproductively-oriented sexualities from the discourse of the nation."[19]

In short, homosocial attractions among men serve to bind men not just to each other but to an object we call the nation. Underscoring this point, recent studies of high art of the late eighteenth century by Thomas Crow and others call attention to the proliferation of feminized images of male beauty, intended for a male viewer. As Abigail Solomon-Godeau insists, however, the fascination with the sensual ephebe or the androgyne in neoclassical art production *coexisted with* misogynistic and homophobic public discourses, "which are signaled by their obsessive invocation of the threat of effeminacy and emasculation." In addition, she adds, such feminized forms of male subjectivity—"non-phallic" or "castrated"—may accompany and even work to shore up male power by incorporating the threat posed by women to the patriarchal gender order. "If the exploration of male trouble teaches us anything," Solomon-Godeau writes, "it must surely be that the imagery of feminized and vulnerable manhood is as much an index of the resilience of patriarchy as it is a sign of its fragility."[20]

In any event, while the dynamics of fraternal love may explain a great deal about the forms of masculine privilege in a period of political turmoil, there is much more to be said about the gender orientations of men and women within the political erotics of the nation-state. During the same years when revolutionary artists were fascinated by masculine beauty, the political canvas continued to be populated with allegorical images of beautiful female bodies—occasionally nude, but more often in a state of partial undress. Paralleling androgynous representations of the male body in high art is the strikingly unfeminine appearance of many female political personifications in revolutionary print culture.[21] In such cases, one is tempted to see *La Patrie* as a disguise for what is after all the masculine (collective) subject of the nation and its virile values, an occasion for the manifestation of homosocial desire.[22] But it would be misleading to conclude that *La Patrie* is nothing but a crossdresser. Despite such androgynous appearances, certainly the most striking feature of the countless allegories of the nation—and the other virtues—is the nation's incorporation in the body of an exceptionally alluring woman. As I have discussed earlier, by itself an iconographic explanation of this phenomenon is insufficient, not least because it is by no means self-evident why Old Regime allegorical traditions were carried over into the revolutionary culture. Nor is it enough to say, as do Lynn Hunt and Maurice Agulhon, that the masculine and feminine representations of Republic, as well as Republic's active and passive poses, are indications of the active and passive stages of the revolutionary movement or of the fortunes of women within the Revolution.[23]

Regrettably, the most fruitful explanations of the conspicuous presence of female representations of the nation offered to date call attention away from what remains the most decisive feature of the national body—*her* sex. Rather than ignore this fact, I contend that the circuit of heterosexual desire between the seductive feminized object of the nation-state and the male patriotic subject offers a useful point of departure for considering what Doris Sommer has termed "the mutual incitement of love and country." As Sommer explains, "If there were no erotic or sentimental investment in the state, if our identities as modern sexually defined subjects did not take the state to be a primary object and therefore the partner on whom our identity depends, what could explain our passion for 'la patria?'" In other words, love and patriotism may evoke the same rush of belonging and possession.[24] While I do not deny that patriotic love can and does take a homoerotic form, I maintain that this does not exhaust the sentimental contents of public and private passion on the national scene. By exploring the consolidations of such heterosexual investments in the nation's body, we may be in a better position to understand how sexuality and nationalism worked to crystallize a new national sexual identity—one deeply insinuated in a gendered construction of public morality and family life at a particular historical moment.[25]

Discussing education's central role in the formation of national identity in "Consideration on the Government of Poland," Rousseau posits such a connection between public and private life—particularly between maternal love and patriotic citizenship. He calls on a familiar—that is, a family—"scene" or visual metaphor in order to anchor patriotism in the strongest of all human emotions—that of an infant's love for his or her mother. Accordingly, he refers to the baby/patriot's first and last sight, of his mother and of his "mother" country:[26]

> It is education that must give to souls a national shape, and guide their opinions and tastes so that they will be patriotic out of inclination, out of passion, out of necessity. A baby first opening its eyes must see the mother country [*la patrie*] and until death must only see her. The true republican sucks love of his mother country [*la patrie*] with his mother's milk, that is to say, laws and liberty. This love makes up his entire existence, he sees only the mother country [*la patrie*], he lives only for her, as soon as he is alone, he is nothing; as soon as he has no more mother country [*patrie*], he is no longer, and if he is not dead, it is for the worse.[27]

Rousseau's intuition into the connection between patriotism and the family—or better yet, his idealized love—has been affirmed in recent scholarship. Sommer finds in novels the key to "sentimentalized" men's attachment to the state, whereas Benedict Anderson focuses on the role of the press and print capitalism in explaining the logic of national identification. Both writers, however, stress the bonds worked by language in the construction of a national community. Anderson ponders the effects of patriotic love, wherein language joins faceless men together in an imaginary fellowship: "It may appear paradoxical that the objects of all these attachments are 'imagined'—anonymous, faceless fellow-Tagalogs, exterminated tribes, Mother Russia, or the *tanah air*. But *amor patriae* does not differ in this respect from the other affections, in which there is always an element of fond imagining. . . . What the eye is to the lover—that particular, ordinary eye he or she is born with—language—whatever language history has made his or her mother-tongue—is to the patriot. Through that language, encountered at mother's knee and parted with only at the grave, pasts are restored, fellowships are imagined, and futures dreamed."[28]

I agree with Anderson on the critical role played by language, and especially printed words, in the formation of national consciousness, although it is important to recall that the modern printing press also facilitated the dissemination of images on a previously unprecedented scale. Moreover, "mechanical reproduction of art," to follow Walter Benjamin's important insight, was a critical factor in the greater democratization of culture.[29] The image's multiple reproduction—in newspapers, broadsides, and engravings—contributed to the loss of the aura possessed by a singular aesthetic object, but at the same time, the image gained a greater usefulness and publicity. In any event, a one-sided focus on print culture begs the question of the persistent female iconography of modern nationalism.[30] Although important, words are not the only influential dimension of the nationalist project. A more complete explanation of this phenomenon might consider how the lover's eye is engaged in patriotic love. (Here we must not lose track of the male definition of the citizenry in France.) In other words, the patriot is a lover, not just a reader or writer of texts, although Anderson did not explore the erotic dimension of this claim.

In the French context, revolutionary enthusiasm was redolent with effusive exclamations of love. As Robespierre avowed on one occasion, "Republic is not a vain word; it is the character of the citizens. The soul of the Republic is virtue, that is, love of *la patrie*; the magnanimous devotion that mixes all the private interests into the general interest."[31] For Robespierre and his compatriots, citizenship did not operate only on the level of intellect. The multiple faces of *la patrie* appearing in the revolutionary public sphere reinforced their many verbal declamations.

Possession

In an etching from 1789, *Necker Has a Man of the Third [Estate] Take Measurements for France's New Costume* (Figure 4.1), a crowned naked woman representing France is being measured by a tailor for a new costume under the supervision of the popular minister to the king, Jacques Necker. In many respects, France's nudity is unexceptional. Contemporary viewers would have had no difficulty placing her alongside the numerous naked women and men who populated the baroque and classical arts of early modern Europe, drawn to evoke pleasure or ideal beauty. Nor would they have been unacquainted with the lofty signification that the nude body bore within traditional mythological and religious subject matter. France was not an invention of the revolutionary period. She belongs to a long-standing iconographic tradition whereby desiderata and values came to be represented allegorically by feminine personifications.[32] The conventions of allegorical art require that the viewer consent to see France as both a woman and a symbol for a political entity, the body politic of France. In contrast to older images, however, France's body after 1789 came to figure as an emblem of the newly reformed French nation. Her nakedness stood for the return of France to a wholly natural condition, before the country's subjection to the overreaching power of a venal ruler.

European audiences from Columbus's day to the eighteenth century had absorbed the shock of explorers' reports of encounters with peoples who not only possessed vastly different dress and customs but who also dispensed with clothing altogether. Though nakedness could also be a mark of iniquity, in enlightened opinion it served as a trope for the innocent state of nature and the virtuous condition of savagery. In contrast, excessive clothing, perfumes, powdered wigs, corseted bodies, or women who refused to nurse their infants all symbolized the vices of the overly civilized world of European societies. Sympathetic viewers of this print would have no difficulty, then, interpreting this naked figure of France as a defense of natural liberty and equality. The figure of naked Truth further guaranteed that the values of the new regime were free from any taint of historicity. The print's message is clear: France must first be undressed—stripped of all artificial conventions and habits, decayed political and social fashions, and remnants of Old Regime power—before she can be redressed in the garments of virtue. It is also highly significant that the tailor who takes her "measure" is a man of the third estate—*un homme du tiers*. He will

Figure 4.1. Chez Sergent, *Necker Has a Man of the Third [Estate] Take Measurements for France's New Costume*. 1789. Courtesy of the Bibliothèque Nationale de France.

fashion for France new garments that have nothing in common with the sartorial styles of aristocratic society.

In the many female allegories of the French state within Old Regime iconography, France appeared as an escort or companion to the king. Even in his absence, France was understood to symbolize the real source of power in the realm—and signs of royalty were abundant in Old Regime culture. In traditional iconography, many emblems—the crown as well as the throne, the sun, the lion, the ermine robe, or the fleur-de-lis—could represent the state or power; each also metonymically associated with kingship. It was not uncommon for multiple symbols to appear conjointly in order to magnify the omnipotence of royalty. In absolutist France, offenses against majesty—including its representations—were judged with deadly seriousness. The *Encyclopédie* article on the crime of *lèse-majesté* explained why an "offense committed against a king or other sovereign" would be considered a very serious crime, "given the fact that sovereigns [claimed they] are the images of God on earth, and that all power comes from God."[33] Everything from an attack on the person of the king to the king's defamation in libels or broadsides, sedition and rebellion, and even counterfeiting (as coins of the realm bore the king's image) fell within the scope of this grave crime.

Therefore, in this early revolutionary print it is striking that there is only a modest reference to monarchy in the crown that France wears. In contrast to its role as a kind of royal placeholder in Old Regime iconography, here the crown identifies France as a symbol for the new nation—inside of which the people still happily embraced their king.[34] Put another way, without her crown, France could easily be mistaken for any of the standard female figures in the Western iconographic tradition who were also appearing on the revolutionary stage. On the other hand, for any artist to imagine, let alone describe, the bare body of the monarch would be to risk conviction under the crime of *lèse-majesté*. The king of France would be nothing without his clothes: to divest him of garments would be to strip his body of all of the sacred, social, and political powers on which the historical claims of the Christian monarchy were based.

Yet in 1789, the process of divestment that would climax in the trial and execution of the king in 1793 was already under way. By constituting themselves as a National Assembly, the former representatives of the third estate violated the Old Regime's hierarchical principles of power and staked a historic claim to popular sovereignty. At this point in time, Necker was widely regarded as the people's protector in the government, the guarantor of bread supplies, and the third estate's champion. Rumors of his dismissal by the king on 11 July precipitated popular demonstrations in Paris, culminating in the insurrection at the Bastille on 14 July. His recall on 17 July was hailed widely as a sign of the irreversible course set by the revolutionary events. So, on one reading of this image, Necker appears to be bringing the third estate (the tailor) into the political process. On the other hand, it is the tailor—the people as a whole, not one individual no matter how great—who is the maker (theorist) of both the civil and the political contracts.[35] The great insight of liberal political philosophy embraced by revolutionaries is that civil society, political society, and the family are all the products of contractual relations. All are freely entered into, not despotically willed. Against this background, it is even more important that France appears alone. She is the symbol of the nation, a free and sovereign community, not an auxiliary of absolutist power.

France is a political metaphor. Her body is a political body, or body politic.

Yet there is something unsettling about a reading of this image that entirely suppresses its sexual connotations. This figure of France is exceptionally life-like and desirable. An artist well schooled in rococo treatments of the female nude draws her beautiful body to agreeable human proportions. She is tall but not monumental, as would frequently be the case in the developing canon of officially authorized revolutionary art. She stands erect, gently leaning her bent elbow on Necker's shoulder. He directs the process by which France will be re-suited in conformity with her natural, and no longer artificially adorned, body. But this popular hero is also a man who is helping to bring to life a beautiful woman.

To classically versed audiences, the print might also easily evoke the an-cient story of the sculptor Pygmalion who fashioned a statue so lifelike that only modesty seemed to prevent it from moving—a myth given dramatic form by none other than Jean-Jacques Rousseau in 1762.[36] Pygmalion admired the beauty of his creation so much that he fell in love with it. Taking pity on him, Venus brought the statue to life as Galatea. She was at once his love and his cre-ation. Two among Jean-Michel Moreau le Jeune's illustrations for Arnand Berquin's 1775 edition of Rousseau's *Pygmalion* capture the moment when Galatea first comes to life and when Pygmalion declares his love for her. The first image (Figure 4.2) captures Pygmalion's moment of surprise, even terror: "[He takes courage, and finally picking up his chisel, he gives a tap and is seized with terror, and lets it drop while exclaiming] *Oh Gods! I feel her stirring flesh! She resists the chisel!* [He descends trembling and confused] *Vain terrors of my restless soul! . . . I do not dare, I cannot, and everything leads me to stop. Ah! With-out a doubt, the Gods wish to terrify me: They will have consecrated her at their supreme rank.*"[37] In the second image (Figure 4.3), Moreau le Jeune captures the lovers' rapturous embrace:

Galatea, with a sigh: Me again.
Pygmalion: Yes, dear and beautiful object to which my fire has given birth, Yes, it is you, it is you alone; I gave you my being, I could no longer live but for you.[38]

In the manner of Galatea and Pygmalion, France appears as Necker's cre-ation and love object. He is the new man, an author of the nation. As represen-tative of the male subjects of France, he invests her with a distinct kind of love, patriotic love. By drawing the emerging political relationships as simultaneously relationships of gender, the printmaker posits an erotic dimension for the origi-

Il s'encourage, et enfin présentant son ciseau, il en donne un coup saisi d'effroi, et le laisse tomber en poussant un grand cri.

Dieux ! je sens la chair palpitante !
Elle repousse le ciseau !

Figure 4.2. N. Ponce, after J. M. Moreau le Jeune, "He Takes Courage." In Arnaud Berquin, *Pygmalion; scène lyrique de J.-J.Rousseau.* Reproduction of original edition of 1775. Paris, J. Lemonnyer, 1883, 9.

J. M. Moreau le J.ne del.   N. de Launay sculp. 1773

GALATHÉE *avec un soupir*.

Encore moi.

PYGMALION.

Oui, cher & bel objet que mes feux ont fait naître,

Oui, c'est toi, c'est toi seul; je t'ai donné mon être,

Je ne vivrai plus que par toi.

Figure 4.3. N. de Launay, after J. M. Moreau le Jeune, "Galatea, with a Sigh." In Arnaud Berquin, *Pygmalion; scène lyrique de J.-J.Rousseau*. Reproduction of original edition of 1775. Paris: J. Lemonnyer, 1883, 18.

nal attachments that will bind the French subjects together in their newly fashioned national identity.

The probability of a literary precursor for *Necker Has a Man of the Third
[Estate] Take Measurements for France's New Costume* is underscored by another
feature, for the entire scene takes place on a stage. Behind the central group of
three is a partly drawn theater curtain, and at the edge of the stage—to the
group's left and below their feet—are the men of the pit, or *parterre,* where the
male Parisian theater audience habitually stood for three to four hours.[39] These
men are not just applauding but actively cheering the performance. Their seduction—their patriotic love—is manifest in their raised hands and exuberant
posture. Although this scene demonstrates the interlocking relationship between erotics and patriotism, it is emphatically one-sided: It posits men as the
spectators as well as the authors of the national romance being played on the
national stage.[40] It is only men's love for the nation that will legitimate the new,
postabsolutist French state: Women are curiously absent from the public stage,
although a figure of Woman is presented as the object and foundation of desire for the state. In a parallel fashion, republicans believed that the heterosexual contract grounding a reformed family life would only be secure if women,
like love, were to be contained within rather than allowed to roam free on the
outskirts of the family, as they often did during former times. Although France
is surely an abstraction, an allegory for the equally abstract notion of a sovereign national community, this print suggests how patriotism might elicit men's
love and satisfy, in a strangely circuitous fashion, their passions.

France is just one example of the countless female personifications used by
revolutionary image-makers to figure the abstract values that assisted in the legitimization of power in the new polity. Figures of Republic, Liberty, and *La
Patrie* would soon supplant France herself as the republican movement pro-
ceeded to sever all connections to the Old Regime. Thus, this particular print
registers the optimism of the early Revolution, when it was widely believed
that a constitutional monarchy could coexist with the newly pronounced principles of popular sovereignty and individual rights. I am proposing, however,
that the image, instead of depicting France as a quaint holdover from Old
Regime iconography, both contributes to and reflects the process by which
men claimed their individual rights and simultaneously expressed their political solidarity within, and loyalty to, the nation-state. This image speaks to a
specific historical conjuncture. Like the Old Regime countenance of France,
Necker's popularity would be swept away by successive events.

Several anonymous images from 1789 indicate the shifting politics. These prints, often with the same title ("without you I would have perished"), portray an allegory of France being rescued from the abyss. France's rescuers are either soldiers of the National Guard or (male) representatives of the third estate—usually portrayed in threes, to reinforce for the viewer the central role of the third estate in revolutionary political activity. But the basic melodramatic trope in each of these images is of the rescue of a vulnerable female by valiant young men.[41] The hitherto all-powerful state is reduced to an endangered woman whose very existence is in doubt. Of course, the basic plot is a romance: Her rescue by loving men eroticizes the bond that unites the subjects of the nation-state. In *Without You I Would Perish: To the Glory of the French*, 14 *July* 1789 (Figure 4.4), France, wearing a crown and a royal robe, is being pulled up by her arms by three guardsmen; to the left of the principal action, at least two others appear. An engraved obelisk celebrates the taking of the Bastille, and there are numerous weapons—scythes, pikes, and axes—testifying to the popular mobilization that resulted in this heroic action. The people save France, who is in need of their help. The people, as the printmaker reminds his

La France sauvée de l'Abime par le Patriotisme ou les Abus l'avoient precipitée.

Figure 4.4. *Without You I Would Perish: To the Glory of the French*, 14 *July* 1789. 1789. Courtesy of the Bibliothèque nationale de France.

viewers, are the courageous men of the National Guard units made up of members of the third estate.

Another great achievement of revolutionary men—the "reestablishment" of the rights of man—is affirmed in *France, Accompanied by Minerva, Arrives to Compliment the Republic, in the Presence of the Nation, for Having Reestablished the Rights of Man* (Figure 4.5). A seated, half-nude figure of Republic is equipped with the symbols of Liberty (the pike capped with a red bonnet) and France (the Gallic coq, perched behind her head). Republic is receiving the compliments of France and Minerva. France is crowned but is simply dressed, without the ermine robes in which she appeared in the previous image from early 1789, when the king's popularity was still high. She appears in three-quarter profile. One breast (closest to the viewer) shows through the gauzy

Figure 4.5. *France, Accompanied by Minerva,*
Arrives to Compliment the Republic, in the Presence of the Nation, for Having
Reestablished the Rights of Man. ca. 1793.
Courtesy of the Bibliothèque nationale de France.

material to reveal its fullness and an erect nipple—the transparent signs of her natural, nurturing role as protector of the state, on the one hand, and of her virginal, sacred status, on the other. The Roman goddess of wisdom and patroness of the arts, Minerva, wearing her golden helmet (but not her aegis), stands out in this group of three women. She is a kind of liminal figure. Her more masculine dress and pose contrasts with that of her sister goddesses. Her helmet is a reminder of her status as the goddess of war, protector of the city, but also of woman's fabled Amazonian capacities. She seems to unite the human and allegorical worlds, the practical or active world of men and the celestial or domestic world of women. Like the Greek goddess Athena, with whom she is associated, Minerva presides over the useful and ornamental arts—both of men, such as agriculture and navigation, and of women, such as spinning, weaving, and needlework. Behind these three allegorical figures march a line, perhaps a battalion, of national guardsmen. Ultimately, they are the recipients of Republic's freedom and the true protectors of these three goddesses—above all, the beautiful figure of Republic.

Two allegorical representations by Louis-Simon Boizot—*An Allegorical Figure of the French Republic* (Figure 4.6) and *Republican France/Opening Her Breast to All the French* (Figure 4.7)—were designed to affirm the declaration of the Republic in September 1792 and the fall of the monarchy one month earlier. The second is the more erotic and suggestive, the first the more alluring and sensual. She is young, beautiful, and lifelike. Despite her stolidity and the club she carries—a symbol of strength and power associated with the popular concept of Hercules as representative of the French people—there is a faint air of vulnerability about *An Allegorical Figure of the French Republic*. She peers out (at passersby), inviting attention—not something a demure, virtuous woman could risk doing without losing her reputation! Unmistakably, she asks to be recognized, embraced, and perhaps protected by her male subjects. In comparison, while *Republican France* is young and virginal, her most prominent features are her breasts, and the print's title merely anchors the singular meaning of the image: She presents herself as an offering. She offers her bosom to all Frenchmen. Not surprisingly, this popular image has attracted considerable notice among recent feminist commentators. Regarding the excessive breast imagery of the Revolution as "a fetishistic phenomenon," perhaps not unjustifiably, Madelyn Gutwirth refers to *Republican France* as a "democratic pinup": "Despite her Phrygian bonnet and her level, with her glazed expression and eloquent breasts she proclaims nothing so much as Frenchmen's equality of sexual opportunity. Her wearing of the emblems of freedom and equality is a joke on her: she is reduced to her breasts."[42]

Figure 4.6. Louis-Simon Boizot, *An Allegorical Figure of the French Republic*.
1792. Source: 1789: *French Art during the Revolution*, exhibition organized
and catalog edited by Alan Wintermute (New York: Colnaghi, 1989), 100.

Gutwirth is right to call attention to the obvious sexual content of Boizot's
image. However, the erotic motif does not depend on such an exaggerated portrayal. Indeed, far from just reducing woman to the breast or "an adjunct to
male eroticism,"[43] *Republican France* is no ordinary body but a metaphor for
the body of the nation. Gutwirth is right to detect an erotic charge in this
image, but she limits its effect to the voyeuristic pleasure for the male specta-

Figure 4.7. Alexandre Clément, after Louis-Simon Boizot. *Republican France/Opening Her Breast to All the French*. 1792. Courtesy of the Bibliothèque nationale de France.

tor. Instead, the repetitive presence of a seductive (metaphorical) female body in the imaginary place of the nation may help explain how men are lured to attach deep longings to the state. As the feminine object of men's desire, *La Patrie* is more than the fatherland. She invites the embrace of her male suitors, the emancipated subjects of the newly constituted nation-state. Eros is the glue that binds private passion and public duty. But we need to remember that eros is a longing, always postponed, never wholly achieved. In the curious scenario of deferred passions, erotic life becomes a school for patriotism, while, as we have seen, patriotism may teach a practice of love. To recall Doris Sommer's formulation, the erotic and sentimental investments in the state are far from accidental. Rather, the identities of modern sexually defined subjects are part of the process by which such subjects take the state as a primary object and the partner on whom their identity depends.

Belonging

Speaking of Eros, as well as the physical consequences of love, revolutionary artists often portrayed *La Patrie* in the company of male cupids. These child figures—a standard device in Western art and mythology—refer to the consequences of physical passion while simultaneously embodying desire itself.[44] *Love of the Fatherland* (Figure 4.8) is an excellent example of this ambiguity. In the foreground of this oval image, a flame burns on the altar of the Fatherland; at the rear is an obelisk engraved with a pike adorned with a chain of laurel wreaths. The suggested patriotic ardor is replicated in the erotic charge that accompanies the exchange of looks between the beautiful, lifelike figure of *La Patrie*—her two breasts exposed in the manner of Boizot's *Republican France*—and Cupid, who holds a burning flame. Cupid looks up adoringly to her, but is she his mother or his lover—as improbable as this may be—his intended bride?

In fact, the mythological sources speak of Cupid's mother as well as his bride. In Roman mythology, Cupid is the son of Mercury, the winged messenger of the gods, and Venus, the goddess of love. He is also the husband of the immortal Psyche—with whom he falls in love after Venus's machinations to wreak revenge on the formerly mortal Psyche go awry. Thus, the knowing and adoring glance that passes between *La Patrie* and Cupid associates her with Psyche as well as Venus. The abundant breasts of *La Patrie*—nurturing springs or sexual objects?—further confound the ambiguity surrounding her identity. In any event, the French subject-citizen (Cupid) is shown desiring a female object. By belonging to the new Republic, the citizen is both the issue and lover of the nation. Patriotism might be said to describe the double condition of his "be-longing."

In *Leave Your Arrow and on Some Familiar Tunes Learn My Cherished Moral; Be No Longer the Son of Venus, Become the Lover of the Fatherland* (Figure 4.9), a figure of Republic/*La Patrie* instructs Cupid (the small child) to serve the nation rather than Venus. He is called on to leash passion to the nation: to sublimate his love for his mother within a patriotic bond that will bind him to the fatherland, and to break the chains of frivolous, unbridled love.

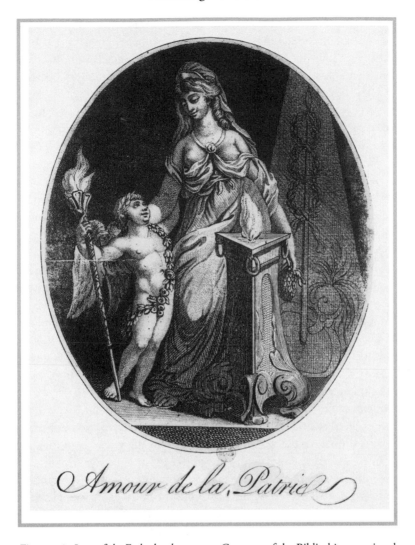

Amour de la Patrie

Figure 4.8. *Love of the Fatherland.* ca. 1793. Courtesy of the Bibliothèque nationale de France.

Certainly, the message of this print resonates with the revolutionaries' condemnation of the voluptuous and libertine culture of the Old Regime. The latter, associated with trifling play and erotic games, has been supplanted by a new order wherein disciplined passion and chastened love is placed in the service of state. Yet Cupid's lesson on patriotic love suggests that incestuous desire may not be so far from its source.

Republican instructions on the new morality are clear. The family is to be the only legitimate locus of love; reproduction, not pleasure, is to be the object of such cherished morals. As a consequence, women were exhorted by some radical republicans not even to leave the home. As Louis Prudhomme's *Révolutions de Paris* insisted, "Coming back to his home, it is from your patriotism, and it is in your arms that the citizen must taste, in the shade of the laws that he decreed at the senate, its chaste pleasures."[45] Similarly, for Jacques-Louis David, republican "moral regeneration" would supplant the gender license of the Old Regime with fertile heterosexuality. In his address to the Convention of 23 Messidor Year II (11 July 1794), proposing a fête to commemorate the deaths of the young martyrs Joseph Bara and Agricola Viala,[46] David advised women, "When you are married, serve the empire that nature has given you. . . learn that true wealth is in having many children who, strong and courageous, will one day defend the nation. As the example of Cornelia shows, they are your jewels and the ornaments of your homes."[47]

Conjugal heterosexual relations were intimately related to the state. Women, symbolized by their breasts, were expected to play a role in both the newly constituted family and state. As nurses and nurturers, women learned to substitute family duty for wayward passion. Motherhood is best understood, therefore, as the vehicle of women's incorporation into the new political order, as an almost primordial incorporation insofar as female traits are what work for and against their full participation in the new polity. The breast itself remained an ambivalent symbol: an enticement to sexual desire but also the most vital instrument of the infant citizen's original survival. Even the latter, however, was the subject of divided opinion, for the breast carried the taint of bad as well as good milk, of the wet nurse's infamy and the virtuous mother's devotion. Furthermore, the breast was the object of an extensive discourse on its proper function: Women were advised on how to nurse their own infants for the child's best welfare and warned to avoid the dangers associated with mercenary care by other women.[48] Injunctions about the improper use of the breast were an indispensable element in the republicans' project of disciplining the female body.

The ambivalence posed by visual depictions of the breast in revolutionary iconography resembles the problems resulting from the presence of nudity in Christian religious iconography. As Mary Miles observes in her study of Renaissance religious iconography,

> nudity or partial nudity in religious paintings creates in viewers tensions of two kinds. First, there is a tension between cultural and natural meanings. The bare-breasted Virgin, for example, evokes visual

Laisse ta fléche, et sur des airs connues
apprends ma morale chérie.
ne sois plus le fils de Vénus;
deviens l'amour de la Patrie.

...Piis.

Figure 4.9. *Leave Your Arrow and on Some Familiar Tunes Learn My Cherished Moral; Be No Longer the Son of Venus, Become the Lover of the Fatherland.* ca. 1793. Courtesy of the Bibliothèque nationale de France.

associations that emphasize her similarity with other women, while popular devotional texts and sermons contradict these evoked associations by insisting on their difference. . . . Second, nudity in religious paintings creates a tension between erotic attraction and religious meaning. . . . On the one hand, then, nudity must be depicted naturalistically enough to evoke the viewer's erotic interest; on the other hand, it must not be dominant enough to render this erotic attraction primary; the religious message must dominate, with the erotic component in a subordinate and supportive role.[49]

Miles is interested in the way in which such erotic potential was blocked in early Renaissance paintings of the Virgin—which were (almost entirely) *men's* images of a woman. Yet quoting Jane Gallop's statement that "the visual mode produces representations as a way of mastering what is otherwise too intense," she also calls attention to the way in which painting both expressed and evoked in viewers highly complex and ambivalent responses. Just as in the Renaissance, then, republican representations of the female body could elicit feelings of threat and of comfort. There is no question, however, that the ideal republican body was a "fantasy of a totally good mother," just like the Virgin in Christian Europe.[50]

The ideal of republican motherhood encouraged women to achieve their patriotic duty through their roles within the family, as mother and wife. A married woman was expected to be fecund, chaste, and respectable. As early as 1789, Candace Proctor reports, a number of the *cahiers*, such as that of the united orders of Rozières, suggested that "women also receive consideration when, by virtuous conduct, they are an example to their sex, and, having married, contribute by their conduct to the maintenance of the fortune of the citizens to whom they are united, and who give to the State healthy and robust children, well trained in the duties of citizens."[51] Similarly, a song written in honor of the Frenchwomen who had labored so hard to prepare for the Festival of the Federation of 14 July 1790 included the following stanza:

> To be worthy of the *Patrie*
> More still do you it owe
> Don't border there your duty
> Give us some little heroes.[52]

Children in republican prints appeared either in allegorical costume, as in the figure of Cupid; as representatives of the new French citizen; or, without any mythological substitution, as small but future citizens.[53] A *"scène de moeurs"* entitled *Republican Schoolteacher* (Figure 4.10) borrows directly from eighteenth-century genre painting. An alluring yet maternal teacher instructs her pupil in the principles of liberty. Together they read—or, more likely, given his age, she reads to him—the Declaration of the Rights of Man and Citizen. Recalling the slipped chiton of so many allegorical goddesses, the woman's

Figure 4.10. Chez L'Epicier, *Republican Schoolteacher*. ca. 1793. Courtesy of the Bibliothèque nationale de France.

exposed left breast accentuates the nurturing role played by the family and the state, to which the boy belongs. The printmaker implies that, like a devoted mother, Republic embraces her sons. It is a school for its subjects. The line between mother and teacher, like that between nature and culture, is bridged in republican ideology, as the natural woman intuitively imparts the principles of liberty to the next generation. In this case, the breast is a confirmation, not a disturbance, of the mother/teacher's place as a figure of authority and rectitude.

In other images, boys play at being republican men—marching like soldiers in parade formation or defending flag and country.[54] Like the boy in the image *Republican Schoolteacher,* they are at home with *La Patrie,* for the nation provides an asylum for its citizens. His duty is to love and honor the state like a parent, and he does this by learning his lessons—the moral and legal principles of republican virtue and freedom. Similarly, a print celebrating the Constitution of 1793, *The Fatherland Instructs Its Children, She Receives All of Them in Her Bosom and Reason Enlightens Them* (Figure 4.11), shows *La Patrie* instructing one child, a Cupid-like figure, in the lessons of the Constitution and the Rights of Man. A sunburst above the Panthéon (inscribed with the word *Reason*) radiates with three enlightened ideas of revolutionary fraternity: Adore the eternal (one), love your brothers, cherish your country.

What, then, does the nation ask of its members? A great deal, it appears. In the words of David, "Let the mother whose son has died on the battle field take pride in the blood that he has shed for the fatherland. Let tears of joy follow those of grief in seeing the honors that the people give in his memory."[55] The engraving *Devotion to the Fatherland* (Figure 4.12) is a complex allegory of the bonds of patriotism and the tribute rendered to heroes. On a pedestal, a seated figure of Republic receives the donations of the French people. A mother, enthusiastically attended by another young son, raises her infant child in dedication to Republic, commemorating the moment when he, too, will offer his life for the fatherland. Two young soldiers volunteer to go to war, while a woman burns incense. In a poignant group at the right, a mother reaches out to embrace her volunteering son, while her husband—twisting in Republic's direction—reaches out toward her, as if to bring her into the ambit of state law and duty in which her son is placed. Of all the subjects in this print, only this woman looks away from Republic, caught between patriotic duty and motherly concern. The iron-willed young man, like his fellow soldier, exhibits no such ambivalence. He is resolved to fight, and if necessary to die for his country. Hinting at the gender divide between virile men and sentimental women that animates David's two famous works—*The Oath of the Horatii* and *Brutus*—*Devotion to the Fatherland* nevertheless elicits women's (even the

Figure 4.11. *The Fatherland Instructs Its Children, She Receives All of Them in Her Bosom and Reason Enlightens Them.* ca. 1793. Courtesy of the Bibliothèque nationale de France.

Figure 4.12. Pierre Antoine de Machy, after Antoine Talamona *Devotion to the Fatherland*. Courtesy of the Bibliothèque nationale de France.

woman who hesitates) as well as men's participation in the glorification of the state. Nonetheless, women's citizenship is qualified, for only men possess the right to defend (the body of) the nation.

In the republican logic of freedom, the motif of death is yoked to life; life is given and taken in the cycle of national reproduction. However, women and men are differently placed in this eternal drama. Women are the bearers of future life; born to achieve greatness, men, by risking their lives, secure the nation's survival. The dead heroes of the Revolution were meant to convey to the people of France "how beautiful it is to die for one's country," as the Commission d'Instruction Publique announced on 12 July 1794.[56] Although women were not expected to sacrifice their lives on the battlefield, they were not exempt from the lessons of heroism. In his address of 23 Messidor Year II, David advised young republican women "to listen to the voice of the fatherland" and called on mothers "to imitate the example" of the dead heroes Bara and Viala:

> Victory brings to you friends worthy of you. . . be careful not to despise these illustrious defenders covered with honorable scars. The scars of the heroes of liberty are the richest dowry and the most durable ornament. After having served their country in the most glorious war, may they taste with you the sweetness of a peaceful life. May your virtues, may your chaste fecundity increase a hundredfold the resources of the fatherland. May each of you be seen in the middle of a

large family, showing you respect and saying with admiration: there is the worthy companion of a virtuous citizen who has lost his arm at the memorable battle of Fleurus. May the offspring of such a father, marching in his tracks, be the implacable enemies of tyranny and the emulators of Barra and Viala.[57]

David (not implausibly, given the political/military context of his address) invents an armless veteran on whom he confers a chaste and honorable wife.[58] It is noteworthy that David's hero is a wounded subject, in the manner of the central figures of his great paintings of this period—*Marat at His Last Breath* and the less familiar *Death of Joseph Bara*. As Alex Potts proposes, "The most intensely moving heroic body is a damaged body, one that has the pathos of a vulnerable yet indomitable subject facing death." Discussing this same speech by David, Potts contends that "beauty enters in by way of the young women of the Revolution. David's celebration of the struggle against despotism turns at the end from the pathos of the dead hero, to the rewards awaiting the battle-scarred heroes who survive. Wounded yet purged in the struggle, they can now enjoy a utopian life of peace and pleasure, prepared by the chaste yet fertile women who await them. However, the most intense beauty achieved in the aftermath of heroic struggle is still in the final analysis located in the damaged male body."[59]

In contrast to the damaged male body, female figures of sensuous beauty or virtue appear whole, but they are remarkably marginal or at least infinitely substitutable. *La Patrie* has many different female bodies, but none are invested with the same heightened tension between desire and ideal subjectivity found in portrayals of virtuous, free male subjects in the high art of the period.[60] Potts is right to insist that while woman functions as a sensuous object of male desire, in the eighteenth-century discourses around the free subject, only the beautiful male body is a sign of ideal subjectivity.[61]

What purpose, then, does the female object of desire play within republicanism, if not that of ideal subjectivity? As I have suggested, the female representation of the state, like the good republican wife, is far from peripheral to the political romance of nationalism. The maternal body of the state and the good wife are two versions of home—both of which efface the material circumstances to which they refer. Just as the products of war are overcome by the glorification of heroic death, so, too, the material circumstances of housework and social labor are submerged within romantic love and its exaltation. Ideally, the feminine visage of the nation, like the domesticated woman to whom the (damaged) hero may return, operates to incite and anchor man's longing for home and country.

The Revolution heightened the association of freedom with the rights and liberties of the Republic—a community conceived on the grander scale of the nation-state, in comparison to the small city-states of Renaissance Europe and antiquity. Ideally, freedom was not just the property of an absolute and solitary will but the condition of a subject who participates in a larger whole. By belonging, the free subject achieved a recognized place and sense of identity within a national homeland. From this perspective, freedom requires a public relationship between self and other. It gestures toward a politics of equal recognition among free citizens of a shared community. So defined, civic freedom helps to explain the enormous power exerted on individuals and groups by "imagined communities"—nationalism, as well as other religious or cultural identities.

Yet, as is now widely acknowledged, such self-referencing and participation may also foster, even require the exclusion, and subordination, of others both inside and outside the community. Certainly, women were (and are) among those groups that have not achieved equal representation in the community, but they are not inessential to the operation of the nation. As we have seen, nationalism is a relational concept, and man's relation to woman is a constitutive element in the creation of a national—ultimately, masculine—subject. In this context, the paradox of a female representation of a masculine state reveals how public and private life came to intersect and support each other in the modern nation. Like the image of *La Patrie*—or, in one of the foundational myths of Western culture, Ulysses' return to the faithful Penelope—woman's place in the family allowed men to posit their desire for home and to reach out for public recognition outside the comfortable space of the family. *La Patrie* remains both mother and wife to her male subjects. David's veteran resembles Rousseau's fictional character Emile. Both need to marry in order to fulfill their destiny as free political subjects within a republican form of government. By establishing a domestic union, man secures the conditions of his public freedom. But in doing so, as Freud proposed, he also gives up his desire to possess his mother.

Both Carole Pateman and Lynn Hunt have drawn suggestively on Freud's arguments in their interpretations, respectively, of the sexual contract and the family romance of the French Revolution.[62] However, both are concerned fundamentally with male-male relationships—specifically men's generative capacities in the political sphere. They both allude to the male fantasy under the regime of modern fraternity that it is possible to give birth to the new order without women. Pateman addresses the shift from classical to modern patriarchy and the persistent political, though naturalized, control that men exercise over women. Hunt focuses on the fragility of the masculine fraternity that results from the competition that breaks out among men after the death of the king—that is, after the overthrow of the old patriarchy. However, Hunt's assessment of incest curiously absents the love of sons for their mothers—Oedipus' fate in the Greek myth and Freud's equally famous account. Instead, she focuses on brother-sister incest. Even the Marquis de Sade, she alleges, skipped over the dynamics of mother-son love. Only in the sensational accusations leveled by radical republicans against the queen does the problem of mother-son love arise: For them, it is a terrifying act, which amounted to the most horrific crime against nature known to mankind. Notably, however, this charge inverts the Freudian scenario. In the trial proceedings against the queen, it is she (the mother) who is charged with incest against her innocent child! For the revolutionaries, there does not seem to be an equivalent possibility—that is, the son's incestuous desire for his mother. Yet the hyperbolic affect surrounding this charge suggests something more than the queen's perversity—doubtless the power of repressed desires for a certain kind of female body.

By yoking man's repressed love for his mother to the abstraction of the nation, men are bound together as citizen-subjects. This is a fatherland without a father—no pope, no king. Still, patriotic devotion to this "hidden god," to borrow Lucien Goldmann's term, is enabled by the charge of man's erotic passion.[63] Supplementing homosocial desires among men, then, the leashing of heterosexual desire to the political requirements of the state helped to produce a political subject who was willing to risk his life for a "higher" cause—not merely his own self-preservation. Instead of confronting his own vulnerability vis-à-vis the all-powerful state, the republican citizen was constituted as a powerful subject in his own right. Citizenship offered men a role as guardians of the allegorical body of the nation—a body that simultaneously incites and conceals the seduction of patriotic love. In the emotionally charged field of the political imagination, this heterosexual position invites the citizen to protect the object of his love from violation by other men (opponents or traitors within the nation) or other states (external threats to the survival of the Republic).

Violation and Protective Love

The iconography of the king's body described the organic relationships between the different estates composing the body politic. The body of the king was masculine, omnipotent, and eternal. While rejecting monarchy, republi-

cans aimed to fashion an equally invulnerable state. But the representation of
the nation as a woman introduced a different impediment: Insofar as it appeared as the body of a woman, the republican nation risked suffering specifically female injuries, frailties, and indignities. As republicans made abundantly
clear by their obsessive concern with modesty (*la pudeur*), sexual vulnerability
was woman's greatest weakness. As if to guard against the consequences of female weakness, republican allegories were routinely endowed by their creators
with masculine attributes, or at least elevated beyond the ordinary world of
feminine concerns.

Figure 4.13. *The Constitution of Year III. . . . By Violating Me Three Times
They Have Caused My Death!!!! May She Rest in Peace.* ca. 1799. Courtesy of
the Bibliothèque nationale de France.

Yet such concerns were never far from the surface of political life, even in the next century. Men's fears for the Republic's survival and their efforts to ward off dangers to its existence were expressed in the eroticized language of violation—the obverse of seduction. *The Constitution of Year III. . . By Violating Me Three Times They Have Caused My Death!!!! May She Rest in Peace* (Figure 4.13) identifies a series of coups against the French Constitution, culminating in Napoléon's coup of 18 Brumaire (9–10 November) 1799, as the rape of Republic. Taken sometimes as an unsympathetic, even counterrevolutionary image, this print operates as well to link republican men's honor to the chastity of a feminized state.

Conversely, the sexualization of the Republic—especially Republic's reduction to a prostitute by her enemies—invited men to associate their political objections to the republican Constitution with an act of sexual aggression. An untitled early twentieth-century print harkening back to 1870 (Figure 4.14) reprises these themes, but this time republicanism is confronted with foreign threats to France's integrity. A French soldier stands guard at France's bedroom, poised to protect her honor against the Prussian predator. This image is an uneasy one, however. The Prussian's vantage point seems more advantageous than that of her national suitor/protector. Door ajar, the Prussian stands ready to enter, while the citizen-soldier is reduced to impotence, listening for intruders from behind a closed door.

Love and Country

Like words, visual images help to create fictions, and both textual and visual versions of reality in the revolutionary period were yoked to nationalist passions. The personification of the nation-state during the Revolution gave license to the love that republicans felt for *La Patrie* and allowed for a more tangible expression of that passion than was expressible through words alone. Visual fictions were at once a holdover of traditional French Catholic and monarchical culture, but they also became the means by which a new political culture was forged. As Maurice Agulhon appreciates, "Once the State became collective and anonymous, it lost the means to be emotive unless it proved possible to reawaken devotion for the ideal that was its inspiration, namely Liberty, or the Republic, (the principles are linked, the names more or less interchangeable). But for Liberty or the Republic to be loved, was it not more or less necessary for them to be personified?"[64]

As faceless men were uniting to form the web we call the nation, the object of their political desires was represented as a beautiful, chaste, and anonymous female body. In the arena of political spectacle, men's fantasies of sexual

Figure 4.14. Untitled. 1914. Source: Maurice Agulhon and Pierre Bonte, *Marianne: Les Visages de la République* (Paris: Gallimard, 1992), 56.

possession were endowed with political meaning. The nation, as potential partner, is a fantastical projection with erotic overtones. Paradoxically, actual sexual possession was being relegated in this period to an increasingly private role—in the Greek sense of privacy, that is, hidden from the public view—and men's sexual passion tied to fatherhood in the republican codes of domesticity and family. Virile man's new partner—the Republic as chaste mother rather than a sister goddess—was desexualized but *not* altogether desensualized. In response to the widespread denigration of the style of the feminine arts, the actions of free (libertine) women, or the gender ambiguities that republicans associated with Old Regime excess, republican men saw the nation as a mother, in a double sense. To bear and nurture the next generation, *La Patrie* needed to elicit from men the desire of a lover as well as the compassion and respect of a son. In this way, the republican citizen was interpolated (to his new role) as a father in and of the fatherland.

Epilogue

Tᴴɪꜱ ʙᴏᴏᴋ began as an attempt to explore anew the consequences of a central problem in the history of representation: the substitution of a classical female goddess for a male icon, but one who was always metonymically tied to a particular person, either living or dead.[1] The shift from the body of the king to the body of the nation was all the more surprising because of the exclusion of women, at the same historical moment, from the most characteristic form of modern political organization in France as elsewhere—the all-male elective and representative assembly. Yet what is to be made of the fact that despite strong cultural currents and legal compulsions that allied women with nature and domesticity, images of women were everywhere present in the public realm? Additionally, a metaphorical body, not the portrait of a publicly recognized woman, stood for the most privileged and universalizing form of public life, the state and its institutions. These paradoxes led me to consider the interaction between visual and political argument, to regard representations of the body politic as a site of "graphic politics" in revolutionary France. By this formulation, I meant to capture the way in which images, like words, had the power to persuade, to take sides in political argument, and to encourage viewers to do so as well. Rather than treating the image as a (second-rate) illustration of ideas, an accompaniment to or surplus for a printed text (present or absent), I set out to look at the image on its own terms.

Before long, then, these intersecting issues of gender, politics, and imagery became part of a larger set of questions about the workings of visual culture in the passage from Old Regime to revolutionary society. An important obstacle to be addressed was the widespread prejudice against the image and the related assumption that the Revolution marked a turning point in the establishment of a modern regime of writing and texts, which in turn supplanted an older visual order. Just as François Furet once accused his fellow twentieth-century historians of repeating the gestures of Jacobinism, it could be said that recent scholarship on the Revolution carries over the linguistic biases of the revolutionary generation—thanks in no small measure to the enormous impact of Furet on contemporary history. The efforts of revolutionary leaders to replace images with texts and rational argument have been amply noted. I have sought instead to counterpose their statements to the unprecedented proliferation of political images during the revolutionary period. I am interested in the revolutionaries' willingness to exploit the power of images, even to adopt the tactics of their Catholic adversaries, whom they labeled superstitious mystifiers. Similarly, in response to influential proponents of the linguistic turn in revolutionary studies, I have aimed to demonstrate the persistence of the visual in this revolutionary transition, and not just as a faint shadow of its once radiant semblance. In place of a naïve view of the image as copy or metaphysical presence, I am encouraged by W. J. T. Mitchell's argument on behalf of picture theory as "a postlinguistic, postsemiotic rediscovery of the picture as a complex interplay between visuality, apparatus, institutions, discourse, bodies, and figurality. The realization that *spectatorship* (the look, the gaze, the glance, the practices of observation, surveillance and visual pleasure) may be as deep a problem as various forms of *reading* (decipherment, decoding, interpretation, etc.) and that 'visual experience' or 'visual literacy' might not be fully explicable in the model of textuality."[2]

The visual prints of the French Revolution satisfied a wide range of needs and motives—commercial, political, documentary, and pedagogical. They were intended to demean and elevate, to humor and mollify. Revolutionary print culture was both a medium of information and an early expression of mass culture. However, "the very element that makes visual imagery of all kinds distinct from texts," as Nicholas Mirzoeff explains, is the "undeniable impact on first sight that a written text cannot replicate." For David Freedberg, the image has the surprising ability to arouse "admiration, awe, terror and desire."[3] Such was the case, as I have sought to demonstrate, when female images were paraded openly within the revolutionary public sphere. And let us not forget, as well, that no matter how tame, sanctioned, or elevated the representation of a female body might have been, femininity—especially when openly displayed—always carried within it a charge of illicit pleasure and taboo desire, of partiality and difference against the universal's claim to speak for the whole—that is, for no one in particular. To observe the power of the image is also to confront the limitations of the utopian architectonics of Jürgen Habermas's model of the "bourgeois public sphere" as "an openly visible place or stage in which everything may be revealed, everyone may see and be seen, and in which everyone may speak and be heard."[4] Rather than imagining the public sphere as a sphere of free conversation, I have sought to present a model of public life that is more constrained, but at the same time more discordant.

Still, as a mechanically reproduced art form, in Walter Benjamin's justly famous formulation, the revolutionary print was part and parcel of the development of democratic culture. Although much has been written about the power of print and the dissemination of printed words through the market to serve as vehicles of democratic and nationalizing communication, so the same could be said of the mechanically reproduced image. In broadsides, engravings, or newspapers, images had the potential, which Benjamin attributes to the photograph in the nineteenth century, to diminish art's aura, even as it helped to make art more public and more useful. The multiply reproducible image was therefore ideally suited to the project of nationalism. To paraphrase Benedict Anderson on the fellowship that comes from reading a common print language, so, too, did fellow viewers, in their connection through printed images, form, in their secular, particular, and visible invisibility, the embryo of the nationally imagined community.[5]

Like all cultural productions, visual imagery and its reception are embodiments of mind and expressions of human intelligence. On my account, no outcomes are foreordained, nor does granting power to the image foreclose human agency. Although I have aimed to address the ways in which images may force or reinforce certain ideals, I hold open the possibility that individual viewers may respond to an image in unexpected ways. Similar violations— what, from the standpoint of the dominant culture, might be termed a "perverse" reading—challenged the efforts of those who sought through words to encode the image with a stable meaning. Whereas images are powerful instruments in shaping how individuals come to see themselves as members of a given nation-state, this does not preclude the possibility that image-makers' desired norms can be subverted in a resistant reading. Yet neither should we assume that image-makers' intentions are all of a piece or that the image is entirely transparent. From my perspective, the image is both multivalent and porous. It is always a site of contestation, of instability and excess. Not only in caricature, the most obvious case, but also in documentary and allegorical images, contrasting meanings may coincide or clash. In addition, it is important to allow for the heterogeneous mix of words and image within any specific work. Thus, in focusing on revolutionary images featuring women's bodies, I am frankly less interested in providing further evidence of women's victimization in the social and political order than I am in capturing the oppositional energies released within the regimes of both politics and vision.

I have suggested parallels between the resistance of the image to the text within the new discursive order established by the revolutionary break with the old regime, on the one hand, and the anomalous position of women in the new political order, on the other. Apart from whatever protests women may have registered against their political, legal, and social inequality—or against their prescribed disappearance from public affairs and arenas—it could be said that women (re)appeared in the graphic domain: even if, as far as we know, men were making most of the representations.

The age of print was steeped in strong traditions of visual representation. French men and women of the revolutionary period would have had a vast visual repertoire to draw on—from familiar Catholic sacred images in churches to cheap devotional prints hawked by colporteurs, from royal imagery displayed on coins, books, and broadsides to spectacular royal fêtes. Of course, all of these traditions were for revolutionaries the source of the problem. From our perspective, however, in an age in which the visual domain was gendered as feminine and demoted in relation to the more prestigious and reasonable work of the text, we can hardly count attacks on the image as innocent. In any event, it seems as if revolutionaries themselves discovered the limits of radical iconoclasm. We might hope that they came to understand that to textualize everything is to cut off one's head, that human cognition is in considerable measure the evolutionary inheritance of a complex visual apparatus. More likely, their motives were solely pragmatic. The very same politicians who denigrated the visual arts as sensual, seductive, dangerous, or feminine grasped the efficacy of the image. Like their predecessors, they relied on widely circulated allegories and caricatures to embody both their ideals and fears. To admit this is not, however, to imply that nothing had changed.

As I have argued in this book, to underscore the persistence of female allegories across the revolutionary divide is misleading. The same could be said about the deployment of prerevolutionary metaphors of female vice and danger. For example, although the new female representations may have looked like antique goddesses, they signified an altogether new relationship of the subject to the nation—one no longer rooted in the partiality and privilege that characterized Old Regime authority. Whether we are speaking of a shift from allegory to symbol, as Samuel Taylor Coleridge and the Romantics believed, or merely a shift in emphasis, there is no question that the new female body of the nation served to legitimate something novel—the individual's participation, irrespective of status, in a universal or collective whole. On the other hand, Benjamin's insistence on the narrative dimension of allegory is just as important. As the nation came to be embodied in the allegorical form of a female that same body could serve as a vehicle for history. What else is nationalism but the promise of a historical future (and past) for the members of the national community? And how convenient that the pledge was vested in the reproductive body of the republican mother?

All of these matters led me to question the broader meanings carried by the image in this age of discourse and text. Is it too far-fetched, I ask, to surmise that the image conveyed a sort of revenge of the feminine on the masculinization of politics and public life, on the one hand, or on the textualization of representation, on the other? I have not attempted to answer these questions. By posing them, I simply aim to suggest the possible stakes raised by the gendered representation of the national body of France. At the very least, what is at work here is a strong connection between visualization and the embodiment of ideas.

I have suggested that representations of the female body were a powerful motif in shaping ideas of the nation, including the roles of male and female citizens. In addition, I proposed that the imaged female body had a role to play in consolidating the erotic dimension of patriotism, which distinguished its function greatly from that of being a mere adornment to power, as in old regime iconography. Pointing to parallels between the domestic and public spheres, I elaborated on the ways in which a female embodiment of the nation elicited men's desire, and on how Eros helped to bind private passion to public duty. On these terms, republican citizenship offered men the opportunity to become guardians of the nation's allegorical body, to venture their lives for an abstract ideal. While not denying the (homoerotic) ties that bound men together in the forging of modern nationalism, I nevertheless insist that heterosexual desire was a potent force, which could be aroused by images of female vulnerability, beauty, and motherhood.

As for women, I have proposed the ways in which they, too, formed attachments to the nation-state, and, as political subjects, their subjectivity was also shaped in relation to the Republic's iconographic traditions. Doubtless it was frustrating to confront the paucity of evidence concerning women's relation to the image—not just as creators but also as spectators. What we do know suggests that women were not exempt from the powerful forces of nationalism; nor were their subjectivities any less well-consolidated or more fragile than men's. Moreover, family relationships were fraught with political meanings. To be a daughter, friend, wife, mother, or lover was also to live one's life as a national subject, but it was not only this. To the public meanings that attach to any given body are also a whole range of unconscious projections and identifications. But here I have been concerned to stress the former, to interrogate the way in which visual and political cultures coincide and collide. If we agree with the premise that nationalism is a relational concept, we need to know as much about woman's relationship to man as about man's relation to woman, and about how cross-sex relationships were mediated by same-sex or intergenerational attachments. In the interim, I gain some satisfaction from having demonstrated that the visual display of the female body had a good deal to do with how individuals forged their own sense of themselves as individual subjects and as members of a larger community that we still call the nation.

Notes

Introduction

1. Anne Norton, *Reflections on Political Identity* (Baltimore, 1988), 39.

2. Doris Sommer, *Foundational Fictions: The National Romances of Latin America* (Berkeley, 1991), 40–41.

3. The most comprehensive inventory of political prints remains *Un Siècle d'histoire de France par l'Estampe, 1770–1871: Collection de Vinck*, 4 vols. (Paris, 1909–29). Two other critical sources of French and British materials from the period are Georges Duplessis, *Inventaire de la collection d'estampes relatives à l'histoire de France léguée à la Bibliothèque nationale par M. Michel Hennin*, 5 vols. (Paris, 1881–84), and Mary Dorothy George, *Catalogue of Political and Personal Satires preserved in the Department of Prints and Drawings in the British Museum*, vols. 5–11 (London, 1935–52). For an overview of revolutionary print culture, see the following exhibition catalogs and critical works: Michel Vovelle, *La Révolution française: Images et récit, 1789–1799*, 5 vols. (Paris, 1986); Musée Carnavalet, *La Révolution française: Le Premier Empire* (Paris, 1982); Antoine de Baecque, *La Caricature révolutionnaire* (Paris, 1988); Claude Langlois, *La Caricature contre-révolutionnaire* (Paris, 1988); *French Caricature and the French Revolution, 1789–1799*, ed. James Cuno (Los Angeles, 1988); Claudette Hould, *Images of the French Revolution* (Quebec, 1989); *Representing Revolution: French and British Images, 1789–1804* (Amherst, Mass., 1989); Musée Carnavalet *L'Art de l'estampe et la Révolution française* (Alençon, 1980); James Leith and Andrea Joyce, *Face à Face: French and English Caricatures of the French Revolution and Its Aftermath* (Toronto, 1989); David Bindman, *The Shadow of the Guillotine: Britain and the French Revolution* (London, 1989); Emmett Kennedy, *A Cultural History of the French Revolution* (New Haven, Conn., 1989); Maurice Agulhon, *Marianne into Battle: Republican Imagery and Symbolism in France, 1789–1880*, trans. Janet Lloyd (Cambridge, 1981); Lynn Hunt, *Politics, Culture, and Class in the French Revolution* (Berkeley, 1984); Hunt, "Engraving the Revolution: Prints and Propaganda in the French Revolution," *History Today* 30 (1980): 11–17; Hans-Jürgen Lüsebrink and Rolf Reichardt, *The Bastille: A History of a Symbol of Despotism and Freedom*, trans. Norbert Schürer (Durham, N.C., 1997); Klaus Herding and Rolf Reichardt, *Die Bildpublizistik der Französischen Revolution* (Frankfurt am Main, 1989); *Aux armes et aux arts! les arts de la Révolution 1789–1799*, ed. Philippe Bordes and Régis Michel (Paris, 1988).

4. As in France, North American audiences had the chance to visit the major exhibition of French revolutionary caricatures, as well as notable exhibits at several locations, including the Library of Congress, the University of California at Los Angeles, the New York Public Library, the Musée du Québec, and other Canadian venues. Additionally, it is particularly gratifying that in just a decade more printed and digitalized sources have become available for teaching and consultation. Cf. *Images of the French Revolution Videodisk and Catalogue Co-produced by the Bibliothèque Nationale and Pergamon Press*, vol. 1 (Paris, 1990); Jack R. Censer and Lynn Hunt, *Liberty, Equality, Fraternity: Exploring the French Revolution* (University Park, Pa., forthcoming); *Sklavin Oder Bürgerin? Französische Revolution und Neue Weiblichkeit 1760–1830*, ed. Viktoria Schmidt-Linsenhoff (Frankfurt, 1989).

5. Studies of the body and representation in recent scholarship are too numerous to cite in full. However, *Fragments for a History of the Body*, ed. M. Feher, 3 vols. (New York, 1989), offers an example of the application of body history in numerous fields and historical periods. These trends are further illustrated by the founding of the journal *Representations* in 1983 by an interdisciplinary group of scholars. In the specific case of Old Regime and revolutionary France, there is a rich literature on which to draw, including Ernst Kantorowicz, *The King's Two Bodies: A Study in Medieval Political Theology* (Princeton, N.J., 1957); Marc Bloch, *The Royal Touch: Sacred Monarchy and Scrofula in England and France*, trans. J. E. Anderson (London, 1973); Norbert Elias, *The Court Society*, trans. Edmund Jephcott (New York, 1983); Michel Foucault, *Discipline and Punish: The Birth of the Prison*, trans. Alan Sheridan (New York, 1977); Joan B. Landes, *Women and the Public Sphere in the Age of the French Revolution* (Ithaca, N.Y., 1988); Dorinda Outram, *The Body and the French Revolution: Sex, Class, and Political Culture* (New Haven, Conn., 1989); Madelyn Gutwirth, *The Twilight of the Goddesses: Women and Representation in the French Revolutionary Era* (New Brunswick, N.J., 1992); Antoine de Baecque, *The Body Politic: Corporeal Metaphor in Revolutionary France, 1770–1800*, trans. Charlotte Mandell (Stanford, Calif., 1997); Nicholas Mirzoeff, *Bodyscape: Art, Modernity, and the Ideal Figure* (London, 1995); *From the Royal to the Republican Body: Incorporating the Political in Seventeenth- and Eighteenth-Century France*, ed. Sara E. Melzer and Kathryn Norberg (Berkeley, 1998); Peter Brooks, *Body Work: Objects of Desire in Modern Narrative* (Cambridge, Mass., 1993); Abigail Solomon-Godeau, *Male Trouble: A Crisis in Representation* (London, 1997); and Ewa Lajer-Burcharth, *Necklines: The Art of Jacques-Louis David after the Terror* (New Haven, Conn., 1999).

6. Antoine de Baecque, "The Allegorical Image of France, 1750–1800: A Political Crisis of Representation" *Representations* 47 (Summer 1994): 139; Barbara Stafford, *Good Looking: Essays on the Virtue of Images* (Cambridge, Mass., 1996), 11. Cf. James A. Leith, "The Terror: Adding the Cultural Dimension" in *Symbols, Myths, and Images of the French Revolution: Essays in Honor of James A. Leith*, ed. Ian Germani and Robin Swales (Regina, Saskatchewan, 1998), 3–16.

7. W. J. T. Mitchell, *Picture Theory: Essays on Verbal and Visual Representation* (Chicago, 1994), 5.

8. Brian C. J. Singer, *Society, Theory, and the French Revolution: Studies in the Revolutionary Imaginary* (New York, 1986), 102.

9. "Declaration of the Rights of Man and Citizen," trans. Keith Michael Baker, in *University of Chicago Readings in Western Civilization*, vol. 7, *The Old Regime and the French Revolution* ed. Keith Michael Baker (Chicago, 1987), 238.

10. See Hannah Arendt on the paradox of grounding universal human rights in the nation-state: *The Origins of Totalitarianism* (New York, 1979).

11. Hunt, "Freedom of Dress in Revolutionary France," in *From the Royal to the Republican Body*, 224–49; Jennifer Harris, "The Red Cap of Liberty: A Study of Dress Worn by French Revolutionary Partisans, 1789–1794," *Eighteenth-Century Studies* 14:3 (1981): 283–312.

12. See Marcel Garaud, with Romuald Szramkiewicz, *La Révolution française et la famille* (Paris, 1978). Shanti Singham offers an astute comparison of universalist absences in "Betwixt Cattle and Men: Jews, Blacks, and Women, and the Declaration of the Rights of Man," in *The French Revolution and the Idea of Freedom: The Old Regime and the Declaration of Rights of 1789*, ed. Dale Van Kley (Stanford, Calif., 1994), 154–98.

13. Jean-Jacques Rousseau, *Les Confessions*, in *Oeuvres complètes* (Dijon, 1959), 404–5, cited in Hunt, *Politics, Culture, and Class in the French Revolution*, 1.

14. In October 1793 the Convention introduced a revolutionary calendar to supplant the Christian calendar. The twelve months of the year were each divided into three ten-day weeks or *décades*, each poetically named for the weather—e.g., Brumaire for fog, Nivôse for snow, Floréal for spring flowers. The first year of the new calendar was dated from the establishment of the Republic on September 22, 1792. Thus, Year I of the Republic corresponded to 1792–93, Year II to 1793–94, and so on.

15. National Convention, session of 9 Brumaire Year II (30 October 1793), and General Council of the Commune of Paris, session of 27 Brumaire Year II (17 November 1793), in *Women in Revolutionary Paris, 1789–1795: Selected Documents Translated with Notes and Commentary*, ed. Darline Gay Levy, Harriet Branson Applewhite, and Mary Durham Johnson (Urbana, Ill., 1979), 212–20. Dominique Godineau suggests that the demand for direct democracy by the Society for Revolutionary Republican Women may have been an important factor in the Jacobin repression of women's organized political activity in October–November 1793. Dominique Godineau, *The Women of Paris and Their French Revolution*, trans. Katherine Streip (Berkeley, 1998), 158–74. Cf. Applewhite and Levy, "Women, Radicalization, and the Fall of the French Monarchy," in *Women and Politics in the Age of the Democratic Revolution*, ed. Harriet B. Applewhite and Darline G. Levy (Ann Arbor, Mich., 1990), 81–107; William H. Sewell, Jr., "Le citoyen/la citoyenne: Activity, Passivity, and the Revolutionary Concept of Citizenship," in *The Political Culture of the French Revolution*, ed. Colin Lucas (Oxford, 1988), 105–123; Christine Fauré, *Democracy without Women: Feminism and the Rise of Liberal Individualism in France*, trans. Claudia Gorbman and John Berks (Bloomington, Ind., 1991); Joan B.Landes, *Women and the Public Sphere*; Elisabeth G. Sledziewski, *Révolutions du Sujet* (Paris, 1989).

16. Dominique Godineau, "Political Practice during the French Revolution," in *Women and Politics in the Age of the Democratic Revolution,* 68.

17. Session of 9 Brumaire Year II of the National Convention, in *Réimpression de l'Ancien Moniteur,* vol. 18, 298–300, cited in *Women in Revolutionary Paris, 1789–1795,* 216–17.

18. George Mosse, *Nationalism and Sexuality: Middle-Class Morality and Sexual Norms in Modern Europe* (Madison, Wis., 1985).

19. As is now well appreciated, French women did not achieve equal citizenship with men in the new nation, and it was only in the last half of the twentieth century that they began to secure full rights in the political, social, and familial spheres.

20. Landes, *Women and the Public Sphere,* 67. I make a similar argument in two earlier published versions of Chapter 2, "Political Imagery of the French Revolution," in *Representing Revolution,* 13–21, and "Representing the Body Politic: The Paradox of Gender in the Graphic Politics of the French Revolution," in *Rebel Daughters: Women and the French Revolution,* ed. Sara E. Melzer and Leslie W. Rabine (Oxford, 1992), 15–37. Similarly, Sarah Maza states, "In the old symbolic order, the spotlight was on the stage, on the theatrical display of power at the core of which was the sacred body of the king; in the new, the focus was on the public, which was both the ultimate repository of power and that which needed to be taught, convinced, and controlled" (*Private Lives and Public Affairs: The Causes Célèbres of Prerevolutionary France* [Berkeley, 1993], 314). Maza and I are both indebted to Habermas on this point, particularly his contrasting discussion of the absolutist and bourgeois public spheres. From the perspective of Furet and Foucault, Marie-Hélène Huet discusses a similar development. See her account of the emphasis on language in the French Revolution, in *Rehearsing the Revolution: The Staging of Marat's Death, 1793–1797* (Berkeley, 1982).

21. See Jeffrey Ravel, "Seating the Public: Spheres and Loathing in the Paris Theaters, 1777–1788," *French Historical Studies* 18, no. 1 (Spring 1993): 173–210, and his *The Contested Parterre: Public Theater and French Political Culture, 1680–1791* (Ithaca, N.Y., 1999).

22. Maurice Agulhon, *Marianne au combat: L'Imagerie et la symbolique républicaines de 1789 à 1880* (Paris, 1979); *Marianne au pouvoir: L'Imagerie et la symbolique républicaines de 1880 à 1914* (Paris, 1989). The third volume of Agulhon's research was presented by the author in *Annales historiques de la Révolution française* 289 (1992); volume is published in English as *Marianne into Battle: Republican Imagery and Symbolism in France, 1789–1880,* trans. Janet Lloyd (Cambridge, 1981). Lynn Hunt, "Hercules and the Radical Image in the French Revolution," *Representations* 1, no. 2 (Spring 1983): 95–117; Hunt, *Politics, Culture, and Class in the French Revolution;* Hunt, *The Family Romance of the French Revolution* (Berkeley, 1992).

23. Marina Warner, *Monuments and Maidens: The Allegory of the Female Form* (New York: 1985); Madelyn Gutwirth, *The Twilight of the Goddesses.*

24. James A. Leith, "Ephemera: Civic Education through Images," in *Revolution in Print,* 270–89; Leith, *Space and Revolution: Projects for Monuments, Squares, and Public Buildings in France, 1789–1799* (Montreal, 1991); Leith, *The Idea of Art as Propaganda in France, 1750–1799: A Study in the History of Ideas* (1965; Toronto, 1969); Leith, *Media and Revolution: Moulding a New Citizen in France during the Terror* (1968; Toronto, 1974). The papers from a collo-

quium held to honor Leith's contribution to the study of visual imagery, propaganda, and cultural dimensions of the Revolution are collected in *Symbols, Myths, and Images of the French Revolution.*

25. Michel Vovelle, *La Révolution française: Images et récit,* 5 vols. (Paris, 1986); *Les Images de la Révolution française,* ed. Michel Vovelle (Paris, 1988); Antoine de Baecque, *La Caricature révolutionnaire;* de Baecque, "The Citizen in Caricature: Past and Present," in *The French Revolution and the Meaning of Citizenship,* ed. Renée Waldinger, Philip Dawson, and Isser Woloch (Westport, Conn., 1993); Langlois, *La Caricature contre-révolutionnaire;* Herding and Reichardt, *Die Bildpublizistik der Französischen Revolution;* Lüsebrink and Reichardt, *The Bastille.*

26. De Baecque, "The Allegorical Image of France," 138–39n9.

27. Nevertheless, see his discussion of "The Body of Liberty: Prophecy of a Completed Revolution," in *The Body Politic,* 320–23.

28. Gutwirth, *Twilight of the Goddesses,* xix, 383, 389n. 36.

29. "Women lost their erotic aura as goddesses of the high culture and entered modernity stripped of energy and aspiration, as man's mere, inferior, piously viewed, complement." Ibid., 384.

30. According to de Baecque, three forms emerged during the Bicentennial: "1) the return of the *enigma of the thinking and acting subject,* exemplified in the renewal of biography and textual studies (especially Kantian and Rousseauian); the recognition of the unpredictability of individual choice and of the complexity of the contract linking the individual and the community, especially in a time of revolution; 2) the *struggle of representations,* or the idea that what defines and unifies groups is not so much a class interest as a perception, a 'representation' of the self as belonging to a community and of the enemy as foreign to it; the Revolution in this sense may be described as an immense and quickly evolving form of introspection, aimed at shaping a representation of the socio-political body that could define who was to be included and who excluded; 3) the *primacy of the political,* understood as the most global instance of the organization of society, even more than the economic" ("The Allegorical Image of France," 140). Cf. Roger Chartier, "The World as Representation," in *Histories: French Constructions of the Past,* ed. Jacques Revel and Lynn Hunt, trans. Arthur Goldhammer and others (New York, 1995), 544–58 (originally published in *Annales* 44 [November–December 1989]: 1505–20).

31. Stafford, *Good Looking,* 5.

32. See Lynn Hunt, ed., *The New Cultural History* (Berkeley, 1989); Peter Burke, ed., *New Perspectives on Historical Writing* (University Park, Pa., 1992).

33. See Michel Foucault, *The Archaeology of Knowledge,* trans. A. M. Sheridan Smith (New York, 1972). For further considerations on the role of language, from outside the French tradition, which have also influenced Keith Baker, see J. G. A. Pocock, "Introduction: The State of the Art," in *Virtue, Commerce, and History* (Cambridge, 1985), 1–34; Quentin Skinner, "Meaning and Understanding in the History of Ideas," *History and Theory* 7 (1969): 3–53.

34. Keith Michael Baker, *Inventing the French Revolution: Essays on French Political Culture in the Eighteenth Century* (Cambridge, 1990), 4–5. I use Baker to exemplify the way in

which contemporary historians are indebted to both Furet and Foucault, on the one hand, and Habermas, on the other. But he is not alone in this respect. Since 1989, there has been a powerful revival of interest among French historians, influenced by French linguistic theories, in Habermas's account of public opinion.

35. Baker, *Inventing*, 7. See François Furet, *Interpreting the French Revolution*, trans. Elborg Forster (Cambridge, 1981).

36. Baker, *Inventing*, 9. Baker points out here that Hunt's effort to revise Furet's approach by characterizing the Revolution as a period in which language itself became charismatic is caught in a similar ambiguity: for instance, "How far (and in what manner) is the linguisticality of the French Revolution its 'special, temporary condition,' rather than 'a status it shares with any and all events'?" (*Inventing*, 8–9). See Hunt, *Politics, Culture, and Class*, and Hunt's review of Furet's *Penser la Révolution française* in *History and Theory* 20 (1981): 313–23.

37. Jürgen Habermas, *The Structural Transformation of the Public Sphere: An Inquiry into a Category of Bourgeois Society*, trans. Thomas Burger; Cambridge, Mass., 1989). The French translation of *Strukturwandel der Öffentlichkeit*, titled *L'Espace public: Archéologie de la publicité comme dimension constitutive de la société bourgeoise*, trans. Marc B. de Launay (Paris, 1978), was published in France in the same year as Furet's *Penser la Révolution française*. The title was given a splendid Foucauldian twist by its French translator and publisher, further testifying to the widespread influence that Foucault enjoyed among French academics in those years.

38. Habermas, *Structural Transformation*, 24.

39. In the second "structural transformation of the public sphere" under the conditions of advanced capitalism, Habermas points to the leading role played by advertising and 'public opinion' as we know it today as a function of publicity. Gone is the original liberal conception of the oppositional bourgeois public sphere in which publicity performed critical functions. In its place, opinion-making is monopolized by the state in conjunction with the goals of capitalist industry, and an older print culture is superceded in a media-tized public sphere. It is the Situationists who best bring out the role of the spectacle in modern society. And a good deal of poststructuralist and postmodernist cultural criticism has been devoted to charting this trend in public life. In other words, from a number of directions, scholars insist that the model of a discursive regime derived from eighteenth- and early nineteenth-century society is no longer suited to describing contemporary conditions. In place of discourse, one can point to a sort of "second coming" of the visual in today's market-driven, commodified, and media-saturated public sphere.

40. The phrase is Stafford's, *Good Looking*, 11.

41. Philip Stewart, *Engraven Desire: Eros, Image, and Text in the French Eighteenth Century* (Durham, N.C., 1992), xi–xii.

42. In *Politics, Culture, and Class*, Hunt provides an excellent account of the choice of Liberty for the seal of the first Republic, as well as subsequent efforts by the radical revolutionaries to promote the adoption of Hercules as an image of Republic. In "The Allegorical Image of France," de Baecque elaborates on Jacques-Louis David's proposal to the Convention on 17 Brumaire Year II, for a colossal statue of the French people, as well as the official

use of Liberty as a figure of republican administration during the Revolution. In turn, I am concerned with the impact of an even broader deployment of female imagery within revolutionary republican culture.

43. Whereas I have not chosen images for their documentary features, allegorical and caricatural images may document and record events. Moreover, revolutionary prints blurred the received generic distinctions between caricature and documentary, or even allegory and documentary. As Sura Levine remarks on the problem of documentary and caricature, "We usually think today of these two representational modes as wholly distinct, the one devoted to satirical or exaggerated renderings and the other to objective depictions. The images that survive from the Revolution suggest, however, how difficult it is to sustain such clear-cut divisions. Like caricatures, documentary images from the period are highly codified, stylized representations of the events they portray. And like documentary images, revolutionary caricatures possess a commemorative function, depicting historical figures and actions from the viewpoints and interests of particular social classes. Both kinds of images, then, construct their materials as much as they simply report on them. Setting the visual terms through which an event was to be understood, informing thereby the constantly changing political and social circumstances that they represent, revolutionary prints can productively be viewed as 'events' in their own right, as key moments in the consolidation of the new French nation" (Levine, "Print Culture in the Age of the French Revolution," in *Representing Revolution*, 7).

44. Claudette Hould offers the outlines of a history of revolutionary engraving and engravers that, as she says, has yet to be written ("Revolutionary Engraving," in *Images of the French Revolution*, 63). In *La Caricature révolutionnaire*, de Baecque identifies some six hundred caricatures produced during 1789 and 1792, five hundred of which are anonymous.

45. See *Representing Revolution*, cat. 9.

46. On Citoyenne Rollet, see Jules Renouvier, *Histoire de l'art pendant la Révolution: Considéré principalement dans les estampes* (Paris, 1863), 243–44. The paired abolitionist images are reproduced in Hugh Honour, *The Image of the Black in Western Art*, vol. 4, parts 1 and 2, *From the American Revolution to World War I* (Cambridge, Mass., 1976), 83–34 and 218 n. 203. In an unpublished paper, Paul T. Werner argues that the real intent of the female version of *Moi libre aussi* was not to commemorate the abolition of slavery but to draw an analogy between the newfound freedom of blacks and the still nonexistent freedom of women. "Brother Other: Blacks and Civil Rights in the French Revolution," paper presented to the Socialist Scholar's Conference, New York, 1995.

47. In his survey, Jules Renouvier (*Histoire de l'art pendant la Révolution*) also discusses the painters Adelaide Guyard (Labille-Guillard), Marguerite Gerard, and Mme Benoit (Benoiste, Mlle le Roux de la Ville). For further remarks on the numbers of women active in the arts in France during the eighteenth century, despite their very limited presence among the illustrious artists of the day, see Mary D. Sheriff, *The Exceptional Woman: Elisabeth Vigée-Lebrun and the Cultural Politics of Art* (Chicago, 1996), 262–63.

48. Nicolas Mirzoeff, "Revolution, Representation, Equality: Gender, Genre, and Emulation in the Académie Royale de Peinture et Sculpture, 1785–93," *Eighteenth-Century Studies* 31, no. 2 (1997–98): 153, 169. Labille-Guiard—like her better known associate, Elisabeth

Vigée-Lebrun, who went into exile during the Revolution—was admitted to the Academy in 1783, a period of artistic reform. Although women were admitted to the Academy at that time, their numbers were restricted to four—an issue that was protested in the artistic reform campaigns of the early Revolution. As for the early revolutionary period of artistic experimentation, including demands for gender equality, this directly parallels the period of gender possibility during the early years of the Revolution, which in 1793 was ended by the placing of restrictions on women's political freedom.

49. On the underrepresentation of women in the visual arts in the early modern period, and the position of one significant female artist of the period, compare Linda Nochlin, "Why Have There Been No Great Women Artists?" in *Women, Art, and Power and Other Essays* (New York, 1988), and Sheriff, *The Exceptional Woman*. Sheriff agrees with Nochlin that lack of education, not the lack of natural faculties, explains why women contributed so little to cultural developments in this period. Both Sheriff and Nochlin, however, are concerned primarily with the "high" rather than the "low" arts, with painters rather than printmakers.

50. Sheriff, *The Exceptional Woman*, 106.

51. *Lettres analitiques [sic], critiques et philosophiques sur les tableaux du Sallon (Paris, 1791)*, 13, cited in Mirzoeff, "Revolution, Representation, Equality"? 167.

52. Simone de Beauvoir, *The Second Sex*, cited in Rosemary Betterton, "How Do Women Look? The Female Nude in the Work of Suzanne Valadon," in *Visibly Female: Feminism and Art*, ed. Hilary Robinson (London, 1987).

53. John Berger, *Ways of Seeing* (London and Harmondsworth, 1989), 47. For a contrasting view, see Kenneth Clark, *The Nude: A Study in Ideal Form* (Garden City, N.Y., 1959).

54. Laura Mulvey, "Visual Pleasure and Narrative Cinema," *Screen* 16, no. 3 (1975): 11.

55. Michel Foucault, *The History of Sexuality*, vol. 1, *An Introduction*, trans. Robert Hurley (New York, 1978); Foucault, *Discipline and Punish*. Cf. Gilles Deleuze, *Foucault*, trans. Sean Hand (Minneapolis, 1988).

56. Lynda Nead, *The Female Nude: Art, Obscenity, and Sexuality* (London, 1992), 10.

57. See Joan DeJean, "Looking like a Woman: The Female Gaze in Sappho and Lafayette," *L'Esprit Créateur* 28 (Winter 1988): 35, cited in Mary Sheriff, "Letters: Painted/ Penned/Purloined," *Studies in Eighteenth-Century Culture*, vol. 26, ed. Syndy M. Conger and Julie C. Hayes (Baltimore, 1998), 30. Sheriff argues that to be "'oppositional'—rather than merely willful, wishful, or fanciful—an interpretation must, with political purpose, analyze, occupy, and strategically redeploy the signifiers at work in a specific historical image. An oppositional reading is most effective when it moves into and cites the same discourses engaged by an image, both describing how the image is shaped by those discourses and looking for the subversive possibilities within them" ("Letters: Painted/Penned/Purloined," 30).

58. Richard Leppert, *Art and the Committed Eye: The Cultural Functions of Imagery* (Boulder, Colo., 1996), 215. Leppert summarizes Marcia Pointon's insight into the "female nude as a form of rhetoric in which the subject is not fully contained or controlled either by the (male) artist, or the 'author,' or by the (male) spectator, or the 'reader'" in the following way: "In essence, the female nude *exceeds* her characterization by men, and this excess is not simply the result of external analysis by feminist spectators but in fact is inherent in the object itself. Put

perhaps too simply, the female nude, even (perhaps especially) in its most objectified and objectionable form—usually what we call pornographic—constitutes an acknowledgment by men of the ability of women to satisfy a desire that men cannot satisfy themselves. Moreover, the female nude represents an *imaginary* female body to which the male spectator has access only psychically, not physically. In representation, she remains explicitly out of reach, except in fantasy. In other words, the desire to look, and to 'possess' by looking, in the end only demonstrates that looking is *not* the same as 'having'" (*Art and the Committed Eye*, 214). Cf. Marcia Pointon, *Naked Authority: The Body in Western Painting, 1830–1908* (Cambridge, 1990).

59. On the distinction between symbol and allegory, see *The New Princeton Encyclopedia of Poetry and Poetics*, ed. A. Preminger and T. V. F. Brogan (Princeton, N.J., 1993); Fletcher, *Allegory*; and Terence Hawkes, *Metaphor* (London, 1972). In *The Origin of German Tragic Drama*, trans. John Osborne (London, 1963), Walter Benjamin contests the "symbolizing mode of thought" that took root around 1800—by this he would include both romanticism and neoclassicism —as foreign to allegorical expression in its original form. Thus, he counters Samuel Coleridge's formulation, which I am adopting here in order to make sense of the very movement of the symbol that Benjamin finds so objectionable in the modern period. Instead, Benjamin proposes to take allegory back to the baroque, before its neoclassical reinvention, in order to recapture the expressive and narrative dimension of the form. There he discovers a "strange combination of nature and history" and refers to the "violence of the dialectical movement in the allegorical depths" (*Origin of German Tragic Drama*, 167, 166). As he states, "Whereas in the symbol destruction is idealized and the transfigured face of nature is fleetingly revealed in the light of redemption, in allegory the observer is confronted with the *facies hippocratica* of history as a petrified, primordial landscape. Everything about history that, from the very beginning, has been intimately sorrowful, unsuccessful, is expressed in a face—or rather in a death's head. And although such a thing lacks all 'symbolic' freedom of expression, all classical proportion, all humanity—nevertheless, this is the form in which man's subjection to nature is most obvious and it significantly gives rise not only to the enigmatic question of the nature of human existence as such, but also to the biographical historicity of the individual" (*Origin of German Tragic Drama*, 166).

60. See Hunt, "Hercules and the Radical Image in the French Revolution."

61. Warner, *Monuments and Maidens*, xx.

62. Kaja Silverman, "Liberty, Maternity, Commodification," *New Formations* 5 (Summer 1988): 78. I borrow this formulation from Silverman. However, insofar as she stresses the deeroticization of the subject's relationship to Liberty, her analysis of Frédéric-Auguste Bartholdi's nineteenth-century Statue of Liberty differs from my own. Silverman emphasizes the foreclosure of sexuality and the resanctification of motherhood. Writing of the experience of entering into and climbing inside Bartholdi's statue, Silverman states, "It is crucial to understand that at some very important level Liberty is precisely an extension of the desire to 'return' to the inside of the fantasmatic mother's body without having to confront her sexuality in any way. Her 'contents' are erotic only in the sense that a bachelor machine or one of

Hans Belmer's '*poupées*' might be said to be; they are all system and structure" ("Liberty, Maternity, Commodification," 82).

63. Barbara Maria Stafford, *Body Criticism: Imaging the Unseen in Enlightenment Art and Medicine* (Cambridge, Mass., 1991), 12. See the marvelous image (13) accompanying Stafford's remarks: T. McLean, *The Body Politic or the March of the Intellect* (1836).

64. This is, of course, a central theme of de Baecque's outstanding contribution, *The Body Politic*. Cf. Marcel Gauchet, *La Révolution des droits de l'homme* (Paris, 1989), and *La Révolution des pouvoirs: la souveraineté, le peuple et la réprésentation 1789–1799* (Paris, 1995).

65. I borrow this phrase from Norman Bryson. See his "Gericault and 'Masculinity,'" in *Visual Culture: Images and Interpretation*, ed. Norman Bryson, Michael Ann Holly, and Keith Moxey (Hanover, N.H., 1994), 231. On this point, see Pierre Bourdieu, *Outline of a Theory of Practice*, trans. Richard Nice (Cambridge, 1977).

66. See Warner, *Monuments and Maidens*; Agulhon, *Marianne into Battle*; and Hunt, *Politics, Culture, and Class*.

67. Hunt adds, it was not a threatening femininizing force and hence not incompatible with republicanism. *La Nation* was, in effect, a masculine mother, or a father capable of giving birth" (*The Family Romance*, 99).

68. Mabel Berezin pursues a similar set of issues in her study of Italian fascism. See her "Political Belonging: Emotion, Nation, and Identity in Fascist Italy," in *State/Culture: State Formation after the Cultural Turn*, ed. George Steinmetz (Ithaca, N.Y., 1997).

69. "La patrie . . . la mère commune." Cited in Patrice Higonnet, *Goodness beyond Virtue: Jacobins during the French Revolution* (Cambridge, Mass., 1998), 144. *La patrie* may be translated in a number of ways—most commonly, the fatherland, but also homeland, native land, and mother country. The gender of the French noun motivates a feminine identification, whereas *patrie* from the Latin *patria*, from *patrius*, refers to the fatherland. As I discuss throughout this book, especially in Chapter 4, the doubled gender associations are an important component of the emotional affect of patriotism.

70. For a similar perspective, see Joan Wallach Scott, *Only Paradoxes to Offer: French Feminists and the Rights of Man* (Cambridge, 1996).

CHAPTER I

IMAGE AS ARGUMENT IN REVOLUTIONARY POLITICAL CULTURE

1. Jean-Antoine-Nicolas de Caritat, marquis de Condorcet, *Sketch for a Historical Picture of the Human Mind*, trans. June Barraclough, intro. Stuart Hampshire (New York, 1955), 37, 39. Condorcet's *Sketch* was first published by the French Republic at its own expense in an edition of three thousand copies in the Year III (1795). It was an improved version of the hastily written manuscript titled *Prospectus d'un tableau historique des progrès de l'esprit humain*, found after Condorcet's death. When Condorcet's complete works appeared in 1847, the editor M. F. Arago indicated that he had revised the manuscript of the *Esquisse*. It is thought that the manuscript to which he referred may have been one in the possession of

Condorcet's daughter, who was his collaborator in the publication of her father's works. (See "Note on Works" in Ibid., xiii–xiv). See *Esquisse d'un tableau historique des progrès de l'esprit humain* in *Oeuvres complètes de Condorcet*, ed. A. Condorcet O'Connor and M. F. Arago, vol. 6 (Paris, 1947).

2. Condorcet, *Sketch.*

3. In light of claims to the primacy of the discursive and the secondary nature of the visual, see Walter D. Mignolo's admirable effort to link the privileging of European forms of literacy to the conquest of America (*The Darker Side of the Renaissance* [Ann Arbor, Mich. 1995]). In this context, he contrasts Amerindian and European writing systems, demonstrating how alphabetic writing is linked with the exercise of power, and considers the role of the book in colonial relations. He addresses deep-seated "humanist biases"—against the visual and in favor of print. Thus, Renaissance humanism is identified as one of the factors that predisposed Europeans to conquer native peoples of the New World, not just because they were naked (as I point out in Chapter 4), but because they had no written language.

4. Condorcet, *Sketch*, 11, 42.

5. *Ibid.*, 100 (my emphasis).

6. *Ibid.*, 101–102.

7. *Ibid.*, 99.

8. It is striking how far Condorcet diverges from Leonardo da Vinci's defense of painting against poetry because of its superiority of "natural likeness" ("Paragone: Of Poetry and Painting," in *Treatise on Painting, (Codex urbinas latinus 1270)*, trans. and annotated by A. Philip McMahon [Princeton, N.J., 1956]). Cf. W. J. T. Mitchell, *Iconology: Image, Text, Ideology* (Chicago, 1986).

9. Barbara Stafford points to the widespread use during the eighteenth century of metaphors of "graphic despotism." Such metaphors registered the change in "northern Europe (especially France, Germany, the Low Countries, and Great Britain). . . from an oral, visual, and aristocratic culture to a market-centered, democratic, print culture. Supposedly ignorant listeners and gullible onlookers had to be molded into silent and solitary readers" (*Artful Science: Enlightenment Entertainment and the Eclipse of Visual Education* [Cambridge, Mass., 1994], 1).

10. Roger Chartier, "General Introduction: Print Culture," in *The Culture of Print: Power and the Uses of Print in Early Modern Europe*, trans. Lydia G. Cochrane (Princeton, N.J., 1989), 1.

11. Elizabeth Eisenstein, *The Printing Press as an Agent of Change: Communications and Cultural Transformations in Early-Modern Europe*, vols. 1 and 2 (Cambridge, 1979), 67–70. Cf. Walter Benjamin, "The Work of Art in the Age of Mechanical Reproduction," in *Illuminations*, ed. Hannah Arendt, trans. Harry Zohn (New York, 1968); Chandra Mukerji, *From Graven Images: Patterns of Modern Materialism* (New York, 1983); Kristin Eldyss Sorensen Zapalac, *"In His Image and Likeness": Political Iconography and Religious Change in Regensburg, 1500–1600* (Ithaca, N.Y., 1990); Tessa Watt, *Cheap Print and Popular Piety, 1550–1640* (Cambridge, 1991); Philip Stewart, *Engraven Desire: Eros, Image, and Text in the French Eighteenth*

Century (Durham, N.C., 1992). On the varieties of print culture during the French Revolution, see *Revolution in Print: The Press in France, 1775–1800*, ed. Robert Darnton and Daniel Roche (Berkeley, 1989).

12. See Louis Marin, *Le Portrait du roi* (Paris, 1981). On propaganda functions of the monarchy, see Joseph Klaits, *Printed Propaganda under Louis XIV: Absolute Monarchy and Public Opinion* (Princeton, N.J., 1976); Christian Jouhaud, "Readability and Persuasion: Political Handbills" and "Printing the Event: From La Rochelle to Paris," in *The Culture of Print*, 235–60, 290–333. On royal ceremony as another instance, see Lawrence M. Bryant, *The King and the City in the Parisian Royal Entry Ceremony: Politics, Ritual, and Art in the Renaissance* (Geneva, 1986); Ralph Giesey, *The Royal Funeral Ceremony in Renaissance France* (Geneva, 1960).

13. Chartier, "Political Persuasion and Representation: Introduction," in *The Culture of Print*, 233.

14. However, see Marie-Hélène Huet's compelling discussion of Robespierre's antirepresentational impulses in "The End of Representation," in *Mourning Glory: The Will of the French Revolution* (Philadelphia, 1997), 32–58.

15. "Peut-être, pour faciliter le passage de l'erreur à la vérité, convient-il, dans ces premiers moments de substituer, par ménagement pour d'anciennes habitudes, une sorte de culte éphémère des êtres moraux à celui de la Vierge immaculée, des patrons et des patronnes, des saints et des saintes de l'ancien calendrier. Mais si nous voulons amener le peuple au culte pur de la Raison, loin de favoriser son penchant à réaliser des abstractions, à personnifier des êtres moraux, il faudra nécessairement le guérir de cette manie, qui est la principale cause des erreurs humaines; il faudra que les principes métaphysiques de Locke et de Condillac deviennent populaires, que le peuple s'habitue à ne voir dans une statue qu'une pierre, et dans une image qu'une toile et des couleurs; sans cela, je ne serais point surpris de voir une espèce de polythéisme s'établir parmi nous" (*Annales patriotiques et littéraires*, vols. 16–17 [Paris, 23 Brumaire, Year II], 1467; cited in Alphonse Aulard *Le Culte de la Raison et Le Culte de l'Etre Suprême (1793–1794): Essai historique* [Paris, 1904], 87). See the commentaries on Salaville's pronouncements by Antoine de Baecque, "The Allegorical Image of France, 1750–1800: A Political Crisis of Representation," *Representations* 47 (Summer 1994): 133, and Lynn Hunt, "Pourquoi la république est-elle une femme?: La Symbolique républicaine et l'opposition des genres, 1792–1799," in Michel Vovelle, ed., *République et Révolution: L'Exception française* (Paris, 1994).

16. See Hunt's influential discussion of these issues in *Politics, Culture, Class in The French Revolution* (Berkeley, 1984), especially chap. 3, "The Imagery of Radicalism." Significantly, the revolutionary embrace of the allegorical image was prefigured in earlier aesthetic struggles over the role of figurative imagery in the arts, by such art critics as Denis Diderot, Johann Joachim Winckelman, Johann Georg Sulzer, Jean-François Marmontel, Antoine Court de Gébelin.

17. Jules Michelet points out that for fear of creating a new form of idolatry, a living image was substituted in the Festival of Reason at Notre-Dame: "It was objected that a fixed

simulacrum might remind the people of the Virgin *and create another idolatry.* So a mobile, live, animated image was preferred. This image, changing with every festival could not become an object of superstitious adoration. The founders of the new cult, who in no way intended to trivialize it, expressly recommended in their newspapers, that those who would like to have a festival in other cities, *chose, to fill this august part, persons whose characters made their beauty respectable, whose heartfelt behavior and modest gaze discouraged licentiousness and filled the heart with pure and honest feelings"* (cited in Huet, *Mourning Glory,* 43; emphasis in original). The discussion of festivals is a major theme in revolutionary scholarship since the pathbreaking studies by Aulard and by Mona Ozouf, *Festivals and the French Revolution,* trans. Alan Sheridan (Cambridge, Mass., 1988). For a further exploration of these themes, see Huet, *Mourning Glory*; Lynn Hunt, *Politics, Culture, and Class.* On Rousseau's ideas, see Jean Starobinski, *Jean-Jacques Rousseau: La Transparence et l'obstacle, suivi de sept essais sur Rousseau* (Paris, 1971).

18. "Nous ne concevons rien que par des images: dans l'analyse la plus abstraite, dans la combinaison la plus métaphysique, notre entendement ne se rend compte que par des images, notre mémoire me s'appuie et ne se repose que sur des images" (*Rapport fait à la Convention Nationale dans la séance du second mois de la seconde année de la République française au nom de la Commission chargée de la Confection du Calendrier*; cited in Ernst Gombrich, "The Dream of Reason: Symbolism of the French Revolution," *British Journal for Eighteenth Century Studies* 2, no. 3 [1979]: 192).

19. Henri Grégoire, *Rapport fait au Conseil des Cinq-Cents, sur les sceaux de la République* (Paris 11 Pluviose, Year IV [31 Janvier 1796]); cited in de Baecque, "The Allegorical Image," 134.

20. Henri Grégoire, *Rapport sur les moyens de rassembler les matériaux nécessaires à former les Annales du civisme, et sur la forme de cet ouvrage; par le citoyen Grégoire (Séance du 28 septembre 1793)*; cited in Lynn Hunt, "The Political Psychology of Revolutionary Caricatures," in *French Caricature and the French Revolution, 1789–1799,* ed. James Cuno (Los Angeles, 1988), 34.

21. "Toi, sainte Liberté, viens habiter ce temple, Sois la déesse des Français!" This description of the festival is drawn from Gombrich, "The Dream of Reason," 188.

22. "Législateurs! Le fanatisme a cédé la place à la raison. Aujourd'hui un peuple immense s'est porté sous ces voûtes gothiques, qui pour la première fois ont servi d'écho à la verité. Là les Français ont célébré le seul vrai culte, celui de la liberté, celui de la raison. . . là nous avons abandonné des idoles inanimées, pour cette image animée, chef d'oeuvre de la nature." Hébert, an active promoter of the de-Christianization movement, spoke of the woman as "une femme charmante, belle comme la déesse, qu'elle représentait." Cited in Gombrich, "The Dream of Reason," 188–89.

23. "Déese de la Raison! L'homme sera toujours homme, en dépit des raffinements de l'orgueil et de l'opiniâtre fatuité de l'égoisme; toujours il lui faudra des images sensibles, pour l'élever aux objets insensibles. Tu nous offres avec tant de naturel la Raison, dont tu es l'emblème, que nous serions tentés de confondre la copie avec l'original. Tu réunis en toi les moyens physiques et moraux pour la rendre aimable" (*Le Discours républicain prononcé le dernier*

decadi frimaire, jour de l'inauguration du temple de la Raison, par le citoyen Jacques-Antoine Brouillet, prédicateur de morale nommé par la Société des Amis de la République une et indivisible, séante à Avize, et l'un de ses membres, S.I., an II; cited in Aulard, *Le Culte de la Raison*, 88).

24. The de-Christianization campaign soon succumbed to the changing political climate. In its place a return to religion was advanced, without any of the forms of Old Regime Christianity. Robespierre led an attack on the Cult of Reason and its promoters, and a decree was passed announcing the new official belief in a Supreme Being and the immortality of the soul. Nonetheless, the deistic and patriotic Festival of the Supreme Being of 8 June was not free of images or theater. The artist Jacques-Louis David staged a series of topoi to mark the erasure of the Cult of Reason, beginning with Robespierre's burning of a statue representing atheism.

25. "[Q]ue les sens et l'imagination des philosophes se trouvent également choqués et de l'idée d'une *femme* représentant la *Raison* et de la jeunesse de cette femme. Dans les femmes, cette faculté si pure s'identifie pour ainsi dire à la *faiblesse*, aux *préjugés*, aux *attraits* même de ce sexe enchanteur. Chez l'homme, son empire est dégagé de toute erreur: la *force*, l'*énergie*, la *sévérité* y forment un cortège. Mais surtout la raison est *mûre*, elle est *grave*, elle est *austère*, qualitiés qui siéraient fort mal à une jeune femme. J'ai donc cru devoir appliquer l'idée de *jeune* à la *Liberté*, dont l'empire commence" (cited in Aulard, *Le Culte de la Raison*, 88– 89).

26. Etienne Bonnot, Abbé de Condillac, *Essay on the Origin of Human Knowledge,* in *Philosophical Writings of Etienne Bonnot, Abbé de Condillac*, trans. Franklin Philip, 2 vols. (Hillsdale, N.J., 1982), vol. 2. Originally published as *Essai sur l'origine des connaissances humaines*, in *Oeuvres*, vol. 3 (Paris, 1795–1801). Cf. the valuable study by Isabel Frances Knight, *The Geometric Spirit: The Abbé de Condillac and the French Enlightenment* (New Haven, Conn., 1968). In the following discussion, I am indebted to the excellent portrayal of the gender implications of Condillac's and Roussel's thought in Mary Sheriff, *Exceptional Woman Elisabeth Vigée-Lebrun and the Cultural Politics of Art* (Chicago, 1996), 20–25. On these issues, cf. Michelle Le Doeuff, *The Philosophical Imaginary* (Stanford, Calif., 1989), and Ludmilla Jordanova, *Sexual Visions: Images of Gender in Science and Medicine between the Eighteenth and Twentieth Centuries* (Madison, Wis., 1989).

27. Sheriff, *Exceptional Woman*, 23.

28. Ibid., 24.

29. Cited in ibid., 24. See Pierre-Jean-George Cabanis, *On the Relations between the Physical and Moral Aspects of Man*, trans. Margaret Duggan Saidi, ed. George Mora, intro. Sergio Moravia and George Mora, 2 vols. (Baltimore, 1981); originally published as Pierre-Jean-Georges Cabanis, *Rapports du physique et du moral de l'homme* (Paris, Year X–XIII [1802–05]); and Pierre Roussel, *Système physique et moral de la femme* (Paris, 1775).

30. "Je ne sais même si l'idée *d'un temple à la Raison* n'a pas quelque chose de contrastant avec celle que nous avons de la Raison elle-même. Chaque homme n'est-il pas le temple de la Raison? Son culte, n'est-ce pas l'étude?" (cited in Aulard, *Le Culte de la Raison*, 89).

31. Ozouf, *Festivals*, 99.

32. Huet, *Mourning Glory*, 46; Ozouf, *Festivals*, 102; Hunt, *Family Romance*, 154–55. The

program for the festival, according to David's script, specified that the women in the ceremony be all spouses and mothers. Women, young children, and the elderly were to be separated from fathers and sons old enough to bear arms: "The chaste bride braids her dear
daughter's hair with flowers; while the suckling child—a mother's most beautiful ornament—
presses her breast; the son seizes his weapons with a vigorous arm; he wants to receive his
baldric from his father alone. . . . The mothers leave their spouses and sons . . . the fathers
leave their sons armed with swords; both carry an oak branch in their hands" (*Le Moniteur*,
vol. 20, 653; cited in Huet, *Mourning Glory*, 47).

33. Jean-Joseph Goux, *Les Iconoclastes* (Paris, 1978), 12–13, citation and discussion in
Huet, *Mourning Glory*, 46–47 (emphasis in original). On revolutionary iconoclasm, see Stanley J. Idzerda, "Iconoclasm during the French Revolution," *American Historical Review* 60
(1954).

34. Hunt disagrees in part with Huet's reading of the festival. She writes that the Festival
of the Supreme Being and its representations were too abstract to suggest any gender—for instance, an all-seeing eye in the triangle, "a representation that is too abstract to suggest any
gender. In other words, the festival underlined the importance of clear gender boundaries and
of family feeling, but it stopped short of reinstituting a patriarchal family or patriarchal religion. Women had to maintain their proper place within a family that emphasized the natural sentiments of both parents for their children" (*The Family Romance*, 156).

35. Mukerji, *From Graven Images*, 15. Cf. Mukerji's *Territorial Ambitions and the Gardens
of Versailles* (Cambridge, 1997).

36. De Baecque, "The Allegorical Image of France," 134.

37. Cf. Michel Foucault, *Discipline and Punish: The Birth of the Prison*, trans. Alan Sheridan, (New York, 1977); *The Birth of the Clinic: An Archaeology of Medical Perception, trans. A.
M. Sheridan Smith* (New York, 1973).

38. As Jeremy Popkin notes, "Throughout the revolutionary decade newspaper publishers and printers faced very real risks to their persons and property" (*Revolutionary News: The
Press in France, 1789–1799* (Durham, N.C., 1990), 76.

39. On the basis of a study of the engravings of one journal in the first two years of the
Revolution, Jack Censer argues that as a group engravers tended to be politically unsophisti-
cated and sometimes pragmatic in their politics. As he states, the Revolution "found engravers
satisfied financially, somewhat frustrated artistically, and largely untutored in political matters. Yet the Revolution scarcely tolerated neutrality, and most Parisians had to choose one
side or another. . . . Those who allied with the counterrevolutionaries could readily see not
only popular excesses and an end to certain social distinctions that they had enjoyed, but
more important, they could foresee a crushing blow to the luxury trades and their business
prospects in particular. Lacking a long term ideology, they had only dissatisfaction to pro-
claim. On the other hand, those who favored the Revolution were also likely to be exceptionally critical. Once turned against the Old Regime, they could easily find many injustices
in their past condition. Their treatment in the Academies must have been a sore point. In
sum, while the engravers had experienced past inequities, their acquaintance with a positive
revolutionary ideology was new and probably shallow. They had much to complain about but

little constructive to contribute" ("The Political Engravings of the *Révolutions de France et de Brabant*, 1789–1791," *Eighteenth-Century Life* 5, no. 4 [Summer 1979]: 120).

40. Claudette Hould, "Revolutionary Engravings," in Hould *Images of the French Revolution*, (Quebec, 1989), 74. Hould further reports that the charge of the Committee of Public Safety to maintain "the purity of public morality in this great city" led to explicit actions in early 1794: "Carré, the only engraver, and Dien, a printer having done engravings of the Capet family, were handed over to the correctional police tribunal, while print merchants had their works seized: 'In every shop were found not only emblems of royalty but trunks full of kings, queens and dauphins. . . .' Basset, Chéreau, Esnault and Rapilly, Joubert and Depeuille saw engraved copper plates sent to be melted, while 'wagonfuls of engravings of royal effigies' went to the trash can. Despite his political opportunism, six thousand copper plates were examined at Basset's by the Beaurepaire section of the Revolutionary Committee. The bookstores in particular were closely watched. Weber, publisher at the royal Palace, was brought back from the army and jailed at the Conciergerie. His engravings were sent to the Revolutionary Tribunal. On May 20, 1794, he was sentenced to death 'for having published political and obscene writings.' Mercier, Hébert, Desenne and Lallemand were imprisoned, whereas Gattey, the famous merchant of aristocratic brochures was sentenced to death" ("Revolutionary Engravings," 74). Furthermore, artists were victims of denunciations by their fellow artists. The Popular and Republican Society of the Arts heard denunciations of various obscene works by its members, and Hould speculates that the accusations against the celebrated artist [Louis-Léopold] Boilly may have been the result of the hunt for doubtful engravings.

41. The association of engraving and business, along with the frequent charge that engraving amounted to mere copying rather than the more elevated art of imitating nature practiced by painters and sculptors, meant that engravers were long considered a poor relation to the fine arts. Engravers, in turn, objected to this condescension. As Hould reports, on 9 October 1789, the Paris engravers wrote to Abbé de Fontenai, author of the *Journal général de France*, to complain about the painters having poorly hung the engravings at the Salon: "How is it that the academic aristocrats, so proud of their talents, do not show more respect for the artists who make them known? Their works, no matter how beautiful, would be no more than a speck on the horizon if they were not multiplied like poems by our prints?" ("Revolutionary Engravings," 70). On the importance of public exhibitions during the eighteenth-century, see Thomas Crow, *Painters and Public Life in Eighteenth-Century Paris* (New Haven, Conn., 1985).

42. Denis Bruckmann, "Introduction" to *Images of the Revolution (Videodisk and Catalogue) Coproduced by the Bibliothèque Nationale and Pergamon Press*, catalog vol. 1 (Paris, 1990), 8.

43. Hould, "Revolutionary Engravings," 78–79. According to Hould, a 1790 brochure for Camille Desmoulins's *Révolutions de France et de Brabant* states "that each time it is published, fifteen to twenty thousand are distributed in Paris" ("Revolutionary Engravings," 79).

44. Hould finds in Athanase Détournelle's remarks evidence of the fact that engravers

had perhaps less difficulty than other artists in maintaining their economic status during the revolutionary decade. In his plea for government subsidies for the arts, in the context of a contest to be held for the embellishment of Paris (from which engravers would be excluded), Détournelle also suggests the wider social utility of engraving, stating, "If encouraged by the government, Artists will abandon all speculation and concern themselves only with glory. If, as I believe, Painters and Sculptors recount the virtuous acts of the Revolution, Engravers could be requisitioned to multiply and disseminate them throughout the Nation. In this way, the poor will also have the opportunity of owning the beautiful Prints which would otherwise be denied them" (cited in Hould, "Revolutionary Engravings," 67).

45. Hould, "Revolutionary Engravings," 81.

46. At the height of the radical Revolution, in an effort to mount what [Bertrand] Barère called "a vast plan for regeneration," the republican government turned to broad range of media, including festivals, songs, plays, newspapers, paintings, monuments, and caricatures (James Leith, "Historical Introduction" to *Face à Face: French and English Caricatures of the French Revolution and Its Aftermath* [Toronto, 1989], 19).

47. Hould, "Revolutionary Engravings," 67.

48. Pierre Bourdieu, *The Field of Cultural Production*, ed. and intro. Randal Johnson (Cambridge, 1993).

49. Philippe Bordes, "Le Recours a l'allégorie dans l'art de la Révolution française," in *Les Images de la Révolution française*, ed. Michel Vovelle (Paris, 1988), 243–44. Cf. Philippe Bordes, "L'Art et le Politique," in *Aux armes et aux arts! les arts de la Révolution, 1789–1799*, ed. Philippe Bordes and Régis Michel (Paris, 1988), 103–35.

50. "Puisqu'un tableau n'est destiné qu'à me montrer ce qu'on ne me dit pas, il est ridicule qu'il faille des efforts pour l'entendre. . . . Et pour l'ordinaire, quand je suis parvenu à deviner l'intention de ces personnages mystérieux, je trouve que ce qu'on m'apprend ne valait guère les frais de l'enveloppe" (*Histoire du Ciel*, vol. 2, 427; quoted by Ernst Gombrich, "*Icones Symbolicae*: Philosophies of Symbolism and Their Bearing on Art," in *Symbolic Images: Studies in the Art of the Renaissance* (London, 1978), 123.

51. George Richardson, "Introduction" to Ripa, *Iconology; or, a Collection of Emblematical Figures* (1779), 2 vols. (New York, 1979), vol. 1, i. Certainly, it is difficult to retrieve all of the lost symbols and metaphorical associations that such speaking pictures might have conveyed to eighteenth-century audiences. As Philip Stewart (among others) concedes, "We have difficulty assimilating fully the meaning of such double allusions, to the extent that we no longer possess as thoroughly as did their original viewers and readers an internalized repertory of traditional allegorical knowledge—and the classical languages on which they depended—then sometimes referred to as *iconologie*" (*Engraven Desire*, 24). On the other hand, we can be guided by such detailed works as Hubert François Gravelot and Charles Nicolas Cochin's *Iconologie* in understanding the extent to which engravers sought not a perfect resemblance of the (real) world but rather a selective representation of the world in which memory is inscribed.

52. "Discours préliminaire," in Hubert François Gravelot and Charles Nicolas Cochin,

Iconologie par figures ou traité complet des allégories, emblêmes, vol. 1 (Paris, 1791), x–xii.

53. Lester C. Olson, *Emblems of American Community in the Revolutionary Era: A Study in Rhetorical Iconology* (Washington, D.C., 1991), xvi.

54. Jean-François Janinet greeted the Revolution by producing a series of engravings of fifty-six principal scenes from the opening of the Estates-General through March 1791, *Gravures historiques des principaux événements depuis l'ouverture des Etats-Généraux* (Paris, 1789[–90]).

55. Ripa, *Iconology,* vol. 2, 56.

56. Maurice Agulhon, *Marianne, into Battle: Republican Imagery and Symbolism in France, 1789–1880,* trans. Janet Lloyd (Cambridge, 1981), 18.

57. I have drawn the following description of Philibert-Louis Debucourt's print from the excellent catalog entry in *French Caricature and the French Revolution,* cat. 127. For illustrations of Debucourt and Janinet's prerevolutionary works, see the exhibition catalog *Regency to Empire: Printmaking, 1715–1814,* organized by Victor I. Carlson and John W. Ittmann (Baltimore and Minneapolis, 1984).

58. Debucourt was a student of Joseph Marie Vien, David's teacher and holder of the title of first painter to the king and director of the Academy at the time of the Revolution. Although Debucourt was admitted to the Academy in 1781 as a painter, five years later he abandoned painting in favor of printmaking, becoming famous for his colored, multiple-plate intaglio prints depicting the elegant life of Parisian society. This particular work is an example of the single-plate prints that he executed in the English manner, to conform to the economic pressures of the revolutionary period (*French Caricature,* 228).

59. I certainly do not mean to imply that caricaturists were devoid of academic training or unfamiliar with academic guidelines. I mean only to call attention to the more relaxed style of caricatural drawings in contrast to formally posed allegories.

60. See Hans-Jürgen Lusebrink and Rolf Reichardt, *The Bastille: A History of a Symbol of Despotism and Freedom,* trans. Norbert Schürer (Durham, N.C., 1997).

61. See James Cuno, "Introduction," and Ronald Paulson, "The Severed Head," in *French Caricature.* Despite the broader popular appeal and composition of Reformation print culture, cultivated minorities there were also a critical audience for graphic art; and political elites used partisan prints to mobilize the people for one or another cause (Robert Philippe, *Political Graphics: Art as a Weapon* [New York, 1980]).

62. Natalie Zemon Davis, "Women on Top," in *Society and Culture in Early Modern France* (Stanford, Calif., 1975), 131.

63. In another version of this image, *Eh bien J . . . F . . . , dira-tu encore vive la noblesse? Oh non sandisse le Diable me berce* (Well, well, J . . . F . . . , do you still say long live nobility? Oh no, damn! The devil rocks me), the soldier attributes such delusions to the devil's work.

64. Honoré Gabriel Riqueti, comte de Mirabeau, having recognized him on the road, was said to have called out to him, "Passe ton chemin, salope!" ("Pass along, whore") (cited in *Histoire et dictionnaire de la Révolution française, 1789–1799,* ed. Jean Tulard, Jean-François Fayard, and Alfred Fierro [Paris, 1987], 512). See the caricature *Ci-devant duc d'Aiguillon: passe salope* (Paris: Webert , 1792), published in the *Journal de la Cour et de la ville,* January 1792.

65. Of course, in the prerevolutionary pornographic pamphlet literature, the queen is also made the target of such attacks. See Chapters 2 and 3.

66. De Baecque discusses the various versions of "patriotic discipline" in revolutionary caricature from its first appearance in July 1789 as an accompaniment to a pamphlet titled *Dialogue entre un noble et sa femme qui fut fessée au Palais-Royal pour avoir conspué le portrait de M. Necker* (Dialogue between a noble and his wife who was whipped at the Palais-Royal for having spit on a portrait of Monsieur Necker, (*Caricature révolutionnaire*, 97). For noted incidents of spankings, in relation to women's violent behavior, see Gutwirth, *Twilight of the Goddesses*, 312–314.

67. Elisabeth Roudinesco, who presents the competing versions of this incident in contemporary press accounts as well as its place in revolutionary historiography, provides the best account of this event in *Théroigne de Méricourt: A Melancholic Woman during the French Revolution*, trans. Martin Thom (London, 1991), 137–39.

68. Variously translated as "crush bigotry and superstition (the infamous thing)" or "make war on fanatics."

69. Mikhail Bakhtin, *Rabelais and His World*, trans. Hélène Iswolsky (Cambridge, 1968), 317. For discussion of anticlerical and grotesque imagery in revolutionary caricature, see de Baecque, *Caricature révolutionnaire*; Arundhati Virmani, "Ils sont passés ces jours de fête: L'anticléricalisme dans la caricature révolutionnaire," in *L'Image de la Révolution française: Communications présentées lors du Congrès Mondial pour le Bicentenaire de la Révolution, Sorbonne, Paris, 6–12 Juillet 1989*, 3 vols., ed. Michel Vovelle (Paris, 1989), vol. 1, 259–68; and *French Caricature*.

70. Although I do not undertake a psychoanalytic reading of this image, there is much here that would motivate such an effort.

71. James H. Rubin, "Disorder/Order: Revolutionary Art as Performative Representation," in "The French Revolution, 1789–1989: Two Hundred Years of Rethinking," ed. Sandy Petrey, a special issue of *The Eighteenth Century: Theory and Interpretation* (Lubbock, Tex., 1989), 105.

72. Michael de Certeau, *The Practice of Everyday Life*, trans. Steven Rendall (Berkeley, 1984); and Richard Terdiman, *Discourse/Counter-Discourse: The Theory and Practice of Symbolic Resistance in Nineteenth-Century France* (Ithaca, N.Y., 1985).

73. Barbara Maria Stafford, "The Eighteenth-Century: Towards an Interdisciplinary Model," *Art Bulletin* 70, no. 1 (March 1988): 18.

74. Michel Vovelle, preface to *Caricature révolutionnaire*, 11; Claude Langlois, *La Caricature contre-révolutionnaire* (Paris, 1988).

75. Vovelle, preface to *Caricature revolutionnairé*, 11. On the double relationship of revolutionary prints to public opinion, cf. Rolf Reichardt, "Prints: Images of the Bastille," in *Revolution in Print*. On the effects of economic and social conditions on print production, see Daniel Roche, "Censorship and the Publishing Industry," and Carla Hesse, "Economic Upheavals in Publishing," in *Revolution in Print;* and Carla Hesse, *Publishing and Cultural Politics in Revolutionary Paris, 1789–1810* (Berkeley, 1991).

76. Recent research on the history of reading indicates that literacy in France was much

more widespread on the eve of the Revolution than was previously believed. Primary instruction was well implanted in the villages of the northern and northeastern part of the country, where male literacy rates approached 70 to 80 percent. In the estimation of François Furet and Jacques Ozouf, "There was in fact one France that became literate under the *ancien régime* and another that, on the contrary, owed its admission to written culture to the 19th century" (*Reading and Writing: Literacy in France from Calvin to Jules Ferry.* [Cambridge, 1982]), 45. Parisian literacy rates are even more impressive than those for the nation as a whole. However, some qualifications are in order: Many adult readers remained at the lowest stage of literacy, never fully mastering writing, and female literacy rates lagged behind those of men. On the other hand, even nonreaders were exposed to the written or printed word through songs, the books of peddlers (*colporteurs*), signs, posters, programs of civic processions, and, not least, all sorts of pictures that were "almost always accompanied by a text, by hymns, laments, legends, information about the people and places represented" (Daniel Roche, *The People of Paris: An Essay in Popular Culture in the 18th Century,* trans. Marie Evans and Gwynne Lewis [Berkeley, 1987], 222). Cf. Lise Andriès, *Colporter la Révolution* (Montreuil, 1989); Roger Chartier, "Texts, Printings, Readings," in *The New Cultural History,* ed. Lynn Hunt (Berkeley, 1989); Jean-Claude Bonnet, ed., *La Carmagnole des muses: L'Homme de lettres et l'artiste dans la Révolution* (Paris, 1988).

77. On the too often overlooked *performative* dimension of song, see Laura Mason, "Ça ira and the Birth of the Revolutionary Song," *History Workshop* 28 (Autumn 1989): 22–38, and *Singing the French Revolution: Popular Culture and Politics, 1787–1799* (Ithaca, N.Y., 1996). Cf. the important contributions of Richard Leppert, *The Sight of Sound: Music, Representation, and the History of the Body* (Berkeley, Calif., 1993); *Music and Image: Domesticity, Ideology and Socio-cultural Formation in Eighteenth-Century England* (Cambridge, 1988); and *Art and the Committed Eye: The Cultural Functions of Imagery* (Boulder, Colo., 1996).

78. With respect to the staggering volume of printed matter that circulated during the Revolution, Emmett Kennedy nonetheless states that "reading, which foreigners considered widespread in Paris, focused almost exclusively on ephemera—posters, newssheets, pamphlets. . . . Newspapers were often literally fleeting; a fifth of them appeared for only the issue, 80 percent for fewer than a dozen. Newspapers belonged to the seventeenth-century tradition of *feuilles volantes* and *canards* more than to the mass media of the late nineteenth or twentieth centuries" (*A Cultural History of the French Revolution* [New Haven, Conn., 1989], 317).

79. Reichardt, "Prints: Images of the Bastille," 224. Cf. Hans-Jürgen Lusebrink and Rolf Reichardt, "La 'Bastille: Dans l'imaginaire social de la France à la fin du XVIIIe siècle (1774–1799)," *Revue d'histoire moderne et contemporaine* 30 (1983): 196–234.

80. See Rudolf Arnheim, *Art and Visual Perception* (Berkeley, Calif., 1954); E. H. Gombrich, *Art and Illusion* (Princeton, N.J., 1985); E. H. Gombrich "Image and Code: Scope and Limits of Conventionalism in Pictorial Representation," in *Image and Code,* ed. Wendy Steiner (Ann Arbor, Mich., 1981); Michael Fried, *Absorption and Theatricality: Painting and Beholder in the Age of Diderot* (Berkeley, 1980); Ronald Paulson, *Representations of Revolution, 1789–1820* (New Haven, Conn., 1983); Paulson, *Breaking and Remaking: Aesthetic Practice in England, 1700–1820* (New Brunswick, N.J., 1989); Norman Bryson, *Word and Image: French*

Painting of the Ancien Régime (Cambridge, 1981); and Margaret Miles, *Image as Insight: Visual Understanding in Western Christianity and Secular Culture* (Boston, 1985). For summary accounts of research in mental imagery and its implications, see Ronald A. Finke, *Principles of Mental Imagery* (Cambridge, 1989); Richard Mark Friedhoff and William Benzon, *Visualization: The Second Computer Revolution* (New York, 1989); and Mark Rollins, *Mental Imagery: On the Limits of Cognitive Science* (New Haven, Conn., 1989). On the investigation of vision, the now classic study is David Marr, *Vision: A Computational Investigation into the Human Representation and Processing of Visual Information* (San Francisco, 1982).

81. The case of the *Bibliothèque Bleu*—inexpensive books printed in large quantities and sold by peddlers from the early seventeenth century to the Revolution—offers an example of a literature that reached a broad readership. Its contents ranged from religious topics and works of instruction to fairy tales, works of roguery, and practical advice guides. In most cases, a text originating in the learned tradition lay behind the published work. The evidence suggests a much greater overlap between rural and urban readers than has been assumed. According to Roger Chartier, "In the eighteenth century, books from Troyes and equivalent volumes from elsewhere were not (yet) exclusively peasant in their readership. Their city circulation, although difficult to document, must nevertheless have been sizable. It may well be true that the 'notables' in the cities turned away from these books (unless they were collectors), but this was probably not the case for the entire middle level of urban society. More than in the strictly sociological portrait of their public, then, it is in the modes of their appropriation in which the specificity of the 'bluebooks' resides. The reading that they implied or encouraged was not that of the more 'learned' publication. In the acquisition and possession of these books, buyers invested a personal attachment that went well beyond the deciphering of their texts" (*The Cultural Uses of Print*, 262–63). Cf. Lise Andriès's three studies: *Les Contes bleues* (Paris, 1983); *La Bibliothèque bleue au dix-huitième siècle: Une tradition éditoriale*, in *Studies on Voltaire and the Eighteenth Century*, vol. 270 (Oxford, 1989); and *Le Grand Livre des sécrets: Le Colportage en France aux 17e et 18e siècles* (Paris, 1994).

82. We can learn something from the strenuous objections cast by art historians and allied pictorialists to semiotic and textual approaches to the visual object. At the same time, we can profit from the semiotic insight that visual and verbal conventions do interpenetrate— that there is always more than one type of representation at work in an image or a text. See *Visual Theory: Painting and Interpretation*, ed. Norman Bryson, Michael Ann Holly, and Keith Moxey (Cambridge, 1991).

83. W. J. T. Mitchell, *Iconology: Image, Text, Ideology* (Chicago, 1986).

84. Hunt, *Politics, Culture, and Class*, 54; James Leith, "Ephemera: Civic Education through Images," in *Revolution in Print*, 270–89; Ozouf, *Festivals and the French Revolution*, esp. 212–14; de Baecque, *Caricature révolutionnaire*.

85. "In June 1791, when the separation of people from their former head was merely a possibility, the problem for imagemakers was how to express the reordering of the world visually. Two years later, after the king was guillotined and France became a republic, all the devices of carnival were abandoned. The French people had passed beyond the age of liminality" (Vivian Cameron, "The Challenge to Rule: Confrontations with Louis XVI," *Art Journal* 48,

no. 2 [Summer 1989]: 153). Cf. Victor Turner, *From Ritual to Theater: The Human Seriousness of Play* (New York, 1982).

86. Klaus Herding rejects an older tradition (in the work of James Leith or David L. Dowd) of viewing the revolutionary era's graphic arts for their propagandistic effects. See "Visual Codes in the Graphic Art of the French Revolution," in *French Caricature*, 96.

87. Herding, "Visual Codes," 95–96.

CHAPTER 2
REPRESENTING THE BODY POLITIC

1. See the Convention's decree in Marie-Hélène Huet, *Rehearsing the Revolution: The Staging of Marat's Death, 1793–1797*, trans. Robert Hurley (Berkeley, 1982), 6. Cf. Albert Soboul, *Le Procès de Louis XVI* (Paris, 1966); Carol Blum, *Rousseau and the Republic of Virtue: The Language of Politics in the French Revolution* (Ithaca, N.Y., 1986), 169–181; David P. Jordan, *The King's Trial: Louis XVI vs. the French Revolution* (Berkeley, 1979); *Regicide and Revolution: Speeches at the Trial of Louis XVI*, ed. and intro. Michael Walzer, trans. Marian Rothstein (London, 1974).

2. Jean-Jacques Rousseau, *On the Social Contract, with Geneva Manuscript and Political Economy*, ed. Roger D. Masters, trans. Judith R. Masters (New York, 1978), 59, 63. Originally published in 1762 as *Du Contrat social, ou principes du droit politique*. For the definitive modern edition, see Jean-Jacques Rousseau, *Oeuvres complètes*, 5 vols., ed. Bernard Gagnebin and Marcel Raymond, (Paris, 1964), vol. 3.

3. Ernst Kantorowicz, *The King's Two Bodies: A Study in Medieval Political Theology* (Princeton, N.J., 1957). Cf. *From the Royal to the Republican Body: Incorporating the Political in Seventeenth- and Eighteenth-Century France*, ed. Sara E. Melzer and Kathryn Norberg (Berkeley, 1998).

4. Not surprisingly, many have noticed that these actions ushered in a profound genealogical crisis. In the space opened up by the death of the king, who would be his heirs? See Lynn Hunt, *Politics, Culture, and Class in the French Revolution* (Berkeley, 1984).

5. "The Declaration of the Rights of Man and Citizen," trans. Keith Michael Baker in *University of Chicago Readings in Western Civilization*, vol. 7, *The Old Regime and the French Revolution, ed.* Keith Michael Baker (Chicago, 1987), 238. "Le principe de toute souveraineté réside essentiellement dans la Nation. Nul corps, nul individu ne peut exercer d'autorité qui n'en émane expressément," in Maurice Gauchet, *La Révolution des droits de l'homme* (Paris, 1989), ii.

6. Rousseau, On *the Social Contract*, 62. See note 2.

7. Cited in Norman O. Brown, *Love's Body* (New York, 1966), 114. Cf. Ronald Paulson, *Representations of Revolution, 1789–1820* (New Haven, Conn., 1983).

8. See Chapter 1 for further discussion of Jean-Baptiste Salaville's arguments on the question of representation.

9. Rousseau, On t*he Social Contract*, 103. "Sovereignty cannot be represented for the same

reason it cannot be alienated. It consists essentially in the general will, and the will cannot be represented. Either it is itself or it is something else; there is no middle ground. The deputies of the people, therefore, are not nor can they be its representatives; they are merely its agents. . . . The idea of representatives is modern. We get it from feudal government, that wicked and absurd government in which the human species is degraded and the name of man is dishonored. In the ancient republics and even in monarchies, the people never had representatives. The word itself was unknown" (*The Social Contract*, 102).

10. Keith Michael Baker, "Representation Redefined," in Keith Michael Baker eds., *Inventing the French Revolution* (Cambridge, 1990), 251. According to Baker, "[Abbé] Sieyès disengaged the idea of a unitary general will from the communal dream of direct democracy and reconciled it with the practice of representation in a populous modern society. By deriving the practice of representation from the principle of the division of labor and the need for the rational representation of social interests, and combining these elements of the social theory of representation with a modified version of the sovereignty of the general will, he gave an entirely new meaning to the conception of 'representative sovereignty' first introduced by Hobbes" ("Representation Redefined," 250). Sieyes has been the focus of much discussion among students of revolutionary politics and political theory. See William H. Sewell, Jr., *A Rhetoric of Bourgeois Revolution: The Abbé Sieyes and "What Is the Third Estate?"* (Durham, N.C., 1994).

11. At the inaugural meeting of the National Convention on 21 September 1792, delegates demanded the conscious extirpation of all images of royalty. Defying the iconic conventions of royalist patriarchalism, they adopted a female allegorical figure for the seal of the first French Republic. Yet on Jacques-Louis David's recommendation, in 1793 the radical Convention voted to substitute Hercules for Liberty on the seal of the Republic. Even during the Revolution, then, there was no stable solution to the problem of representation, only a continuing struggle over its appropriate content and form. Hercules himself was supplanted by female representations of Liberty and Republic. Although these events have been recounted by many scholars, for one of the best renditions, see Hunt, "The Imagery of Radicalism," in *Politics, Culture, and Class*, 87–119.

12. On the theatrical dimension of Thomas Hobbes's political theory, see Christopher Pye, "The Sovereign, the Theater, and the Kingdome of Darknesse: Hobbes and the Spectacle of Power," in *Representing the English Renaissance*, ed. Stephen Greenblatt (Berkeley, 1988), 279–302; Brown, *Love's Body*; Hanna Fenichel Pitkin, *The Concept of Representation* (Berkeley, 1972); and Bryan Turner, *The Body and Society* (Oxford and New York, 1984). For a seminal discussion of the overlap between bodily metaphors and mechanical imagery in the political thought of Hobbes, Rousseau, and other early modern thinkers, see Otto Mayr, *Authority, Liberty, and Automatic Machinery in Early Modern Europe* (Baltimore, 1986).

13. Thomas Hobbes, *Leviathan*, ed. C. B. Macpherson (Harmondsworth, 1968), 220.

14. Louis Adrian Montrose observes that in her discourse Elizabeth "dwelt upon the womanly frailty of her body natural and the masculine strength of her body politic" ("'Shaping Fantasies': Figurations of Gender and Power in Elizabethan Culture," *Representations* 1, no. 2 [Spring 1983]: 77).

15. Rousseau, *On the Social Contract*, 52. Rousseau also admonishes his readers: "Whoever refuses to obey the general will shall be forced to do so by the entire body; which means only that he will be forced to be free." Furthermore, "the general will is always right, but the judgment that guides it is not always enlightened. . . . Private individuals see the good they reject; the public wants the good it does not see. All are equally in need of guides. The former must be obligated to make their wills conform to their reason. The latter must be taught to know what it wants. Then public enlightenment results in the union of understanding and will in the social body; hence the complete cooperation of the parts, and finally the greatest force of the whole. From this arises the necessity for a legislator" (*On the Social Contract*, 55, 67).

16. Brown, *Love's Body*, 104–5. On the topic of revolution and theater, see Huet, *Rehearsing the Revolution;* Mona Ozouf, *Festivals and the French Revolution*, trans. Alan Sheridan (Cambridge, Mass., 1988); Huet, *Mourning Glory: The Will of the French Revolution* (Philadelphia, 1997); and Frederick Brown, *Theater and Revolution: The Culture of the French Stage* (New York, 1980).

17. On this subject, see Ozouf, *Festivals;* Marie-Hélène Huet, "Le Sacre du Printemps: Essai sur le sublime et la Terreur," *MLN* 103, no. 4 (September 1988): 782–99; and Baker, "Representation."

18. Emmanuel-Joseph Sieyès, "What Is the Third Estate?," trans M. Blondel, in *The Old Regime and the French Revolution*, ed. Keith Michael Baker, 154–79, 157, 156.

19. *Le Tribun du peuple, ou Recueil des lettres de quelques électeurs de Paris avant la Révolution de 1789, pour servir d'introduction aux feuilles de la bouche de fer* (1789; Paris, 1790), 5; cited in Gary Kates, *The Cercle Social, the Girondins, and the French Revolution* (Princeton, N.J., 1985), 20–21.

20. On the Bastille, see Hans-Jürgen Lüsebrink and Rolf Reichardt, *The Bastille: A History of a Symbol of Despotism and Freedom*, trans. Norbert Schürer (Durham, N.C., 1997).

21. Burke described the return from Versailles in the following provocative manner: "Heads were stuck upon spears, and led the procession; whilst the royal captives who followed in the train were slowly moved along, amidst the horrid yells, and shrilling screams, and frantic dances, and infamous contumelies, and all the unutterable abominations of the furies of hell, in the abused shape of the vilest of women" (Edmund Burke, *Reflections on the Revolution in France* [Garden City, N.Y., 1961], 85).

22. "Les Dames de la Halle, réunies en Corps, bientôt suivies des Forts et autres ouvriers, se sont répandues dans les rues, à commencer par celle de la Ferronerie, forçant toutes les femmes de les suivre, et entrant même dans les maisons pour grossir leur nombre. Rendues ensuite à l'Hôtel de Ville, les magasins d'armes et de munitions ont été mis au pillage. De-là ces nouvelles Amazônes, traînant avec elles du Canon, se sont misés en marche pour Versailles." *Courier national, politique et littéraire* (no. 28), 5 October 1789, 229. The journal goes on to applaud the market women's arrival in Versailles, now referring to them as "heroines of liberty": "On ne peut trop admirer le courage et l'ordre de ces Héroïnes de la liberté." Ibid., 230. Indeed, such descriptions of the market women became a common trope in patriotic dis-

course, as is illustrated by the accompanying text of another commemorative print from 1789, *Journée memorable de Versailles le lundi 5 Octobre 1789*: "Nos modernes Amazones glorieuses de leurs Victoire revinrent à Cheval sur les Canons avec plusieurs Messieurs de la Garde Nationale, tenant des branches de Peupliers au bruit des cris réiterés de Vive la Nation, Vive le Roi." (François-Louis Bruel, *Collection de Vinck: Inventaire analytique,* vol. 2 [Paris, 1914], no. 2994).

23. The clergy is here represented by the Abbé Fauchet, revolutionary orator and founder in 1790 of the *Bulletin de la bouche de fer* and creator of the Social Circle or Society of the Friends of the Truth, whose collaborators included Nicolas Bonneville, Jacques-Pierre Brissot, and Jean-Antoine-Nicolas Condorcet. The third estate is represented by Marc-Etienne Populus, deputy from the third estate to the Estates General. Lawyer, political activist, and pamphleteer Guy-Jean-Baptiste Target served as president of the National Assembly in 1790.

24. Carole Pateman, *The Sexual Contract* (Stanford, Calif., 1988), 102, 88. On this issue within republican theory, see Hanna Fenichel Pitkin, *Fortune Is a Woman: Gender and Politics in the Thought of Niccolò Machiavelli* (Berkeley, 1984), and, more generally Mary O'Brien, *The Politics of Reproduction* (Boston, 1981).

25. Hunt, *The Family Romance of the French Revolution* (Berkeley, 1992), 99.

26. "La Révolution non seulement pervertit l'ordre politique, mais plus profondément elle renverse celui de la nature" (Claude Langlois, La *Caricature contre-révolutionnaire* [Paris, 1988], 69). For a disturbing discussion of Théroigne de Méricourt's participation in the Revolution, see Simon Schama, *Citizens: A Chronicle of the French Revolution* (New York, 1989), esp. 873–75.

27. *The Great Rout of The Anti-Constitutional Army* was published in the *Journal de la Cour et de la ville,* 19 February 1792. The text reads "Un detachement de principales Caillette qui ont joué un Role dans la révolution, elles se presentent aux troupes de l'Empereur pour les faire Débander, ce qui leur reussit completement et on cesse d'être étonné de cette Catastrophe lorsqu'on voit la demoiselle Teroig que leur montre sa République, et Medames Sta . . . Dondon. . . Silles . . . Calo. . . Talmouse Condor . . . leur montrent leur Villette—Ce detachement est renforcé par les sans culote et des Jacobins qui presentent au bout de leur piques des Cervelas, des Jambons, des bouteilles des saucisses des Andouilles, etc. etc.. . . [O]n voit dans l'armée que tout y va à la debandade des soldats laissent tomber leur fusils et leur sabres; les drapeau baissent pavillon Le Général Bender meme laisse tomber une de ses Bottes." As Vivan Cameron explains in her extended analysis of this print, apart from the many sexual puns concerning the so-called arms carried by the revolutionary soldiers, the print's text directly attacks women on the Left with revolutionary and political sympathies: They are held responsible for the dispersal of the royalist or anticonstitutional army. "Un detachement de principales Caillette" refers to young women of easy virtue; the Emperor is Leopold II of Austria. Méricourt was known to have organized groups of armed women in France. On her return to her native Belgium, she was imprisoned by the Austrians in January 1791. The list of abbreviated names of the other women in the narrative also refers to other things: "Mesdames Sta . . . Dondon" (a "big lump of a girl"), Silles (probably "eyelash" or the verb "to blink"), Calo (referring to *calot,* meaning "big eye" in popular jargon), Talmouse ("a smack" or "a

punch in the nose"), and Condor ("vulture," but the pun on *con d'or* is also apparent). Although there is a heavy emphasis on the eyes and a bit of nose, the names form a reconstructed face, although the women in the image are essentially faceless. The abbreviations refer specifically to well-known figures in society at the time. Madame de Staël was the daughter of the former finance minister Jacques Necker; Madame Charles de Lameth (former Mademoiselle Picot, known as "Dondon") had connections in the Palais-Royal; Madame de Genlis-Sillery was the former mistress of the Duc d'Orléans and involved in politics; Madame Calon was the wife of the deputy Philibert Calon; Julie Talmouze was the former Julie Soubise; Madame Condorcet's husband had written on the equality of women. Citation and translation in Vivian Cameron, "Political Exposures: Sexuality and Caricature in the French Revolution," in *Eroticism and the Body Politic*, ed. Lynn Hunt (Baltimore, 1991), 91–93.

28. In the same issue of the *Journal de la Cour et de la ville* (19 February 1792) in which this print was published, there appeared an attack on Théroigne Méricourt: "Elle entra dans la boutique d'une marchande de caricatures à qui elle eut l'effronterie de dire que si elle continuait d'étaler celles qui jettaient du ridicule sur d'autres que le pouvoir exécutif, la noblesse ou le clergé, elle viendrait accompagnée de quelques patriotes pour les déchirer" (cited in Langlois, *La Caricature contre-révolutionnaire*, 242).

29. For an excellent discussion of Villette, see Jeffrey Merrick, "The Marquis de Villette and Mademoiselle de Raucourt: Representations of Male and Female Sexual Deviance in Late Eighteenth-century France," in *Homosexuality in Modern France*, ed. Jeffrey Merrick and Bryant T. Ragan, Jr. (New York, 1996), 30–53.

30. *French Caricature*, 213.

31. Ronald Paulson observes, "In the model of the Body Politic the king is the 'head' of state, and so it is appropriate, indeed necessary, that his removal should be accomplished by decapitation" ("The Severed Head: The Impact of French Revolutionary Caricatures on England," in *French Caricature*, 58). Or, as Danton stated at the time, "Kings are struck only at the head" (cited in Huet, *Rehearsing the Revolution*, 5).

32. In early modern Europe, as Bryan Turner (following R. H. Tawney, *Religion and the Rise of Capitalism*, 1938) accurately observes, "the teleological purposiveness of the body was employed to legitimate political and social divisions in society. 'Society, like the human body, is an organism composed of different members. Each member has its own function, prayer, or defence, or merchandise, or tilling the soil. Each must receive the means suited to its station, and must claim no more'" (*The Body and Society*, 177).

33. Ibid., 138. Cf. Otto Gierke, *Political Theories of the Middle Ages*, trans. Frederic William Maitland (Boston, 1958), 66.

34. See Louis Marin, *Portrait of the King*, trans. Martha M. House (Minneapolis, 1988); Marin, "The King's Body," in *Food for Thought*, trans. Mette Hjort (Baltimore, 1989), 189–241; Ralph E. Giesey, *Cérémonial et puissance souveraine: France, Xve-XVIIe siècles* (Paris, 1987); Alain Boureau, *Le Simple Corps du roi: L'Impossible Sacralité des souverains français* (Paris, 1989); Richard A. Jackson, *Vive le Roi! A History of the French Coronation from Charles V to Charles X* (Chapel Hill, N.C., 1984); Lawrence M. Bryant, *The King and the City in the Parisian Royal Entry Ceremony: Politics, Ritual, and Art in the Renaissance* (Geneva, 1986); and

Sarah Hanley, *The Lit de Justice of the Kings of France: Constitutional Ideology in Legend, Ritual, and Discourse* (Princeton, N.J., 1983).

35. See Mikhail Bakhtin's magisterial study, *Rabelais and His World*, trans. Hélène Iswolsky (Cambridge, Mass., 1968). Cf: Peter Stallybrass and Allon White, *The Politics and Poetics of Transgression* (Ithaca, N.Y., 1986); Barbara Babcock, ed., *The Reversible World: Symbolic Inversions in Art and Society* (Ithaca, N.Y., 1978).

36. See, for example, the section on "The Royal Family" in *French Caricature*, 178–98.

37. For a discussion of the unidentified, radical artist Villeneuve, see Annie Duprat, "Autour de Villeneuve, le mystérieux auteur de la gravure *La Contre-Révolution*," *Annales historiques de la Révolution française*, no. 3 (1997), 423–439.

38. In an influential essay, Neil Hertz draws out the Medusan overtones of Villeneuve's provocative representation of the king's head head held aloft by a disembodied arm. See Neil Hertz, "Medusa's Head: Male Hysteria under Political Pressure." *Representations* 4 (Fall 1983): 27–54. On the theme of dismemberment, see Ronald Paulson, "The Severed Head: The Impact of French Revolutionary Caricatures on England," 55–66, in *French Caricature*. On the scatological side of grotesque revolutionary imagery, see Albert Boime, "Jacques-Louis David, Scatological Discourse in the French Revolution, and the Art of Caricature," in *French Caricature, 67–82.

39. Jean-Pierre Guicciardi, "Between the Licit and the Illicit: The Sexuality of the King," trans. Michael Murray, in *'Tis Nature's Fault: Unauthorized Sexuality during the Enlightenment*, ed. Robert Parks Maccubbin (Cambridge, 1985), 96.

40. See James Cuno, "Introduction," esp. Figures 3–6, in *French Caricature*, 13–22; Robert Darnton, *The Literary Underground of the Old Regime* (Cambridge, 1982).

41. There is now an extensive literature on libels directed against the queen, including Chantal Thomas, *The Wicked Queen: The Origins of the Myth of Marie-Antoinette*, trans. Julie Rose (New York, 1999); Thomas, "L'Héroïne du crime: Marie-Antoinette dans les pamphlets," in *La Carmagnole des Muses: L'Homme de lettres et l'artiste dans la Révolution française*, ed. Jean-Claude Bonnet (Paris, 1988); Antoine de Baecque, "Pamphlets: Libel and Political Mythology," in *Revolution in Print: The Press in France, 1775–1800*, ed. Robert Darnton and Daniel Roche (Berkeley, 1989), 165–76; de Baecque, "Le Récit fantastique de la Révolution: Les Monstres aristocratiques des pamphlets de 1789," in *La Révolution du journal, 1788–1794*, ed. Pierre Rétat (Paris, 1989), 235–46; Chantal Thomas, "L'Architigresse d'Autriche: La Métaphore animal dans les pamphlets contre Marie-Antoinette," in *La Révolution du journal, 1788–1794*, 229–34; Annie Duprat, "La Dégradation de l'image royale dans la caricature révolutionnaire," in *Les Images de la Révolution française*, ed. Michel Vovelle (Paris, 1988), 167–76; Lynn Hunt, "The Many Bodies of Marie Antoinette," in *Eroticism and the Body Politic;* Madelyn Gutwirth; *The Twilight of the Goddesses: Women and Representation in the French Revolutionary Era* (New Brunswick, N.J., 1992); Sarah Maza, "The Diamond Necklace Affair: 1785–86," in *Private Lives and Public Affairs: The Causes Célèbres of Prerevolutionary France* (Berkeley, 1993); Jacques Revel, "Marie-Antoinette and Her Fictions: The Staging of Hatred," in *Fictions of the French Revolution*, ed. Bernadette Fort (Evanston, Ill., 1991), 111–29; Elizabeth Colwill, "'Just Another Citoyenne'? Marie-Antoinette on Trial, 1790–1793," *History*

Workshop 28 (1989): 63–87; Colwill, "Pass as a Woman, Act like a Man: Marie-Antoinette as Tribade in the Pornography of the French Revolution," in *Homosexuality in Modern France*, 54–79; Jeffrey Merrick, "Impotence in and at Court," in *Studies in Eighteenth-Century Culture*, vol. 25, ed. Syndy M. Conger and Julie C. Hayes (Baltimore, 1996).

42. Antoine De Baecque, "The Defeat of the Body of the King: Essay on the Impotence of Louis XVI," in *The Body Politic: Corporeal Metaphor in Revolutionary France, 1770–1800*, trans. Charlotte Mandell (Stanford, Calif., 1997), 29–75.

43. *Révolutions de France et de Brabant* nos. 82 and 83, in Camille Demoulins, *Oeuvres*, vol. 8 (München, 1980), 164–65, 187, 204.

44. Burke, *Reflections on the Revolution in France*, 90.

45. See the excellent account by Maza, "The Diamond Necklace Affair: 1785–86." Maza makes an important connection between the licentious connotations of the famous necklace as a *bijou* in this well-known revolutionary caricature and Diderot's most frankly pornographic work, *Les Bijoux indiscrets*, which has the eponymous *bijoux*, female genitalia recounting their adventures (*Private Lives and Public Affair*, 205–6n110).

46. As Hunt remarks, "Representations of the king wearing the cap of liberty and drinking to the health of the nation showed that he was no longer a distant, regal figure. He was now more familiar, more accessible, more like a good bourgeois and much less like a father" ("The Political Psychology of Revolutionary Caricatures," in *French Caricature*, 37).

47. Norman O. Brown comments on the link between the sexual and the political: "A king is erected, *rex erectus est*. A king is an erection of the body politic" (Brown, *Love's Body*, 133).

48. On this theme, see my *Women and the Public Sphere in the Age of the French Revolution* (Ithaca, N.Y., 1988).

49. On the other hand, royalists and counterrevolutionaries were not loathe to borrow republican themes when it came to exploiting issues of gender as we saw in Figure 2.4. *The Great Rout of the Anti-Constitutional Army*. In a particularly mordant series of satirical prints, Targinette (an allegory of the Constitution) is portrayed as dying. Indeed, Langlois prefaces his discussion of the dying Targinette with a reproduction of the print *The Aristocratic Body with the Face of a Woman Dying in the Arms of the Aristocracy*. See La *Caricature contre-révolutionnaire*, 96–100.

50. De Baecque, "Pamphlets: Libel and Political Mythology," in *Revolution in Print*, 173. On antiaristocratic discourse and antinoble sentiment, see Patrice Higonnet, "'Aristocrate,' 'Aristocratie': Language and Politics in the French Revolution," in *The French Revolution, 1789–1989: Two Hundred Years of Rethinking*, ed. Sandy Petrey, a special issue of *The Eighteenth Century: Theory and Interpretation* (Lubbock, Tex., 1989), 47–66; Higonnet, *Class, Ideology, and the Rights of Nobles during the French Revolution* (Oxford, 1981).

51. Witness the centennial celebration of the Statue of Liberty, gift of France to the American nation, as well as the press discussions of the gigantic "Liberty" statue erected by Chinese students at Tiananmen Square, Beijing, in 1989. In conjunction with the Bicentennial celebrations in France, Chanel model Ines de la Fressange, descendant of an old aristocratic family, was elected by the mayors of France to be the new Marianne. She succeeded Brigitte

Bardot, who held the honor in the 1970s, and Catherine Deneuve, who held it in the 1980s. The most recent election of the fashion model Laetitia Casta generated protests by one of the very few female mayors, Françoise Cartron of Artigues-près-Bordeaux, who chided her mostly male peers for using beauty contest criteria to guide their choice.

52. For a fuller discussion of how the exclusion of women from the public sphere is related to the representation of Republic as a woman, see my *Women and the Public Sphere*, esp. chaps. 4 and 5, and Geneviève Fraisse, *Reason's Muse: Sexual Difference and the Birth of Democracy*, trans. Jane Marié Todd (Chicago, 1994). On the symbolic representation of Liberty, her different postures, and some of the reasons inclining the French to choose a female representation of Republic, see Agulhon, *Marianne into Battle*; Hunt, *Politics, Culture, and Class;* Marina Warner, *Monuments and Maidens: The Allegory of the Female Form* (New York, 1985); and Stéphane Michaud, *Muse et madone: Visages de la femme de la Révolution française aux apparitions de Lourdes* (Paris, 1985); Gutwirth, *The Twilight of the Goddesses.*

53. Warner, *Monuments and Maidens,* xix–xx.

54. Hunt, "Political Psychology," 39.

55. I am grateful to Eva Feder Kittay for helping me to clarify this point. For a wide-ranging discussion of this issue, see her "Woman as Metaphor," *Hypatia* 3, no. 2 (Summer 1988): 63–85.

56. Nevertheless, Old Regime artists sometimes did depict their female subjects as muses, and aristocrats enjoyed play-acting as gods and goddesses. But the purpose of all this artifice was to enhance the subject's character. Moreover, these artists and performers addressed a privileged audience of initiates who pleasured in distinguishing the known model from the artful imitation.

57. Dorinda Outram, *The Body and the French Revolution: Sex, Class, and Political Culture* (New Haven, Conn., 1989), 126; cf. 175–84.

58. See Ozouf, *Festivals,* 267, and 262–82.

59. Of course, the revolutionaries did not invent the allegorical tradition to which Liberty belongs. Still, as I am arguing, they made particular use of Liberty as a symbol of their break with the monarchical past. Warner observes that there are two outstanding rationales offered for the strong link between allegory and the female form: (1) Linguistic gender—in the Romance languages, absolute concepts are for the most part feminine; (2) classical myth allotted considerable importance to goddesses, personifications of various virtues (*Monuments and Maidens,* 87 and passim). On the Renaissance tradition, see Cesare Ripa, *Iconology; or, a Collection of Emblematical Figures,* [selected by] George Richardson, 2 vols. (New York, 1979), and the discussion by E. H. Gombrich, "*Icones Symbolicae*: Philosophies of Symbolism and Their Bearing on Art," in *Symbolic Images: Studies in the Art of the Renaissance* (London, 1978).

60. Ozouf, *Festivals,* 280.

61. Ibid., 212–13, 214.

62. See Sumathi Ramaswamy, "Virgin Mother, Beloved Other: The Erotics of Tamil Nationalism in Colonial and Post-Colonial India," in *Thamyris* 4, no. 1 (Spring 1997): 9–39;

Ramaswamy, "Body Language: The Somatics of Nationalism in Tamil India," *Gender and History 10*, no. 1, 78–102; George Mosse, *Nationalism and Sexuality: Middle-Class Morality and Sexual Norms in Modern Europe* (Madison, Wis., 1985); Warner, *Monuments and Maidens*; Mary Ryan, *Women in Public: Between Banners and Ballots, 1825–1880* (Baltimore, 1990); and John Higham, "The Indian Princess and Roman Goddess: The First Female Symbols of America," *Proceedings of the American Antiquarian Society* 100 (1990): 45–79.

63. It would be ridiculous to deny the textual basis of modern French nationalism, and I certainly do not intend to do so. However, readers of my earlier work (including the earlier published versions of this essay) will notice that my view on these matters has evolved. I argued previously that in the new symbolic order wrought by the bourgeois revolution the old hierarchy between icon and sign was reversed. However, I have come to believe that this formulation was too bald. For this reason, I am emphasizing the way in which, far from disappearing or being wholly subordinated by the text, images continued to be a constitutive element of the modern order of representation. See "Political Imagery of the French Revolution," in *Representing Revolution: French and British Images, 1789– 1804* (Amherst, Mass., 1989), 13–21, and "Representing the Body Politic: The Paradox of Gender in the Graphic Politics of the French Revolution," in *Rebel Daughters: Women and the French Revolution*, ed. Sara E. Melzer and Leslie W. Rabine (Oxford, 1992), 15–37.

64. On French emblems, see Michel Pastoureau, *Les Emblèmes de la France* (Paris, 1998). For Vauban's contribution to the creation of France's geometrical, ordered, national boundaries, see Peter Sahlins, *Boundaries: The Making of France and Spain in the Pyrenees* (Berkeley, 1989), 68–71, and Chandra Mukerji, *Territorial Ambitions and the Gardens of Versailles* (Cambridge, 1997), 248–99. On the Gallic cock, see Michel Pastoureau, "The Gallic Cock," in *Realms of Memory: The Construction of the French Past,*. vol. 3, *Symbols*, ed. Pierre Nora, English-language ed. Lawrence D. Kritzman, trans. Arthur Goldhammer (New York, 1992), 405–32. On the Marseillaise, see Michel Vovelle, "La Marseillaise: La Guerre ou la paix," in *Les Lieux de mémoire*, vol. 1, *La République*, ed. Pierre Nora (Paris, 1984), and Laura Mason, *Singing the Revolution: Popular Culture and Politics, 1787–1799* (Ithaca, N.Y., 1996), 93–103. Benedict Anderson writes about the map's achievement of logo status in the context of anticolonial nationalisms, but the same could be said of their European forerunners. Hence, this occurs when maps become so familiar and standardized as to need no explanatory glosses; even "lines of longitude and latitude, place names, signs for rivers, seas, and mountains, *neighbors*" can be removed. As "pure sign. . . the map entered an infinitely reproducible series, available for transfer to posters, official seals, letterheads, magazine and textbook covers, tablecloths, and hotel walls. Instantly recognizable, everywhere visible, the logo-map penetrated deep into the popular imagination, forming a powerful emblem for the anticolonial [*sic*] nationalisms being born" (Benedict Anderson, *Imagined Communities: Reflections on the Origin and Spread of Nation* [London, 1991], 175).

65. Ramaswamy, "Body Language," 102.

66. See *Women and the Public Sphere in the Age of the French Revolution*, 159ff.

67. Agulhon, *Marianne into Battle*, 29, 9.

68. Ibid., 30.

CHAPTER 3
EMBODIMENTS OF FEMALE VIRTUE

1. Edmund Burke, "On Conciliation with the Colonies," speech before the House of Commons, 22 March 1775, in *Burke's Speeches on American Taxation, "On Conciliation with America," and "Letter to the Sheriffs of Bristol,"* ed. F. G. Selby (London, 1897), 80; cited in Michael Kammen, *Spheres of Liberty: Changing Perceptions of Liberty in American Culture* (Ithaca, N.Y., 1986), 40.

2. Linda Orr, *Headless History: Nineteenth-Century French Historiography of the Revolution* (Ithaca, N.Y., 1990), 16.

3. What has been referred to as "embodiment" by Dorinda Outram and others can also be discussed through the problematic of moral virtue within republicanism. On corruption and republican manners, see the important studies by J. G. A. Pocock, *The Machiavellian Moment: Florentine Thought and the Atlantic Republican Tradition* (Princeton, N.J., 1976), and *Virtue, Commerce, and History: Essays on Political Thought and History, Chiefly in the Eighteenth Century* (Cambridge, 1985).

4. In addition to the discussion in Chapter 2, I consider the topic of republican bodies and democratic representation in my *Women and the Public Sphere in the Age of the French Revolution* (Ithaca, N.Y., 1988), chap. 5 and passim. On representation, cf. Hanna Fenichel Pitkin, *The Concept of Representation* (Berkeley, 1972); Nancy L. Schwartz, *The Blue Guitar: Political Representation and Community* (Chicago, 1988); and Anne Norton, *Reflections on Political Identity* (Baltimore, 1988).

5. Philippe Bordes, "Le Recours à l'allégorie dans l'art de la Révolution française," in *Les Images de la Révolution française*, ed. Michel Vovelle (Paris, 1988), 245.

6. Madelyn Gutwirth reminds us that "like the nouns of order and goodness, virtually every word designating disorder and enmity, as a noun expressing quality, is feminine in the French tongue; all, then, are represented as female. Foremost among these . . . is Discord, whom [Hubert] Gravelot and [Charles Nicolas] Cochin [authors of *Iconologie par figures ou Traité complet des allegories emblémes]* in their visual recipe recommend be depicted as a 'malevolent Divinity—with the air of a Medusa, flying through the air, and in her passage pressing out the venom of her fearful snakes.' But all her sisters run amok with her. . . . All of these images convey a sheer destructiveness inherent in female will" (*The Twilight of the Goddesses: Women and Representation in the French Revolutionary Era* (New Brunswick, N.J., 1992), 330–331.

7. For further illustration of such oppositions of virtue and vice, almost always (though not without exception) represented by female figures, see George Richardson's translation of Cesare Ripa's *Iconologia* of 1593, *Iconology; or a Collection of Emblematical Figures* (1779), [selected by] George Richardson, 2 vols. (New York, 1979).

8. For example, see Anon., "Aristocrats digging the Champ-de-Mars, 1790," in *Representing Revolution: French and British Images, 1789–1804* (Amherst, Mass., 1989), 9 (cat. 16).

9. Of equal interest, the text reports that the king never showed at the place on the field where the flags of the 60 batallions from Paris had formed a double line for him to pass

through. Instead, on Lafayette's order, he was carried to the alter by a crowd of soldiers, remaining beyond the view of the vast majority of people who assembled on this occasion. Significantly, the artist chose to depict the scene from afar rather than the close perch of the platform where the important people would be seen in full view. At least in this respect, the artist fails to instantiate the official imagery of the day, which, according to Vovelle, transcribed in terms of neoclassical imagery the union of the king and the laws. See Michel Vovelle, *La Révolution française: Images et récit*, 5 vols. (Paris, 1986), vol. 1, 122.

10. Vovelle includes several such images that may be compared with the print under discussion, and he notes how the panoramic vision, and the visible arrangement of the people facing the altar of the nation, achieve a pedagogic end. Consider the following three prints *Ceremonie de la Confédération nationale au Champ-de-Mars le 14 juillet 1790 au moment où tous les Français ont juré sur l'autel de la Patrie d'être à jamais unis par les liens indissolubles de la Fraternité*; Isidore-Stanislas Helman after Charles Monnet, *Fédération générale des Français au Champs-de-Mars le 14 juillet 1790*, and *Pacte fédératif des Français* (Bibliothèque nationale), all included in Vovelle, *La Révolution française*, vol. 1, 121–23.

11. Annie Renee Michele Jourdan contrasts the "pantheonization" of Mirabeau, Voltaire, Rousseau, and Marat (*Les Monuments de la Révolution française: Le Discours des images dans l'espace parisien, 1789–1804*, academisch proefschrift [Amsterdam, 1993]). Cf. Emmett Kennedy, *A Cultural History of the French Revolution* (New Haven, Conn., 1989).

12. For recent discussions of Curtius and Mme Tussaud, see Lena Johannesson, "Le Yo-Yo, David et Madame Tussaud, Notices Sur L'Iconographie de la Révolution," *L'Art et les révolutions, Section I: L'Art au temps de la Révolution française* (Strasbourg, 1992), 35–83; David Bindman, *The Shadow of the Guillotine: Britain and the French Revolution* (London, 1989); Claudine Mitchell, "Spectacular Fears and Popular Arts: A View from the Nineteenth-Century," in *Reflections of Revolution: Images of Romanticism*, ed. Alison Yarrington and Kelvin Everest (London, 1993), 159–81: Tony Halliday, "David's *Marat* as Posthumous Portrait" in *Jacques-Louis David's Marat*, ed. William Vaughan and Helen Weston (Cambridge, 2000), 56–76.

13. See Ozouf, "The Pantheon," in *Realms of Memory: The Construction of the French Past*, vol. 3, *Symbols*, ed. Pierre Nora, English-language edition ed. Lawrence D. Kritzman, trans. Arthur Goldhammer (New York, 1998). In a fascinating discussion, Ozouf places the Pantheon in the context of the eighteenth-century's admiration for "great men." She, too, underscores the moral lessons that greatness teaches ordinary men, and stresses the collective nature of the idea of greatness: "The great were by nature plural; they formed an assembly" (327). But Ozouf also stresses the difference between greatness and the qualities possessed by either monarchs or heroes: The cult of great men, she writes, was "defended as a counterweight to despotic power, a bulwark against arbitrary government. That the ecumenical celebration of the great possessed this almost militant value is attested by a series of exclusions: the great man was neither a king nor a hero nor even an illustrious man. It was in opposition to all images of splendor and solitude that the eighteenth century constructed its idea of greatness" (327). However, Ozouf underscores that just as the figure of the great man lent itself to a variety of incarnations, it was also difficult to maintain the reputation for greatness.

Ironically, "pantheonization" was as much a process of election as of exclusion—"pantheonization" and "de-pantheonization." Mirabeau's ashes were spirited out a side door at the very moment when Marat's were brought in the main entrance. Marat's ashes were subsequently removed to Saint-Etienne-du-Mont; Lepeletier's were reclaimed by his family (Ozouf, 340–41).

14. Claudette Hould points out that the engraver may have been inspired by Voltaire's lines in *La Pucelle*, when he chose to feature this image of an irreverent Fame: "Fame always has two trumpets/One, applied to her lips in the proper way,/Glorifies the exploits of heroes;/The other is at her beh . . . , since it must be said/That is the one that teaches us/About this jumble of new books" (cited in Hould, "Revolutionary Engravings," in *Images of the French Revolution* [Quebec, 1989], 243).

15. When the Marquis de Pastoret proposed the inscription "aux grands hommes la patrie reconnaissante" (to great men/the fatherland/in recognition), which transformed the Church of Sainte-Geneviève into the Panthéon, he was merely giving voice to a common sentiment, according to Ozouf ("The Pantheon," 326). Cf. Kennedy, *A Cultural History of the French Revolution*, 332–33.

16. Michael Walzer argues against the objection that the killing of a monarch is an instance of imperfect procedural justice. He states that "it was precisely the purpose of the trial to demonstrate that Louis was a traitor, which is to say, *not an enemy* but a citizen who gives aid and comfort to the enemy. An important distinction, for treason has to be proven, while enmity does not. To be sure, legal proof is a matter of principle. Kings had been murdered in the past, assassinated by some private person or hustled off to a remote castle and killed in a corner, out of sight; and then no principle was involved, no legal precedent set. But the point here was to make a point—that the king was, like any other citizen, liable to the law. How could that be done without a trial? And how could the trial of the king be anything but an imperfect (which is not to say a 'sham') trial?" ("The King's Trial and the Political Culture of the Revolution," in *The French Revolution and the Creation of Modern Political Culure*, vol. 2: *The Political Culture of the French Revolution*, ed. Colin Lucas [Oxford, 1988], 189).

17. For this summary discussion of the Cult of Great Men, I am indebted to the excellent account by Jourdan, *Les Monuments de la Révolution française*, 61 and chap. 2 passim. Cf. Paul Bénichou, *Le Sacre de l'écrivain* (Paris, 1973), from whom Jourdan draws the phrase regarding the "excellence of human nature."

18. "Le devoir le plus cher à des coeurs vraiement républicains est la reconnaissance due aux grands hommes. De l'épanchement de cet acte sacré naissent toutes les vertus nécessaires au maintien et à la gloire de l'état." "Discours prononcé à la fête décernée par la Section des Piques aux mânes de Marat et de Lepelletier le 29 septembre 1793," in *Opuscules et lettres politiques* (Paris, 1979), cited in Jourdan, *Les Monuments de la Révolution française*, 61.

19. The print literature abounds with examples of public interest in great men. However, the corpus also reveals how very fragile the reputations of these men were. The images run the gamut from celebratory to defamatory. Concerning the Cult of Great Men from the earliest moments of the Revolution, a particularly interesting image is an aquatint by Jean-François Janinet from the collection Musée Carnavalet, showing the waxmaker Philippe Curtius de-

livering portraits of Jacques Necker and the Duc d'Orléans on 12 July 1789. See *La Révolution française*, ed. M. Vovelle, vol. 1, 82.

20. Thomas Crow recounts a curious event surrounding Louis-Michel Lepeletier's assassination that underscores the French revolutionary repudiation of fatherhood. "The Convention leadership chose to treat the matter as—literally—a death in the family. Five days after the murder, the deputies collectively adopted Lepeletier's young daughter and only child, Suzanne, as the child of the nation. The gesture would have carried enormous resonance at that moment in light of the king's emotionally charged identity as singular father to all of his subjects; the loss of their colleague allowed the representatives of the French people as a whole to assume the role of collective father to this single eleven-year-old, a bid to replace the broken bond with the sovereign through a dizzying reversal of scale and direction" (*Emulation: Making Artists for Revolutionary* France (New Haven, Conn., 1995), 156.

21. On the other hand, Claude Bonnet suggests that as the century progressed, "the domestic increasingly became the touchstone of politics and the father the central figure in the Cult of Great Men" ("Naissance du Panthéon," *Poétique*, no. 33 [February 1978]: cited in Ozouf, "The Pantheon," 329).

22. Cf. Erica Harth, "The Salon Woman Goes Public . . . or Does She?," in *Going Public: Women and Publishing in Early Modern France*, ed. Elizabeth C. Goldsmith and Dena Goodman (Ithaca, N.Y., 1995), 179–93; Carla Hesse, "Kant, Foucault, and Three Women," in *Foucault and the Writing of History*, ed. Jan Goldstein (Oxford, 1994), 81–98.

23. I develop this theme in my unpublished paper "History without Testaments: Storytelling and the Politics of Memory in the Work of Hannah Arendt," prepared for delivery at the conference "Hannah Arendt Twenty Years Later: A German Jewess in the Age of Totalitarianism," 22–23 March 1996, The Program for the Study of Germany and Europe, Minda de Gunzburg Center for European Studies, Harvard University.

24. Jourdan, *Les Monuments de la Révolution française*, 99.

25. In this light, see T. J. Clark's important contribution: "Painting in the Year Two," *Representations* no. 47 (Summer 1994): 13–63.

26. On gendered imagery in republican thought, cf. Hanna Fenichel Pitkin, *Fortune Is a Woman: Gender and Politics in the Thought of Niccolò Machiavelli* (Berkeley, 1984); Linda Kerber, *Women of the Republic: Intellect and Ideology in Revolutionary America* (Chapel Hill, N.C., 1980), and "The Republican Ideology of the Revolutionary Generation," *American Quarterly* 37 (Fall 1985): 474–95; Bloch, "The Gendered Meanings of Virtue in Revolutionary America"; and Carroll Smith-Rosenberg, "Domesticating 'Virtue': Coquettes and Revolutionaries in Young America," in *Literature and the Body: Essays on Population and Persons*, ed. Elaine Scarry (Baltimore, 1988).

27. Jean-Jacques Rousseau, *Emile, or on Education*, trans. Allan Bloom (New York, 1979), 444–45. *Emile ou de l'éducation* was originally published in 1762, just one month after *Du Contrat social*. For the definitive modern edition, see Jean-Jacques Rousseau, *Oeuvres complètes*, 5 vols., ed. Bernard Gagnebin and Marcel Raymond (Paris, 1969), vol. 4. Arthur M. Melzer translates Rousseau as stating that "the word *virtue* comes from *force*," not strength, as in Bloom's translation. In any event, it is clear that Rousseau is intent on emphasizing the

issue of self-discipline or self-forcing, the use of an inner power to conquer the impulses in the interest of law and duty. See Arthur M. Melzer, *The Natural Goodness of Man: On the System of Rousseau's Thought* (Chicago, 1990), 101.

28. On the importance of bodily action in gendered conceptions of virtue, see Dorinda Outram, *The Body in the French Revolution* (New Haven, Conn., 1989).

29. In his project on education for the Legislative Assembly, Condorcet proposed secular, universal primary education—identical for the two sexes. The republican "martyr" Lepeletier, whose proposals on education were adopted by the Convention after his death at the urging of Robespierre, believed that girls ought to be educated at the primary level. They would learn the "three R's" and train their memories by studying civic chants and certain lines of history appropriate for the development of the virtues of their sex and for receiving moral notions of domestic and rural economy. The principal part of a girl's day would be devoted to spinning, sewing, and laundering, or to working in the workshops close to the schools. See D. Julia, *Les Trois couleurs du tableau noir: La Révolution* (Paris, 1981), 330.

30. Elke and Hans-Christian Harten, *Femmes, culture et révolution* (Paris, 1989), 27.

31. In a similar vein, Louis Gauffier's neoclassical painting *Générosité des femmes romaines* translates the women's action into the register of antiquity by finding precedents for their actions in Roman women's generosity. See Vovelle, *La Révolution française*, vol. 1, 205.

32. In summer and fall 1789, Kéralio launched two journals: *Journal de l'état et du citoyen*, followed soon by *Mercure national*, which she undertook jointly with her father and her husband, François Robert.

33. "L'affaire de M. Marat nous a donné occasion de connaître un vrai phénomene politique: c'est un journal sur les affaires publiques, composé par une femme. On avoit dit jusqu'à présent que les femmes n'entendoit d'autre metaphysique que celle de l'amour: mais Mademoiselle de Keralio a prouvé par le titre seul de son journal, que les abstractions les plus ardues ne l'effrayent pas. Son titre est de cette métaphysique qui avoisine de l'obscurité: c'est *le journal d'état et du citoyen*" (*Revolutions de Paris*, vol. 2, no. 14, 34–35).

34. In Chapter 4, I discuss even greater sacrifices—of husbands, sons, and brothers in the national cause.

35. Although in theory the Church was a universal community, its claims to serve all were belied by its evident exclusion of noncommunicants and non-Catholics from membership. Practices that denied full membership to people of limited property (in the period of constitutional monarchy), as well as to Protestants, Jews, blacks, and *"gens de couleur,"* were open points of contention. On citizenship debates, see Shanti Singham, "Betwixt Cattle and Men: Jews, Blacks, and Women, and the Declaration of the Rights of Man," in *The French Revolution and the Idea of Freedom: The Old Regime and the Declaration of Rights of 1789*, ed. Dale Van Kley (Stanford, Calif., 1994), 114–53; David Geggus, "Racial Equality, Slavery, and Colonial Secession during the Constituent Assembly," *American Historical Review* 94, no. 5 (December 1989): 1290–1308; Gary Kates, "Jews into Frenchmen: Nationality and Representation in Revolutionary France," in *The French Revolution and the Birth of Modernity*, ed. Ferenc Fehér (Berkeley, 1990), 103–16.

36. Dominique Godineau, *The Women of Paris and Their French Revolution*, trans. Katherine Streip (Berkeley, 1998), 101.

37. Along with Dominique Godineau, Darline Gay Levy and Harriet B. Applewhite are the most forceful advocates of the view that women's escalating claims to the "rights of militant, democratic citizenship, especially the right to bear arms," blurred and even subverted classical and Rousseauian models of appropriate gender roles. Accordingly, they take issue with feminist readings that overvalue cultural determinations. As they state, "Our interpretation of women's practice of militant citizenship cautions against reading back into the ever-shifting ideological constellations and power struggles in which women were caught up between 1789 and 1793 a repressive linguistic-political-military hegemony that the Jacobins established only in the fall of 1793, and even then, only incompletely." Although my purpose in these essays lies closer to what they would doubtless term a "cultural" explanation, I stress the way in which representations are always risked in action, put to use in surprising and unanticipated ways. Several examples of women's expanded claims for citizenship that I discuss in the following paragraph are developed in great depth in their perceptive account, "Women and Militant Citizenship in Revolutionary Paris," in *Rebel Daughters: Women and the French Revolution*, 91, 86, and passim.

38. See Gary Kates, *The Cercle Social, the Girdondins, and the French Revolution* (Princeton, N.J., 1985), 124; "Etta Palm d'Aelders Proposes a Network of Women's Clubs to Administer Welfare Programs in Paris and Throughout France" ("Lettre d'une amie de la vérité, Etta Palm, née d'Aelders, Hollandoise, sur les démarches des enemies extérieurs et intérieures de la France; suivie d'une addresse à toutes les citoyennes patriotes, et d'une motion à leur proposer pour l'Assemblée nationale, lue à l'Assemblée féderative des amis de la vérité, le 23 mars, 1791 (n.p. n.d.)," in *Women in Revolutionary Paris, 1789–1795: Selected Documents Translated with Notes and Commentary*, ed. Darline Gay Levy, Harriet Branson Applewhite, and Mary Durham Johnson (Urbana, Ill., 1979), 68–69.

39. "A Bordeaux, quatre mille citoyennes, mères de famille, ayant à leur tête Madame Courpon, épouse du major de la garde nationale, se sont rendues au champ-de-Mars; et là, réunies aux défenseurs de la patrie, elles ont juré de mourir pour la défense de la nation et la loi." *Revolutions de France et de Brabant*, in Camille Desmoulins, *Oeuvres*, vol. 8, no. 84 (Munchen, 1980), 281.

40. For a significant account of the provincial Jacobin women's clubs, see Suzanne Desan, "'Consitutional Amazons': Jacobin Women's Clubs in the French Revolution," in *Re-creating Authority in Revolutionary France*, ed. Bryant T. Ragan, Jr., and Elizabeth A. Williams (Brunswick, N.J., 1992), 11–35.

41. "Petition to the National Assembly on Women's Rights to Bear Arms" (Pauline Léon, "Adresse individuelle à l'Assemblée nationale, par des citoyennes de la Capitale, le 6 mars 1791"), in *Women in Revolutionary Paris*, 72–74. This petition is dated by Godineau, *The Women of Paris*, 108, and Levy and Applewhite themselves as being in 1792, not 1791, as it was dated in their earlier publication ("Women and Militant Citizenship in Revolutionary Paris," 88). According to Godineau, "This petition, which constituted the 'official' birth of the Parisian female militants in their first public gesture, was specifically a demand for arms" (*The Women of Paris*, 108).

42. "[P]endant que les ennemis du dehors trouveront la mort sous le fer de leurs époux, elles sauveront l'intérieur de l'empire, des secousses que ménagent, avec tant d'adresse, les instigateurs des troubles qui jettent la méfiance et le désordre au milieu des citoyens qu'une même cause a réunis". (*Journal de Perlet*, no. 159, 8 March 1792).

43. Godineau, *Women of Paris*, 109.

44. *Journal de Perlet*, no. 184, 2 April 1792, 12–13.

45. Levy and Applewhite, "Women and Militant Citizenship," 90.

46. Pierre Alexis Roussel, *Le Château des Tuileries*, 2 vols. (Paris, 1802), vol 2, 34–56, cited in *Women in Revolutionary Paris*, 167–68. As the editors of *Women in Revolutionary Paris* point out, it is the only full record of a regular meeting of the society. "Femme Monic" is identified as the proprietress of a small haberdashery shop, a spy for the Committee of Public Safety, and director of the knitters at the Jacobins.

47. "Nous faisons sucer à nos enfants un lait incorruptible et que nous clarifions à cet effet avec l'esprit naturel et agréable de la liberté," cited in Mary Jacobus, "Incorruptible Milk: Breast-feeding and the French Revolution," in *Rebel Daughters: Women and the French Revolution*, ed. Sara Melzer and Leslie W. Rabine (Oxford, 1992), 54.

48. "Je les ai nourris pour la Patrie—Aux mères fecondes la Patrie reconnaissante." Cited in Harten and Harten, *Femmes, culture et révolution*, p. 154.

49. *Archives parlementaires de 1787 à 1860*, 1st ser., vol. 67 (1905), 614; translated and cited in Marilyn Yalom, *A History of the Breast* (New York, 1997), 115. Cf. Fanny Fay-Sallois, *Les Nourrices à Paris au XIXe Siècle* (Paris, 1980).

50. See Harten and Harten, *Femmes, culture, et révolution*, 154

51. Yalom, *A History of the Breast*, 117.

52. Madelyn Gutwirth concludes that, given the emphasis on this theme in revolutionary ideology, there are relatively few images of nursing mothers (*Twilight of the Goddesses*, 352). Perhaps this is the case if we restrict our search to singular portrayals of this subject. What she overlooks, however, is the extent to which the image of the nursing mother is incorporated within other scenes, in both overt and subtle ways.

53. See *The Natural Goodness of Man*, 22ff.

54. On the connections between urban public life and women in Rousseau's thought, see my *Women and the Public Sphere*, chap. 3.

55. Rousseau, *Emile*, 359.

56. Ibid., 397.

57. Ibid., 358, 369.

58. Ibid., 361.

59. Ibid., 370.

60. This conflation of symbols in revolutionary iconography is not extraordinary. On republican symbolism, see E. H. Gombrich, "The Dream of Reason: Symbolism of the French Revolution," *British Journal for Eighteenth Century Studies* 2, no. 3 (1979): 187–205; James Leith, *Media and Revolution: Moulding a New Citizenry in France during the Terror* (Toronto, 1968); and Maurice Agulhon, *Marianne into Battle: Republican Imagery and Symbolism in France, 1789–1880*, trans. Janet Lloyd (1979; Cambridge, 1981); and Agulhon, "Politics and Im-

ages in Post-Revolutionary France," in *Rites of Power: Symbolism, Ritual and Politics since the Middle Ages,* ed. Sean Wilentz (Philadelphia, 1985).

61. Rousseau is only the most eminent of the many *philosophes,* political writers, government officials, and above all physicians who advocated in the eighteenth-century against wet-nursing and for breast-feeding. For an influential English treatise on the subject, see Dr. William Cadogan's *Essay upon Nursing* (1748). Yalom, in her important book on the topic of the breast in history, reports the stunning fact that "by 1801, it has been estimated that half of all Parisian babies and two-thirds of English babies were nursed by their mothers." In contrast, "in 1700, less than half of British mothers breast-fed their own children. . . . In France, the incidence of wet-nursing was even higher: what had been only an aristocratic practice during the sixteenth century won over the bourgeoisie in the seventeenth and even extended to the popular classes in the eighteenth" (*A History of the Breast,* 105–106). Cf. Mary Jacobus, "Incorruptible Milk: Breast-feeding and the French Revolution," in *Rebel Daughters,* 54–78.

62. Cf. J. E. Cirlot, *A Dictionary of Symbols,* trans. Jack Sage (New York, 1962). It is noted that in Nigeria, the turtle suggests the female sexual organ and is an emblem of lubricity. More generally, the turtle is a symbol of material existence, turgidity, involution, obscurity, slowness, stagnation, and highly concentrated materialism. It is surely significant that *Modesty* is represented here stepping on the turtle, which peeks out from under her robe.

63. For a discussion of the *Encyclopédie* frontispiece as an instance of the dominance of female allegories in the culture of early modern Europe, where not only science but virtually all of the abstract virtues were personified as feminine, see Londa Schiebinger, *The Mind Has No Sex? Women in the Origins of Modern Science* (Cambridge, Mass., 1989), chap. 5.

64. Cited by Kennedy, *A Cultural History of the French Revolution,* 336. Kennedy also remarks on the widespread cult of Marat during the next year. On the latter, cf. Marie-Hélène Huet, *Rehearsing the Revolution: The Staging of Marat's Death, 1793–1797,* trans. Robert Hurley (Berkeley, Calif., 1982) and *La Mort de Marat,* ed. Jean-Claude Bonnet (Paris, 1986).

65. On "Purging the Body Politic," see Carol Blum, *The Republic of Virtue* (Ithaca, 1986), esp. chap. 12; Lynn Hunt, *Politics, Culture, and Class in the French Revolution* (Berkeley, 1984). Blum cites the following observation by Jean Starobinski that analyzes the fatal causative link between the purity of the body politic and the evil of the other, drawing a parallel between Rousseau's thinking and the logic of the Terror: "The autonomy of the self, excessively preoccupied with its own purity, flips over into submission, dependence, and idolatry. It becomes unjust and unreasonable in wishing to hold onto a permanent justification. I am thinking here of the Terror. Certainly not in order to see Rousseau as its theoretician (although Robespierre drew the essential part of his ideas from Rousseau), but because the Terror seems to me to be, on the political level, homologous with what unfolds on the mental level in the autobiographical writings of Rousseau. To safeguard the conviction of his own radical innocence, Jean-Jacques must reject the evil to the outside, to impute it to a universal plot formed by his enemies. It is absolutely necessary that evil come from others and from them alone" (Starobinski, "La Mise en accusation de la sociét," in *Jean-Jacques Rousseau* (Neuchâtel, 1978); cited in Blum, *The Republic of Virtue,* 217–18.

66. Robespierre, *Oeuvres complètes*, vol. 8; cited by Carol Blum, *The Republic of Virtue*, 159.

67. Unfortunately, it is not possible to discuss in detail all the images dedicated to martyr-heroes, or those occasioned by the "pantheonization" of Mirabeau, Voltaire, Lepeletier, Marat, and Rousseau. However, this corpus of work certainly confirms the argument for the significance that the revolutionaries accorded to the Cult of Great Men. Likewise, Jacques-Louis David's The Death of *Marat,* his unfinished work *The Death of Joseph Bara*, and his lost painting *The Death of Lepeletier de Saint-Fargeau,* which he presented as a gift to the Convention on 29 March, an astonishing two months from the day of the funeral, are certainly among the most important demonstrations of the artistic effort to raise fallen men to the level of apotheosis. On the topic of martyrdom and the revolutionary fascination with immortality, see Antoine Schnapper, "A propos de David et des martyrs de la Révolution," in *Les Images de la Révolution française,* 109–17, and these essays *from La Révolution et la mort,* ed. Elizabeth Liris and Jean Maurice Bizière (Toulouse, 1991): Elizabeth Liris, " A propos de l'immortalité révolutionnaire," 107–18: Philippe Goujard, "L'héroïsation en l'an II," 119–26; Jacques Solé, "Robespierre et la politique de la mort (1792–1794)," 127–136; Patrice Higonnet, "Du suicide sentimental au suicide politique," 137–49; and Antoine de Baecque, "Le Corps des martyrs et le discours politique," 151–62.

68. Bara's heroic death in the Vendée was recounted in a letter read at the Convention in December 1793: "Entouré hier par les brigands, a mieux aimé périr que de se rendre et leur livrer deux chevaux qu'il conduisait" (Yesterday, surrounded by brigands he would rather have perished than give up the two horses he led). Thanks to support from Robespierre, Bara obtained the honors of the Panthéon and a fête organized by David. Cited in Bordes, "L'Art et le politique," in *Aux armes et aux arts! les arts de la Révolution, 1789–1799,* ed. Philippe Bordes and Régis Michel (Paris, 1989), 130. David himself portrayed the thirteen-year-old as a nude androgyne in an ecstatic pose of otherworldly beauty. Crow observes that when "it came to the suppression of the genitals—doubly imperative in view of the mandate to David from Robespierre that he represent outraged innocence and the special object of a mother's love— the overall illumination and blond light deprived him of the device of veiling shadow. His response was to take the boy's body and break it in two, simultaneously to figure its suffering and to downplay its sex. The body of Bara is twisted unnaturally at its center" (Crow, *Emulation,* 181). For an essential, and contrasting, perspective on David's and other paintings in the androgyne genre, see Abigail Solomon-Godeau, "Male Trouble: A Crisis in Representation," *Art History* 16, no. 2 (June 1993): 286–312.

69. On the intersection of sexuality, honor, and reputation see Guido Ruggiero, *Boundaries of Eros: Sex Crime and Sexuality in Renaissance Venice* (New York, 1985); and *Binding Passions: Tales of Magic, Marriage, and Power at the End of the Renaissance* (New York, 1993)

70. Jean-Jacques Rousseau, "Letter to M. d'Alembert on the Theatre," in *Politics and the Arts; Letter to M. D'Alembert on the Theatre,* trans. Alan Bloom (Ithaca, N.Y., 1960), 99. Rousseau's *Lettre à M. d'Alembert sur les spectacles* originally appeared in volume 7 of *l'Ency-*

clopédie in 1758. For the definitive modern edition, see Rousseau, *Oeuvres complètes*, vol. 5.

71. Rousseau, *Emile*, 361.

72. Chérieux's print seems to reprise William Hogarth's satirical print *Credulity, Superstition, and Fanaticism* (1762), discussed by Terry Castle in her influential essay "The Female Thermometer." In Hogarth's work, the crowd's spiritual elevation is shown to be indistinguishable from "more primitive forms of excitement." Seen in this light, Chérieux appears to recast religious enthusiasm, thought provoked by female desire and sexual appetite, into political enthusiasm. See Terry Castle, *The Female Thermometer: Eighteenth-Century Culture and the Invention of the Uncanny* (New York, 1995), 28.

73. Rousseau, "Letter to M. d'Alembert," 109.

74. G. W. F. Hegel, *Phenomenology of Spirit*, trans. A. V. Miller (Oxford, 1977). 288.

75. Counterrevolutionary and foreign publics—especially in Britain—enjoyed a caricatural art that attacked both the sansculottes and their women. Later in this chapter I discuss some examples from British caricature that exploit the association of women (of the popular classes) with violence.

76. See Chantal Thomas, "Heroism in the Feminine: The Examples of Charlotte Corday and Madame Roland," in *The French Revolution, 1789–1989: Two Hundred Years of Rethinking*, ed. Sandy Petrey (Special Issue of *The Eighteenth Century: Theory and Interpretation*) (Lubbock, Tex., 1989), 67–82.

77. I develop this connection in *Women and the Public Sphere*, chaps. 4 and 5.

78. On the grotesque, see Mikhail Bakhtin, *Rabelais and His World*, trans. Hélène Iswolsky (Cambridge, Mass., 1968); Peter Stallybrass and Allon White, *The Politics and Poetics of Transgression* (Ithaca, N.Y., 1986); Barbara Babcock, ed., *The Reversible World: Symbolic Inversions in Art and Society* (Ithaca, N.Y., 1978). On the female grotesque, see Mary Russo, *The Female Grotesque: Risk, Excess, and Modernity* (New York: Routledge, 1994).

79. See, especially, Lynn Hunt, "The Many Bodies of Marie-Antoinette: Political Pornography and the Problem of the Feminine in the French Revolution" and Sarah Maza, "The Diamond Necklace Affair Revisited (1785–1786): The Case of the Missing Queen," in *Eroticism and the Body Politic*, 108–30 and 63–89; Betsy Colwill, "Pass as a Woman, Act like a Man: Marie-Antoinette as Tribade in the Pornography of the French Revolution," in *Homosexuality in Modern France*, 54–79.

80. In a 1784 print, *Female Harpy*, the monster is reported to have been discovered in the Spanish royal province of Chile. The text accompanying *Female Harpy* emphasizes the monster's indeterminate sexuality and bestiality: Her general form is said to be closer to that of a male, and she is mustached and bearded like a goat, gross in proportions, with pointed, horned ears. Around her breasts hair grows, as in a man; and though she eats a sheep daily she is said to relish fish, especially eels, one of which she attacks with gusto. Versions of this female harpy—who is variously presented as wending her way into the royal family, depleting the royal treasury, ruining France, defiling the people's liberty, or trampling the Constitution and the Declaration of the Rights of Man and Citizen—were reproduced often in prerevolutionary and revolutionary prints. According to De Vinck, this calumny originated in a pam-

phlet by the Comte de Provence titled *Description historique d'un monstre symbolique pris vivant sur les bords du lac Fagua, près de Santa-Fé, par les soins de Francisco Xaveiro de Meunrios, Comte de Barcelone. Santa-Fé et Paris, 1784* (François-Louis Bruel, *Collection de Vinck: Inventaire analytique,* 6 vols. [Paris, 1914], cat. 1149). The exhibition catalog *French Caricature and the French Revolution, 1789–1799* (Los Angeles, 1988) presents two versions of this print (183). The catalog's editors attribute the origins of the monster symbolizing Marie Antoinette to a satirical sighting of a Chilean monster with a man's face, lion's mane, snake's scales, bull's horns, bat's wings, and two tails, first reported in 1784 in the *Courrier de l'Europe.* This sensational hoax also titillated public interest in reports that Frederick II had produced centaurs and satyrs through experiments with sodomy. In any event, numerous prints of the *Courrier's* monster circulated in Paris and became the "talk of the town." Not long after its appearance, the monster became a symbol of Marie-Antoinette and acquired a more feminine appearance, losing its beard and coming to resemble a harpy, a popular characterization of the queen as noted by De Vinck. (*Collection de Vinck*). For a discussion of prerevolutionary opposition to the queen, see Simon Schama, "Body Politics," in *Citizens: A Chronicle of the French Revolution* (New York, 1989), chap. 6.

81. Antoine de Baecque, *The Body Politic: Corporeal Metaphor in Revolutionary France, 1770–1800,* trans. Charlotte Mandell (Stanford, Calif., 1997), 169.

82. De Baecque, *The Body Politic,* 160–65.

83. See Chantal Thomas, "L'Architigresse d'Autriche. La Mètaphore animale dans les pamphlets contre Marie-Antoinette", and Antoine de Baecque, "Le Rècit fantastique de la Rèvolution: *Les Monstres aristocratiques* des pamphlets de 1789," both in *La Rèvolution du Journal, 1788–1794,* ed. Pierre Rètat (Paris, 1989); and, Chantal Thomas, *The Wicked Queen: The Origins of the Myth of Marie-Antoinette,* trans. Julie Rose (1989; New York, 1999).

84. Lynn Hunt notes that "at least fifteen different prints of the king as pig were printed, and Camille Desmoulins brought the metaphor to everyone's attention in his newspaper: 'The citizens are warned that a fat pig has escaped from the Tuileries; those who run into it are asked to bring it back to its pen'" (*The Family Romance of the French Revolution* [Berkeley, 1992], 51). In addition to the abundant imagery of the king as a pig or swine, he was also portrayed as a cat and an ox as in two anonymous prints, possibly by Villeneuve, as in *Monsieur . . . Le Chat* (Paris, 1790) and *Louis le parjure valet de chambre de M. la baronne de Korf suivant sa maîtresse dans sa fuite* (1791).

86. *Le Moniteur universel,* 19 November 1793, translated and cited in Thomas, "Heroism in the Feminine," in *The French Revolution, 1789–1989,* 79.

86. Robert Darnton, *The Forbidden Best-Sellers of Pre-Revolutionary France* (New York, 1995), 139 and passim, for his engaging account of this work and its wider significance.

87. Sarah Maza, *Private Lives and Public Affairs: The Causes Célèbres of Prerevolutionary France* (Berkeley, 1993), 180–81.

88. "Elles ont vu que dans un état où la liberté politique est entière, il se seroit une révolution dans les moeurs, qui dérangeroit infailliblement la condition privée des femmes; qu'elles pourroient bien être obligées de substituer à leur inoccupation bruyante et frivole, et

à leur indépendance scandaleuse, les autres devoirs d'épouse, de mères, de citoyennes; l'honneur de devenir un jour des Spartiates, ne les a point consolé de la perte des plaisirs d'Athénes; et l'apprehension de voir introduire le divorce a achevé de leur montrer, sous un aspect haïsable, une révolution qui va leur imposer le joug odieux des complaisances, des vertus, des moeurs et de la fidélité." "Pourquoi les femmes sont-elles plus Arisocrates que les hommes?" in *Journal de Perlet*, no. 473, 22 November 1790, 5–6.

89. The second writer expresses surprise at reading the former contribution and objects to the author's anonymity:

> I ask him why he concealed his name when he censures women . . . to dare to write in a century of enlightenment and civility, that women are strangers of a sort to our nation, to liberty, that vanity and fondness for baubles is their only passion; that in the chance of public manners (*moeurs*) and in the great revolution they pay attention only to what interests themselves (*leur amour-propre*), and that they do not seem to regret their particular domination! If these are the truth, I have trouble believing it. I think, on the contrary, that women have ideas of merit (*du beau moral*) to the same degree of perfection, or maybe more perfectly than men; that civic and political virtue can grow in their bosoms as in ours, and that the no doubt respectable writer whom I contest should remember the virtuous Roman women who shredded their clothes, donning mourning dresses in times of misfortune for their nation . . . I love the people as the anonymous author seems to love them; I cherish the frank and disinterested virtues and I admire their patience and goodness, as well as their proud courage. But I hate the populace because it has neither order (*règle*) nor limit (*mèsure*), and it mistakes fanaticism for patriotism, and it is always ready to surmount any barrier: and when class (rang) and dignity have disappeared, I would like still to keep respect for people who had them (*en étoient revêtués*). . . . Finally, I can assure the author . . . that women await with impatience the moment when they can crown with their own hands the conquerors of our generous liberty; and their eagerness to join our august assemblies is again evidence of their natural curiosity, and [I would encourage him] to better think of that still more delicate sentiment, and of the interest they take in our glory, in combining their vote (*suffrages*) with ours in these beautiful hours and glorious moments when men show themselves in all their splendor. Without doubt, I would like to believe that the approval of women and their precious vote are the flattering crowns that even our most austere legislators will not know how to scorn ("Sur l'esprit d'arisocratie qu'on reproche aux femmes," *Journal de Perlet*, no. 485, 3 December 1790, 7–8).

90. "Combien de fois le monarque n'a-t-il pas reçu de ces mêmes femmes, des témoignages d'amour plus flatteurs et plus vrais que les vaïnes flagorneries de ses courtisans, et sur-tout des leçons plus sincères et plus instructives. Espérons qu'à l'avenir toutes nos femmes s'honoreront de devenir, dans ce sens, des femmes du peuple.""Pourquoi les femmes," 7.

91. Gutwirth, *Twilight of the Goddesses*, 267.

92. Patrice Higonnet, "'Aristocrate,' 'Aristocratie': Language and Politics in the French

Revolution," in *The French Revolution, 1789–1989*, 54, 53. More menacingly, along with aristocrats and priests, women—that is, prostitutes—could be the special targets of republican rage. See Schama, "Impure Blood," in *Citizens*, 619–75; and Gutwirth, *Twilight of the Goddesses*, 318–19. For further discussion of the rhetorical construction of "aristocracy," see Patrice Higonnet, *Class, Ideology, and the Rights of Nobles during the French Revolution* (Oxford, 1981).

93. I am grateful to Rico Franses for his wonderfully insightful commentary on my talk "Liberty's Body: Female Virtue, Masculine Rights, and Democratic Sovereignty in the French Revolution," Conference "Ideas of Liberty", 15–17 June 1994, Humanities Research Centre, Australian National University.

94. As David Bindman points out, "the Contrast was probably the most widely disseminated design of the whole anti-radical campaign [in Britain], for it was used on a variety of objects." *The Shadow of the Guillotine: Britain and the French Revolution*, ed. David Bindman (London, 1989), 118. This catalog includes different editions of the print as well as examples of mugs, jugs, and broadsides with the Rowlandson design. Other British images, which make a similar association of Liberty and monstrosity, are Anon., *The Hopes of the Party! or the Darling Children of Democracy!*; James Gillray's *Un petit souper, à la parisienne: or, A Family of Sans-Cullotts refreshing, after the fatigues of the day*; and *A Republican Belle: A Picture of Paris for 1794* (published 10 March 1794). See catalog items #46 and #47 in *Representing Revolution: French and British Images, 1789–1804,* (Amherst, Mass., 1989).

95 *Le Moniteur universel*, 19 November 1793; translated and cited in Thomas, "Heroism in the Feminine," 80. The *Moniteur* actually included a third woman in its censure, Olympe de Gouges, author of *The Declaration of the Rights of Woman*, who also died at the guillotine in the fall of 1793. Of her, the *Moniteur* wrote, "Olympe de Gouges , born with an exalted imagination, took her delirium for an inspiration of nature," cited in Thomas, "Heroism in the Feminine," 80.

96. Jules Michelet wrote about her: "Madame Roland, Robespierre . . . both have the same quirk: they were always writing, they were born scribes" (cited and translated in Thomas, "Heroism in the Feminine," 77).

97. "Nous n'avons eu que trop d'occasions de comparer la cour de Roland et de sa femme, depuis le 10 août jusqu'au commencement de février, avec celle de Louis Capet et de Marie-antoinette pendant les six mois précédents" ("Circulaire de la Société des Amis de la Liberté et de l'égalité, séante au ci-devant Jacobins-Saint-Honoré a Paris, du 26 Mars 1793, l'an IIe de la République française," in F.-A. Aulard, *La Sociéte des Jacobins: Recueil de Documents*, vol. 5 (January 1793–March 1794) (Paris, 1895), 102.

98. For a fuller description of Roland, see the excellent portrayals in Thomas, "Heroism in theFeminine," 33–46; Dorinda Outram, *The Body and the French Revolution: Sex, Class, and Political Culture* (New Haven, Conn., 1989); and Gita May, *Madame Roland and the Age of Revolution* (New York, 1970).

99. The print's title deliberately mocks an earlier celebratory image titled *The Triumph of Marat* and a flock of images from the period of the popular revolution that portrayed Marat at the height of his political influence.

100. Of course, this in turn echoes Rousseau's famous opening line of the *Social Contract*: "Man is born free and everywhere he is in chains." ("l'homme est né libre, et partout il est dans les fers").

101. Cited in "Women and Militant Citizenship in Revolutionary Paris," 93–94. Darline Gay Levy and Harriet Branson Applewhite emphasize the Jacobins' initial vacillation toward women's political claims. Moreover, despite the pronounced misogyny that they exhibited in the repression of October 1793 banning women's clubs and thereafter, the Jacobin men were not always the first to object to politically active women, as Gorsas's remarks indicate. During the insurrection of 31 May to 2 June 1793, the Jacobin leaders as well as sansculotte section officials lauded the members of the Society of Revolutionary Republican Women for the "purest civic mindedness" ("Women and Militant Citizenship in Revolutionary Paris," 80, 93).

102. Godineau remarks that "this phantasm of women armed to the teeth can be found in the accounts of the rebellion [of 31 May–2 June] given by the Girondins: Gorsas, Bergoeing, and Lanjuinais all insisted on this point, in a veritable delirium. It is true that the Revolutionary Republican Women had decided to organize in 'companies of amazons' to fight the Girondins and that the rebels had armed themselves with the first weapons at hand, such as work tools or the knives that women of the people carried in their pockets. Thus the phantasm of women carrying weapons probably had a real basis that was encouraged by the Girondin deputies' desire to frighten their readers by describing the arming as horrible, anarchic, and indecent. But this also suggests an unreasonable male fear that goes beyond concrete reality and touches on the domain of *mentalités*" (Godineau, *The Women of Paris*, 130).

103. Condorcet is an important exception, having written the defense of women's rights in his *Essai sur l'admission des femmes au droit de cité* (1790). Nevertheless, he remained silent on the issue of women's rights when presenting his introductory report on the draft constitution to the Convention in early 1793—the period following the removal of the distinction between active and passive voters, so that the denial of women's rights was made more explicitly a matter of gender difference than one of property or class position. This was also the period of accelerating women's activism in the streets and in the galleries of the Convention, and during which an antifeminine campaign in the revolutionary press was already well advanced. Despite Condorcet's equivocation, his own friends and political allies did respond, however unsuccessfully. David Williams—friend of the Girondins, participant in Sophie de Condorcet's salon, author of *Lettres sur la liberté politique*, and participant in the preparatory work for the Constitution—wrote his *Observations sur la dernière constitution de la France avec des vues pour la formulation de la nouvelle constitution*. Williams supported education for women, their right to testify in cases involving members of their own sex, and political rights for single women, spinsters as well as widows. In addition, during April 1793, the constitutional draft commission discussed an appeal for women's voting rights (entitled "le Partisan de l'égalité des droits et de l'inégalité en fait") by deputy Pierre Guyomar. Guyomar compared prejudice in sexual matters to those of race, calling for its outright abolition and accusing the Declaration of the Rights of Man and Citizen of perpetuating an aristocracy of men and

smuggling in Old Regime principles. Yet the commission concluded that women lacked sufficient education to participate in the nation's political life, and referred them to their own devices to shake off the various yolks that still restrained them. See Elisabeth Roudinesco, *Theroigne de Méricourt: A Melancholic Woman during the French Revolution*, trans. Martin Thom (London, 1991), 129–30.

104. See Geneviève Fraisse, *Reason's Muse: Sexual Difference and the Birth of Democracy*, trans. Jane Marie Todd (Chicago, 1994). Peter Brooks calls Sylvain Maréchal's October 1793 play, *Le Jugement dernier des rois*, the "representative melodrama of the Terror." See Peter Brooks, "The Revolutionary Body," in *Fictions of the French Revolution*, ed. Bernadette Fort (Evanston, Ill., 1991), 40ff; and his translation of the play in the *Yale Review* 78, no. 4 (1990): 583–603.

105. As Fraisse further explains, "Reading is dangerous because it leads directly to writing. Women would write not just letters—women's private correspondence, even when elevated to the status of a literary genre, offended neither men nor society as a whole—but also novels, satires, political essays, texts that transformed a woman into a woman author, in which case it was not even certain that she was still a woman" (*Reason's Muse*, 11). For a contemporary woman's response to Sylvain Marechal, see Albertine Clément-Hémery, "Les Femmes vengées de la sottise d'un philosophe du jour" (1801), in *Opinions de Femmes: De la Veille au lendemain de la Révolution française*, preface by Geneviève Fraisse (Paris, 1989), 81–128.

106. Brooks, "The Revolutionary Body," 39.

107. He continues, "But as for holding a needle, that they always learn gladly." He also advocates restricting girls' education: "In general, if it is important for men to limit their studies to useful knowledge, it is even more important for women, because the latter's lives, although less laborious are—or ought to be—more attached to their cares and more interrupted by various cares. Thus their lives do not permit them to indulge themselves in any preferred talent to the prejudice of their duties" (Rousseau, *Emile*, 368).

108. Antoine de Baecque, *Caricature révolutionnaire* (Paris, 1988), 40–41.

109. Brooks, "The Revolutionary Body," 42.

110. Ibid., 43. Ironically, as Outram underscores, the new controlled, autonomous, impermeable, stoic body, which was "of vital importance to its users and its audience at a time when the first use in French history of state terror on a mass scale was demonstrating how, on the contrary, in reality the body was frail, vulnerable, ultimately disposable" (cited in Brooks, "The Revolutionary Body," 37).

111. Brooks, "The Revolutionary Body," 44.

112. Alain Corbin discusses some of these factors with respect to postrevolutionary France in "The Secret of the Individual," in *A History of Private Life*, vol. 4, *From the Fires of Revolution to the Great War*, ed. Michelle Perrot, trans. Arthur Goldhammer (Cambridge, Mass., 1990), 457–667. For English women in this period, see Mary Poovey, *The Proper Lady and the Woman Writer: Ideology as Style in the Works of Mary Wollstonecraft, Mary Shelley, and Jane Austen* (Chicago, 1984).

CHAPTER 4

POSSESSING *La Patrie*

1. William Church, "France," in *National Consciousness, History, and Political Culture in Early-Modern Europe*, ed. Orest Ranum (Baltimore, 1975), 65. I am telescoping in these short remarks a long, complex set of developments in order to underscore how the rejection of monarchy became possible in 1792. Certainly, the king remained in initial good favor with the revolutionaries, hailed as "the restorer of French liberty," even if his ministers were denounced for their despotism. Yet the monarchical constitution did not succeed, and the rhetorical grounds for republicanism were established in the last decades of the Old Regime.

2. In an anthropological perspective, Anderson offers the following definition of the nation: "It is an imagined political community—and imagined as both inherently limited and sovereign." First, "it is *imagined* because the members of even the smallest nation will never know most of their fellow-members, meet them, or even hear of them, yet in the minds of each lives the image of their communion." Second, "the nation is *limited* because even the largest of them, encompassing perhaps a billion living beings, has finite, if elastic, boundaries, beyond which lie other nations. No nation imagines itself coterminous with mankind." Third, "it is imagined as *sovereign* because the concept was born in an age in which Enlightenment and Revolution were destroying the legitimacy of the divinely-ordained, hierarchical dynastic realm . . . nations dream of being free, and, if under God, directly so." Last, "it is imagined as a *community*, because, regardless of the actual inequality and exploitation that may prevail in each, the nation is always conceived as a deep, horizontal comradeship. Ultimately it is this fraternity that makes it possible, over the past two centuries, for so many millions of people, not so much to kill, as willingly to die for such limited imaginings" (*Imagined Communities: Reflections on the Origin and Spread of Nationalism*, rev. ed. [London, 1991], 6–7). On the French conception of modern citizenship, see Rogers Brubaker, *Citizenship and Nationhood in France and Germany* (Cambridge, Mass., 1992), and Liah Greenfield, *Nationalism: Five Roads to Modernity* (Cambridge, Mass., 1992).

3. "Le philosophe sait que ce mot vient du latin *pater*, qui représente un pere et des enfans, et conséquemment qu'il exprime le sens que nous attachons à celui de *famille*, de *société*, d'*état libre*, dont nous sommes membres, et dont les lois assurent nos libertés et notre bonheur. Il n'est point de *patrie* sous le joug du despotisme." Jaucourt, "Patriotisme," *Encyclopédie ou Dictionnaire raisonné des sciences, des arts et des métiers, par une société de gens de lettres*, 3d ed., vol. 12 (Paris, 1765), 161.

4. George Mosse, *Nationalism and Sexuality: Middle-Class Morality and Sexual Norms in Modern Europe* (Madison, 1985), 1. Cf. Linda Colley's excellent account of the cult of prolific maternity in the forging of British nationalism: *Britons: Forging the Nation, 1707–1837* (New Haven, Conn., 1992), 240 and passim; and Randolph Trumbach's inquiry into the reconstruction of homosexual desire in eighteenth-century England: *Sex and the Gender Revolution*, vol. 1, *Heterosexuality and the Third Gender in Enlightenment London* (Chicago, 1998).

5. There is now an impressive literature on these topics, including Richard Rand, "Love, Domesticity, and the Evolution of Genre Painting in Eighteenth-Century France," and Sarah Maza, "The 'Bourgeois' Family Revisited: Sentimentalism and Social Class in Prerevolution-

ary French Culture," both in *Intimate Encounters: Love and Domesticity in Eighteenth-Century France,* ed. Richard Rand (Princeton, N.J., 1997); Maza, *Private Lives and Public Affairs: The Causes Célèbres of Prerevolutionary France* (Berkeley, 1993); Carol Duncan, "Happy Mothers and Other New Ideas in Eighteenth-Century French Art," in *Feminism and Art History: Questioning the Litany,* ed. Norma Broude and Mary D. Garrard (New York, 1982), 201–20; Ben Barker-Benfield, *The Culture of Sensibility: Sex and Society in Eighteenth-Century Britain* (Chicago, 1992); David Denby, *Sentimental Narrative and the Social Order in France, 1760–1820* (Cambridge, 1994); Roddey Reid, *Families in Jeopardy: Regulating the Social Body in France, 1750–1910* (Stanford, Calif., 1993).

6. "Cet art de plaire, ce desir de plaire à tous, cette envie de plaire plus qu'une autre, ce silence du coeur, ce déréglement de l'esprit, ce mensonge continuel appellé *coquetterie*, semble être dans les *femmes* un caractere primitif, qui né de leur condition naturellement . . . Son bonheur est d'ignorer ce que le monde appelle *les plaisirs*, sa gloire est de vivre ignorée. Renfermée dans les devoirs de *femme* et de mere, elle consacre ses jours à la pratique des vertus obscures: occupée du gouvernement de sa famille, elle regne sur son mari par la complaisance, sur ses enfans par la douceur, sur les domestiques par la bonté: sa maison est la demeure des sentimens religieux, de la piété filiale, de l'amour conjugal de la tendresses maternelle, de l'ordre . . . Elle a un caractère réserve et de dignité qui la fair respecter." "Femme (Morale)," in *Encyclopédie,* vol. 6, 440–42.

7. "Mais que les méres daignent nourrir leurs enfans, les moeurs vont se réformer d'elles-mêmes, les sentimens de la nature se réveiller dans tous les coeurs, l'Etat va se repeupler; ce prémier point, ce point seul va tout reunir. L'attrait de la vie domestique est le meilleur contrepoison des mauvaises moeurs" (Jean-Jacques Rousseau, *Emile,* book 1, in *Oeuvres complètes,* vol. 4, ed. Bernard Gagnebin and Marcel Raymond (Paris, 1969), 258.

8. "Les hommes, destinés aux affaires, doivent être élevés en public. Les femmes, au contraire, destinées à la vie intérieure, ne doivent peut-être sortir de la maison paternelle que dans quelques cas rares . . . [Jean-Jacques Rousseau] étoit fortement pénétré de cette vérité si familière aux peuples anciens, que l'homme et la femme, jouant un rôle entièrement différent dans la nature, ne pouvoient jouer le même rôle dans l'état social, et que l'ordre éternel des choses ne les faisoit concourir à un but commun, qu'en leur assignant des places distinctes. La constitution robuste de l'homme, et les habitudes actives, énergiques, hardies, persévérantes qui doivent en résulter, déterminent le caractère de ses travaux: tous ceux qui demandent une force considérable, des courses lointaines, du courage, de la constance, des discussions opiniâtres, le regardent exclusivement. C'est lui qui doit labourer, négocier, voyager, combattre, plaider ses droits et ceux de ses frères, les autres humains, dans les assemblées publiques." *Discours de Monsieur Mirabeau l'Aîné, sur l'education nationale* (Paris, 1791), 39 –41. Mirabeau, a man of enormous appetites and size, was of course best known before the Revolution for his scandalous life, his debaucheries, and the duels that landed him several trips to prison. But then again Mirabeau's revered Rousseau was himself hardly a paragon of private virtue. Indeed, his personal failings may even have endeared him to his readers, helping them (flawed human beings like himself) to take to heart his moral pronouncements. In any event, Mirabeau's sentimental Rousseauism was not exceptional. François Furet captures the man

when he writes, "Mirabeau bungled everything, yet fate would smile on him. This dissipated, inconsistent, unfaithful, venal man managed to grasp the opportunity of a lifetime: to become the voice of the new nation" ("Mirabeau" in *A Critical Dictionary of the French Revolution*, ed. François Furet and Mona Ozouf, trans. Arthur Goldhammer [Cambridge, Mass., 1989], 267). Indeed, something of his rhetorical force, so powerfully voiced as a deputy of the new nation, is evident also in the way he mobilizes Rousseauian ideas on the family and puts them to work on behalf of morality, education, and the law. In any event, as Furet also states, "All his life he had plundered the works of others, and the Revolution did not alter his habits" ("Mirabeau, 268).

9. "La constitution délicate des femmes, parfaitement appropriée à leur destination principale, celle de faire des enfans, de veiller avec sollicitude sur les époques périlleuses du premier âge, et dans cet objet si précieux à l'auteur de notre existence, d'enchaîner à leurs pieds toutes les forces de l'homme par la puissance irrésistible de la foiblesse; cette constitution, dis-je, les borne aux timides travaux du ménage, aux goûts sédentaires que ces travaux exigent, et ne leur permet de trouver un véritable bonheur, et de répandre autour d'elles tout celui dont elles peuvent devenir les dispensatrices que dans les paisibles emplois d'une vie retirée." *Discours de Monsieur Mirabeau l'Aîné, sur l'éducation nationale*, 41. Mirabeau's phrase "d'enchaîner à leurs pieds" is interesting in this context, as it conjures up the chains that bound chattel slaves to their masters, restricting their movement and denying them human liberty and dignity. In the domestic universe that Mirabeau imagines, however, it is men who are bound by sentiment to women—that is, by the "irresistible power of weakness." In turn, woman's bondage—to her husband, children, and domestic situation—is dictated by the harmony of nature. It is a result of the symbolic chains of love, not the iron chains of (real) slavery. And, just as likely, the result of magnetic attractions between family members—a possibility that would have appealed to a writer like Mirabeau, who participated in mesmerist circles on the eve of the Revolution. See note 10 for a further exploration of this last connection. On mesmerism, see Robert Darnton, *Mesmerism and the End of the Enlightenment in France* (Cambridge, Mass., 1968).

10. The legal briefs in the last years by the Old Regime of Nicolas Bergasse—future deputy to the National Assembly, friend and attorney for the Baron Guillaume Kornmann in his very public divorce struggle with his wife in the late 1780s—offers a consummate example of how private morals, the law, and the political principles of government could be tied together in the hands of a talented political pamphleteer. Certainly, Bergasse may have been exaggerating in 1788 in claiming the circulation of 100,000 copies of all his briefs on behalf of Kornmann. Still, in her excellent account of the Kornmann affair, Sarah Maza confirms the enormous popularity and impact of Bergasse's sentimentalized briefs. Robert Darnton has identified the "Kornmann group" as including, besides Bergasse and Kornmann, another banker, Etienne Clavière, and three writers with radical inclinations: Jacques-Pierre Brissot, Jean-Louis Carra, and Antoine Gorsas—all besides Kornmann future journalists and leaders of the Girondin faction. Less central members of the group included Mirabeau and the Marquis de Lafayette. The Kornmann group's ideology was a peculiar mixture of Rousseau and the "magnetic" theories of Franz Anton Mesmer, combined with hostility to "les grands" or

established authorities of all sorts. For them, the institution of the family, the source of true morality (*les moeurs*), was founded in the laws of nature. Moreover, the attraction of family members for each other, and even a mother breast-feeding her child, according to Brissot, was thought to be the result of the harmonious action of magnetic fluids (Darnton, "Trends in Radical Propaganda on the Eve of the French Revolution [1782–1788]," Ph.D. diss. [Oxford, 1964], 73–76). Maza points out that these ideas came together in the trial briefs written for Kornmann: "Rousseauean aspirations to natural morality, idealizations of the family, and denunciations of the men in power and their agents." At heart, the Kornmann affair was simply a case of a wife's adultery—although Kornmann's defenders conveniently chose to forget the fact that Catherine Kornmann's affair was begun with her husband's permission and encouragement. Much more than a peccadillo, as it was regarded by society in his own day, adultery was decried by Bergasse as "the crime whose consequences are most deadly and usually most irreparable." As Maza explains, "Bergasse argued in classic contractual fashion, the bond between man and woman, and the family that resulted from that bond, were the expressions of the first laws of nature and the foundations of society. Since adultery was the crime that most threatened the family, it should therefore be considered the transgression most dangerous to society." Furthermore, in his provocatively political discussion of adultery, Bergasse applauded those who chose public freedom and paid the price of constraints on their personal life, while lambasting the tolerance of "unfreedom for the sake of shallow pleasures, passing connections, and the empty display of wit." Sarah Maza, *Private Lives and Public Affairs*, 301, 309–10, and chap. 6 passim. On the Kornmann affair, see also Thomas Crow, *Painters and Public Life in Eighteenth-Century France* (New Haven, Conn., 1985), 224–26. On the theme of women's disinterest in their children and their disinclination toward maternity in the novels of adultery, see Tony Tanner, *Adultery in the Novel: Contract and Transgression* (Baltimore, 1979).

11. These ranged from the 1761 unified Prussian Frederician Code and William Blackstone's *Commentaries on the Laws of England* of 1756 to the civil and political reforms in France during the 1790s and the Napoleonic Code of 1804.

12. See Annik Pardailhé-Galabrun, *The Birth of Intimacy: Privacy and Domestic Life in Early Modern Paris*, preface Pierre Chaunu, trans. Jocelyn Phelps (Philadelphia, 1991). In the preface to this detailed study of the changes in Parisian material culture, including public and private space, between the seventeenth and eighteenth centuries, Pierre Chaunu remarks, "The average ordinary house changed more between the first and last quarters of the eighteenth century than it had during the two preceding centuries or during the century that followed. By the end of the reign of Louis XV, it took 29 tons of materials, 41 tons including earthworks, to house one Parisian in accordance with the new standards and expectations for average to high-quality housing. That meant a fireplace in every room; with the same amount of wood, these fireplaces would reflect four times as much heat into the room as those broad, straight, gaping fireplaces that predated the progress made by heating technology. That was one of the modest steps made in the eighteenth century, the century of privacy, toward the earliest form of well-being, or *confort*, to use a word taken almost intact from English: a more intelligent use was made of effort and there was a greater economy of movement" (x–xi).

13. Anderson, *Imagined Communities,* 5. Though Anderson fails to develop his insight into the relationship between gender and nationalism, it has been the focus of considerable debate by feminist scholars, including Doris Sommer, *Foundational Fictions: The National Romance of Latin America* (Berkeley, 1991); Ann McClintock, "Family Feuds: Gender, Nationalism, and the Family," *Feminist Review* 44 (Summer 1993): 62–79; and many of the contributors to *Nationalisms and Sexualities,* eds. Andrew Parker, Mary Russo, Doris Sommer, and Patricia Yeager (New York, 1992).

14. Editor's Introduction, *Nationalisms and Sexualities,* 5.

15. Hence, the sad paradox that the granting of women's citizenship was often opposed by supporters of working-class suffrage and black (male) emancipation throughout the Western world. Only in the mid- and late-twentieth century, in the constitutions of nations that came into existence as a result of the defeat of Western colonialism, did women, like ethnic minorities, achieve formal citizenship simultaneously with men.

16. As Linda Colley points out, ideally the doctrine of separate spheres was profoundly contractual: "Women refrained, at least in theory, from invading the public sphere, the realm of action, on the understanding that their moral influence would be respected and recognised. They accepted a vulnerable position in life, on condition that men would maintain and respect them" (*Britons: Forging the Nation, 1707–1837* [New Haven, Conn., 1992], 263). For a discussion of nineteenth-century France in this context, cf. Michelle Riot-Sarcey, *La Démocratie à l'épreuve des femmes: Trois figures critiques du pouvoir, 1830–1848* (Paris, 1994).

17. "Sans doute la femme doit régner dans l'intérieur de sa maison, mais elle ne doit régner que là; par-tout ailleurs elle est comme déplacée; la seule manière dont il lui soit permis de se faire remarquer ailleurs, c'est par un maintien qui rappelle la mère de famille, ou qui caractérise tout ce qui rend digne de le devenir. La jurisdiction d'une femme respectable n'en est pas pour cela moins étendue: au contraire son époux l'honore autant qu'il la chérit; il la consulte dans les occasions les plus difficiles; ses enfans ont pour elle la soumission la plus tendre et la plus religieuse." *Discours de Monsieur Mirabeau l'Aîné, sur l'education nationale,* 42–43 (emphasis added).

18. Ann McClintock, "No Longer in a Future Heaven: Women and Nationalism in South Africa," *Transition* 51 (1991): 120; cited in *Nationalisms and Sexualities,* 6.

19. *Nationalisms and Sexualities,* 6. (Anderson and Mosse cited in *Nationalisms and Sexualities* as well.) Although among recent French historians, Lynn Hunt has done the most to call attention to the "fraternal" dimension of French revolutionary culture, she surprisingly omits the impact of France's nearly constant involvement in war for the better part of three decades in explaining this development.

20. Abigail Solomon-Godeau, *Male Trouble: A Crisis in Representation* (New York, 1997), 40–41; Thomas Crow, *Emulation: Making Artists for Revolutionary* France (New Haven, Conn., 1995); Alex Potts, "Beautiful Bodies and Dying Heroes," *History Workshop* 30 (Autumn 1990): 1–21; Potts, *Flesh and the Ideal: Winckelmann and the Origins of Art History* (New Haven, Conn., 1994).

21. In fact, the androgynous representations that have caught the attention of recent scholars appear to be a high cultural phenomenon; they are nearly absent in the popular prints of the period.

22. For our purposes, it is possible to speak simultaneously of *La Patrie* and Republic, as well as Liberty, who is often indistinguishable from Republic, or France, who is an even older representation of the French nation. I am interested in embodiments of the French nation-state, all of which I subsume under the general rubric of *La Patrie*.

23. Lynn Hunt, *Politics, Culture, and Class in the French Revolution* (Berkeley, 1984); Maurice Agulhon, *Marianne into Battle: Republican Imagery and Symbolism in France, 1789–1880*, trans. Janet Lloyd (Cambridge, 1977); Aghulhon and Pierre Bonte, *Marianne: Les Visages de la République* (Paris, 1992).

24. Sommer, *Foundational Fictions* 41, 32, ix.

25. By following a semiotic approach to national imagery, my objective is not to reduce, but rather to expand on the meanings that patriotism elicits, to address what Solomon-Godeau terms "the polysemic or multi-signifying aspect of imagery." As she states, "The meanings of a work are thus never reducible to its contents, its subject, its style and mode of execution, but are equally bound to its context and its reception which may or may not be available to historical reconstruction" (*Male Trouble*, 30).

26. In this passage I have intentionally translated *la patrie* as "mother country" rather than "fatherland" in order to underscore the gendered resonances of the ties between mother love (*l'amour de sa mère*) and love of country (*l'amour de sa patrie*). Although French syntax, like that of other Romance languages, certainly facilitates this understanding, Rousseau has in mind much more than a simple grammatical connection. As the passage indicates, he is describing the relationship between the male patriot and his "mother"—that is, mother country. For the Jacobin counterpart to Rousseau's femininization of *la patrie*, see note 69 in the Introduction.

27. "C'est l'éducation qui doit donner aux âmes la forme nationale, et diriger tellement leurs opinions et leurs goûts, qu'elles soient patriotes par inclination, par passion, par nécessité. Un enfant, en ouvrant les yeux, doit voir la patrie, et jusqu'à la mort ne doit plus voir qu'elle. Tout vrai républicain suça avec le lait de sa mère l'amour de sa patrie: c'est-à-dire, des lois et de la liberté. Cet amour fait toute son existence; il ne voit que la patrie, il ne vit que pour elle; sitôt qu'il est seul, il est nul; sitôt qu'il n'a plus de patrie, il n'est plus; et s'il n'est pas mort, il est pis" (Jean-Jacques Rousseau, "Considérations sur le Gouvernement de Pologne et sur sa réformation projetée" (April 1772), in *The Political Writings of Jean Jacques Rousseau*, vol. 2, ed. C. E. Vaughan (New York, 1962), 437.

28. Anderson, *Imagined Communities*, 154.

29. Walter Benjamin, "The Work of Art in the Age of Mechanical Reproduction" in *Illuminations*, ed. Hannah Arendt, trans. Harry Zohn (New York, 1968).

30. John Bull and Uncle Sam are exceptions to the more general rule of female representation. Even in the case of Britain and the United States, there are competing figures—Britannia and Columbia or, even earlier, the Native American Princess.

31. "Ce n'est point assez d'avoir renversé le trône; ce qui nous importe, c'est d'élever sur ses débris la sainte égalité et les droits imprescriptibles de l'homme. Ce n'est point un vain mot qui constitue la république, c'est la caractère des citoyens. L'âme de la république, c'est la vertu; c'est-à-dire, l'amour de la patrie, le dévouement magnanime que confond tous les in-

térêts privé dans l'intérêt général" (*Oeuvres de M. Robespierre*, vol. 5, *Lettres à ses commetans*, ed. Gustave Laurent (Gap, 1961), 17.

32. Marina Warner, *Monuments and Maidens: The Allegory of the Female Form* (New York, 1985), xix.

33. *Encyclopédie*, 9:400a, cited in George Armstrong Kelly, *Mortal Politics in Eighteenth-Century France* (Waterloo, Ontario, 1986), 217.

34. Agulhon addresses the conflation of symbols accompanying the various goddesses associated with revolutionary values, stating, "Even if the new iconologists, the Republican artists and educated patriots were capable of making distinctions and translating the specific meanings of different symbols, the perception of the people was inevitably much simpler. At a cultural level where the concepts of allegory and symbolism were non-existent, and where mythology and Graeco-Latin traditions were unknown, it was clearly not possible to see anything much more than a *single* majestic woman clad in draperies. She had appeared on the scene since the Revolution and through the Revolution and was associated with the sentiments evoked by the Revolution" (*Marianne into Battle*, 22). While Agulhon's point is well taken, to draw such a strong boundary between popular and elite culture may be misleading, as I discuss in Chapter 1. Furthermore, as I argue in this chapter, we need to not lose sight of the allegorical dimension of the visual as well as the political culture of nationalism.

35. I am grateful to Carole Pateman for helping me to clarify this point. On the "original" or sexual contract, see her *The Sexual Contract* (Stanford, Calif., 1988). On a related theme, see Charles W. Mills, *The Racial Contract* (Ithaca, N.Y., 1997). My argument is that man's attachment to the contract cannot be secured on the basis of reason and interest alone—that is without passion.

36. Jean-Jacques Rousseau, "Pygmalion," in *Oeuvres complètes*, vol. 2 (Paris, 1961); *Pygmalion, a poem. Trans. from the French of J.J. Rousseau* (London, 1779). A nineteenth-century reprint of the illustrated 1775 edition is available as Arnaud Berquin, *Pygmalion; scène lyrique de J.-J.Rousseau. Illustrations by Moreau le Jeune.* Reproduction of original edition of 1775 (Paris, 1883). Rousseau referred to his work as a *scène lyrique*, not a melodrama (a musico-dramatic technique, in which spoken text alternates with instrumental music, or more rarely, is recited against a continuing music background). However, his *Pygmalion*, with music by Rousseau and Horace Coignet, is regarded as the first significant example of a work constructed entirely as a melodrama. It was sketched in the 1760s and first performed in 1770 in Lyons. The text was provided with new music by Franz Asplmayr (Vienna, 1772) and Anton Schweitzer (Weimar, 1772); a German translation was set by Georg Benda (Gotha, 1779). *The New Harvard Dictionary of Music*, ed. Don Michael Randel (Cambridge, Mass., 1986), 481.

37. "[Il s'encourage, et enfin présentant son ciseau, il en donne un coup saisi d'effroi, et le laisse tomber en poussant un grand cri] *Dieux*! Je sens la chair palpitante! Elle repousse le ciseau! [Il descend tremblant et confus] Vaines terreurs de mon ame égarée! . . . Je n'ose, je ne puis, tout me vient arrêter. Ah! sans doute, le Dieux veulent m'épouvanter: A leur suprême rang ils l'auront consacrée" (Berquin, Pygmalion; scène lyrique de J.-J.Rousseau, 9).

38. "GALATHÉE, avec un soupir. Encore moi. PYGMALION, Oui, cher et bel objet que mes feux ont fait naître, Oui, c'est toi, c'est toi seul; je t'ai donné mon être, Je ne vivrai plus que par toi" (Berquin, *Pygmalion; scene lyrique de J.-J. Rousseau*, 18).

39. Jeffrey Ravel, "Seating the Public: Spheres and Loathing in the Paris Theaters, 1777–1788," *French Historical Studies* 18, no. 1 (Spring 1993): 173–210. Ravel points out that this practice contrasted with that of other public playhouses in Europe that had seated the spectators in the pit for most of the century. Interestingly, he observes that the purchasers of the cheap tickets in the pit—amounting to 55 to 70 percent of the paid spectators—were exclusively male. Noted for its social heterogeneity and raucous behavior, that is, the crowd in the *parterre* was not sexually heterogeneous, as was true of the seated occupants in the playhouse. Confident of their newfound commercial access to hitherto privileged culture, the *parterre* firmly believed they had also purchased the right to pass critical judgment on an evening's performance, though their raucous behavior was at odds with the dispassionate exercise of reason. Indeed, the mercurial nature of *parterre* spectators even led enlightened voices (playwrights, men of letters, architects) to call for the installation of benches in the pit.

40. See the splendid discussion of erotics and politics in Doris Sommer's *Foundational Fictions*, chap. 1, part 2, "Love and Country: An Allegorical Speculation," 30–51. Kathryn Norberg explores related issues during the French Revolution. She proposes that the public contract among republican men was accompanied by a new ordering of the private sphere: "'Love and Patriotism': Gender and Politics in the Life and Work of Louvet de Couvrai," in *Rebel Daughters: Women and the French Revolution*, ed. Sara E. Melzer and Leslie W. Rabine (New York, 1992), 38–53. Doris Sommer recalls that patriotic passion has a long history. Summarizing Ernst Kantorowicz's masterful account of the progressive reconquest of classical patriotism, she remarks, "The early Middle Ages denied an earthly patria; then made it (France is his prime example) parallel to Jerusalem; shifted the mystical body of the church to the corporate body of the state; understood corporation as the nation's body with the king at its head; and finally left the king behind. But in this return, the ancient *patria* (city, polis) is substituted by the idea of inclusive nation as it developed during the Middle Ages" (Sommer, *Foundational Fictions*, 336n. 11). Cf. Ernst H. Kantorowicz, "*Pro Patria Mori* in Medieval Political Thought," in *Selected Studies* (Locust Valley, N.Y., 1965), 308–24.

41. On the theme of melodrama, see Peter Brooks, *The Melodramatic Imagination: Balzac, Henry James, Melodrama, and the Mode of Excess* (New Haven, Conn., 1995); Maza, *Private Lives and Public Affairs*.

42. Madelyn Gutwirth, *The Twilight of the Goddesses: Women as Representation in the French Revolutionary Era* (New Brunswick, N. J., 1992), 365.

43. Ibid.

44. Cupid—the counterpart of the Greek god Eros—usually appeared as a winged infant carrying a bow and a quiver of arrows, whose wounds inspired love or passion in his every victim. He was sometimes portrayed wearing armor like that of Mars, the god of war, perhaps to suggest ironic parallels between warfare and romance or to symbolize the invincibility of love.

45. De l'influence de la révolution sur les femmes," *Révolutions de Paris*, vol. 7, no. 83, 12 February 1791, 231, cited in Candace Proctor, *Women, Equality, and the French Revolution* (New York, 1990), 56.

46. The festival to celebrate the transfer of the dead Bara and Viala to the Panthéon never took place because of the anti-Jacobin coup of 9 Thermidor Year II (27 July 1794).

47. "Quand votre destinée sera unie à celle d'un époux, servez-vous de l'empire que vous a donné la nature pour étèndre dans son ame celui de la vertu républicaine . . . apprenez que la vraie richesse est de posséder beaucoup d'enfans, qui, forts & courageux, seront un jour les défenseurs de la patrie; qu'à l'exemple de Cornélie, ils soient votre parure et l'ornement de vos maisons" (Jacques-Louis David, *Rapport sur la fête héroique pour les honneurs du Panthéon à décerner aux jeunes Barra & Viala, Séance du 23 messidor [11 Juillet], an 2 de la République (Imprimé par ordre de la Convention Nationale)*. David's speech is also reproduced in Daniel Wildenstein and Guy Wildenstein, *Documents complémentaires au Catalogue de l'oeuvre de Louis David* (Paris, 1973), 108–11. David was not alone in exhorting women to follow the example of the Roman matron Cornelia—who devoted herself to her sons' education after her husband's death, turning down repeated offers of marriage. Her name was invoked repeatedly by revolutionaries as a model for virtuous Frenchwomen.

48. Similarly, Margaret Miles finds the image of the nursing Virgin in Tuscan religious imagery of the fourteenth century to be an ambivalent symbol, evoking for men danger and delight, and for women, "the emotional quandary surrounding the nursing of babies." See Miles's "The Virgin's One Bare Breast: Nudity, Gender, and Religious Meaning in Tuscan Early Renaissance Culture," in *The Expanding Discourse: Feminism and Art History*, ed. Norma Broude and Mary D. Garrard (New York, 1992), 34. Cf. Elisabeth Badinter, *Mother Love: Myth and Reality*, foreword Francine du Plessix Gray (New York, 1981); George D. Sussman, *Selling Mothers' Milk: The Wet-Nursing Business in France, 1715–1914* (Urbana, Ill., 1982).

49. Miles, "The Virgin's One Bare Breast," 33. Cf. Anne Hollander, *Seeing through Clothes* (New York, 1978).

50. Miles, "The Virgin's One Bare Breast," 34–35; Jane Gallop, *The Daughter's Seduction: Feminism and Psychoanalysis* (Ithaca, N.Y., 1982), 35.

51. *Archives parlementaires*, vol. 4, 90, art. 47; cited by Proctor, *Women, Equality, and the French Revolution* (New York, 1990), 58; cf. Beatrice Frye Hyslop, *French Nationalism in 1789, according to the General Cahiers* (New York, 1934), 182.

52. *Hommage rendu au dames françaises, sur leur patriotisme pour accélérer la fete civique du 14 Juillet 1790* (Paris, n.d.), 6, cited in Proctor, *Women, Equality, and the French Revolution*, 58.

53. Hunt claims that in the caricatures of the republican period, "the revolutionaries tended to portray themselves as young people without parents. They imagined themselves as part of no lineage. In a sense, this was a family romance with the notion of parentage taken out; only brothers and sisters remained" ("The Political Psychology of Revolutionary Caricatures," in *French Caricature and the French Revolution*, ed. James Cuno [Los Angeles, 1988] 39). Despite the ample presence of children in caricatures, allegorical, and genre images, I still find few are illustrations of girls. When an image of a child is called for, representations of boys abound. Very rarely, if ever, is a girl shown to represent the class of children in general. Furthermore, girls are rarely featured in the company of small boys—notwithstanding Hunt's observation that, in imagery of the radical period, Liberty and other goddesses play a sisterly role to Hercules, the masculine allegory of the French people.

54. See the two lovely etchings by E. Bericourt, after G. Orrebow, *La Marche des petits patriotes*, (1789) and *Point d'honneur* (1789) in *Images of the French Revolution* (Videodisk and Catalog) *Coproduced by the Bibliothèque Nationale and Pergamon Press*, vol. 1 (Paris, 1990), # 10011 and #10013.

55. "Que la mère dont le fils est mort au champ de bataille, s'enorgueillisse du sang qu'il a versé pour la patrie; que des larmes de joie succèdent aux larmes de la douleur, en voyant les honneurs que le peuple reconnoissant rend à sa mémoire" (David, *Rapport sur la fête héroique pour les honneurs du Panthéon à décerner aux jeunes Barra & Viala*, 9–10).

56. "Qu'il est beau de mourir pour la Patrie"; cited in Alex Potts, "Beautiful Bodies and Dying Heroes: Images of Ideal Manhood in the French Revolution," *History Workshop* 30 (August 1990): 15.

57. Et vous, jeunes républicaines, écoutez la voix de la patrie: c'est en vous qu'elle a mis ses plus douces espérances; vos méres ont donné le jour à des héros, vous imiterez leur exemple. La victoire va vous ramener des amies dignes de vous. . . gardez-vous de dédaigner ces illustres défenseurs couverts d'honorables cicatrices. Les cicatrices des héros de la liberté sont la plus riche dot et l'ornement le plus durable. Après avoir servi leur pays dans la guerre la plus glorieuse, qu'ils goûtent avec vous les douceurs d'une vie paisible. Que vos vertus, que votre chaste fécondité centuplent les ressources de la patrie; que chacun vous voyant au milieu d'une nombreuse famille, vous porte respect et dise avec admiration: voilà la digne compagne d'un citoyen vertueux qui a perdu ses bras à la mémorable journée de Fleurus; que les rejetons d'un tel père, marchant sur ses traces, soient les implacables ennemis de la tyrannie, et les émules des Barra et des Viala! (David, *Rapport sur la fête héroique pour les honneurs du Panthéon à décerner aux jeunes Barra & Viala*, 10)

The victory at the Battle of Fleurus, 8 Messidor Year II (26 June 1794), achieved the supremacy of the republican armies and led to the reconquest of Belgium by 9 Thermidor Year II (27 July 1794).

58. In the account of the fall 1793 meeting of Society of Revolutionary Republican Women offered by Pierrre Roussel, Olympe de Gouges is reported to have struck a very similar theme to David's, promising to the returned warrior a mistress. But she goes further, suggesting that only men willing to sacrifice themselves for their country will have the rewards of a woman; and she calls for women's control of festivals, marriages, and education:

"There will have to be public festivals; confide the direction and regulation of them to us [women]. A lovely woman at the head of a crowd of citizens, charged, for example, with inciting young men to fly to the defense of the Fatherland, would say to one of them: Depart, and upon your return, the hand of your mistress will be the reward for your exploits. Whoever hesitates to fight the enemy will hear her voice speaking these words to him: Stay, you cowardly soul; but never count on being united with your lover; she has sworn to reject the desires of a man who is useless to his country. The art we possess to move the souls of men would produce the salutary effect of enflaming all spirits. Nothing can resist our seductive organ. The warrior would be happy to receive laurels from the hand of beauty; young husbands would believe their chains more fitting if they were forged by the hands of a woman.

Let us request the direction of festivals and marriages, and that we be the only ones charged with the education of youth." "Account of a Session of the Society of Revolutionary Republican Women" in *Women in Revolutionary Paris,* 169–70

59. Potts, "Beautiful Bodies and Dying Heroes," 15.

60. I am calling attention to the variety or anonymity of female representations of the nation. However, I agree with Nicholas Mirzoeff that one of the achievements of the French Revolution was to detach the power, or violence, of the state from any one individual's body, as was the case in the Old Regime identification of the state with the body of the king. Furthermore Mirzoeff speaks of a new representation of the state, in accord with new notions of biology, which came to be seen as the reproduction of an interaction between the feminine and the masculine (*Bodyscape: Art, Modernity, and the Ideal Figure* [New York, 1995], 83).

61. Potts asks whether the body that gives the most intense pleasure can also be the one that most powerfully evokes a free expansive subjectivity produced by political freedom. He argues that "the gendering which operated in both Winckelmann's and David's time made the male body the only possible focus for such a conjuncture. This is a simple factor of the casual exclusion of the feminine from radical eighteenth-century discourses around the free subject. The ideal female body in art conventionally had a relatively simple function as a signifier of sensuous beauty, as the object of desire, uncomplicated by association with more austere ideas of freedom and heroism. It was only in the representation of an ideally beautiful male body that tensions between the body as the sign of pleasure and desire, and an ethical investment of the body as the sign of an ideal subjectivity, the ideal subjectivity of the virtuous and free republican subject, could be played out" ("Beautiful Bodies and Dying Heroes," 8).

62. Lynn Hunt, *The Family Romance of The French Revolution* (Berkeley, 1992); cf. Pateman, *The Sexual Contract.*

63. Lucien Goldmann, *The Hidden God: A Study of Tragic Vision in the Pensées of Pascal and the Tragedies of Racine,* trans. Philip Thody (London, 1964).

64. Agulhon, *Marianne into Battle,* 31. Agulhon notes the convention in the rhetorical style for allegories to be customarily introduced by addressing them as persons. Even more important, he observes, for people unacquainted with the allegorical tradition of classical culture or its conventions, Liberty may have been likened to a new festival queen or a patron saint—who was also represented by a statue, carried in procession as a bust and addressed in hymns.

Epilogue

1. Abigail Solomon-Godeau makes an important observation about the resort to classical imagery in times of greater democratic impulse—which are all times of widening liberties for men and greater constraints on women. In her words, "the male nude has been privileged in periods traditionally viewed as fostering new freedoms and possibilities (fifth-century Greece, the Renaissance, the French Revolution, for example), which have not necessarily extended to women. . . . Hence too, the imaginative identification with classical antiquity that figures so prominently in Neoclassical and revolutionary culture, producing its characteristic

expressions of ideal manhood, requires consideration of what 'Other' has been repressed in the celebration of the radiant One" (*Male Trouble: A Crisis in Representation* (London, 1997), 13.

2. W. J. T. Mitchell, *Picture Theory: Essays on Verbal and Visual Representation* (Chicago, 1994), 16.

3. Nicholas Mirzoeff, "What Is Visual Culture?," in *The Visual Culture Reader*, ed. Nicholas Mirzoeff (London, 1998), 9; David Freedberg, *The Power of Images: Study in the History and Theory of Response* (Chicago, 1989), cited in Mirzoeff, "What Is Visual Culture?," 9.

4. Mitchell, *Picture Theory*, 364.

5. Speaking of print languages as the bases for national consciousness, Anderson writes, "They created unified fields of exchange and communication below Latin and above the spoken vernaculars. . . . . In the process, they gradually became aware of the hundreds of thousands, even millions, of people in their particular language-field, and at the same time that *only those* hundreds of thousands, or millions, so belonged. These fellow-readers, to whom they were connected through print, formed, in their secular, particular, visible invisibility, the embryo of the nationally imagined community" (*Imagined Communities: Reflections on the Origin and Spread of Nationalism*, rev. ed. [London, 1991], 44).

Bibliography

CATALOGS, COLLECTIONS, AND OTHER VISUAL MATERIALS

Andriès, Lise. *Colporter la Révolution.* Montreuil: Robert-Desnos, 1989.

Baecque, Antoine de. *La Caricature révolutionnaire.* Paris: CNRS, 1988.

Baltimore Museum of Art. *Regency to Empire: Printmaking, 1715–1814.* Organized by Victor I. Carlson and John W. Ittmann. Baltimore: Baltimore Museum of Art, 1984.

Bibliothèque nationale, départment des estampes. *Images of the French Revolution (Videodisk and Catalogue) Coproduced by the Bibliothèque nationale and Pergamon Press.* Paris: Bibliothèque nationale, 1990.

———. *Un Siècle d'histoire de France par l'estampe, 1770–1871: Collection de Vinck.* 4 vols. Paris: Imprimerie nationale, 1909–29.

Bindman, David. *The Shadow of the Guillotine: Britain and the French Revolution.* London: British Museum, 1989.

Bordes, Philippe, and Alain Chevalier, eds. *Catalogue des peintures, sculptures, et dessins.* Vizille: Musée de la Révolution Française; Paris: Réunion des Musées Nationaux, 1996.

Boyer de Nîmes. *Histoire des caricatures de la révolte des français. Par M. Boyer de Nîmes, J.-Marie Boyer-Brun author of "Journal du peuple."* Paris: Imprimerie Journal du Peuple, 1792.

Brown University, Department of Art. *Caricature and Its Role in Graphic Satire.* Providence, R.I.: Brown University, 1971.

Carlson, Victor I., and John W. Ittmann. *Regency to Empire: Printmaking, 1715–1814.* Baltimore: Baltimore Museum of Art; Minneapolis: Minneapolis Institute of Arts, 1984.

Champfleury. *Histoire de la caricature sous la République, l'Empire, et la Restauration.* 2d ed. Paris: E. Dentu, 1877.

Collection complète des tableaux historiques de la Révolution française. 3 vols. Paris: Auber, Imprimerie Pierre Didot l'Aîné, 1802.

Collection de quinze estampes sur les principales journées de la Révolution française. Engraved by Isidore Stanislas Helman from drawings by Charles Monnet. 1790–1802.

Cuno, James, ed. *French Caricature and the French Revolution, 1789–1799.* Los Angeles: University of California, Grunwald Center for the Graphic Arts, Wight Art Gallery, 1988.

Darnton, Robert, and Daniel Roche, eds. *Revolution in Print: The Press in France, 1775–1800.* Berkeley: University of California Press in collaboration with the New York Public Library, 1989.

Donald, Diana. *The Age of Caricature: Satirical Prints in the Reign of George III.* New Haven, Conn.: Yale University for the Paul Mellon Center for Studies in British Art, 1996.

Duplessis, Georges. *Inventaire de la collection d'estampes relatives à l'histoire de France léguée à la Bibliothèque Nationale par M. Michel Hennin.* 5 vols. Paris: Bibliothèque Nationale, Départment des Estampes et de la Photographie, 1881–84.

Fauchet, Claude, et al. *Collection complète des tableaux historiques de la Révolution française.* 2 vols. Paris: Pierre Didot l'Aîné, 1798.

George, Mary Dorothy. *Catalogue of Political and Personal Satires Preserved in the Department of Prints and Drawings in the British Museum.* Vols. 5–11. London: British Museum Publications, 1935–52.

Gravelot, Hubert François, and Charles Nicolas Cochin. *Iconologie par figures ou traité complet des allégories, emblêmes.* Vol. 1. Paris, 1791.

Gravures historiques des principaux événements depuis l'ouverture des Etats-Généraux de 1789. Paris: Janinet, Cussac, 1789[–91].

Hould, Claudette. *Images of the French Revolution.* Quebec: Musée du Québec, Les Publications du Québec, 1989.

Langlois, Claude. *La Caricature contre-révolutionnaire.* Paris: CNRS, 1988.

Leith, James, and Andrea Joyce. *Face à Face: French and English Caricatures of the French Revolution and Its Aftermath.* Toronto: Art Gallery of Ontario, 1989.

Menestrier, Claude François. *La Philosophie des images* (Paris, 1682). New York: Garland, 1979.

Musée Carnavalet. *L'Art de l'estampe et la Révolution française.* Alençon: F. D. Imprimerie Alençonnaise, 1980.

———. *La Révolution française—Le Premier Empire: Dessins du Museé Carnavalet.* Paris: Musée Carnavalet, 1982.

Musée de la Révolution française. *Premières collections: 4 juillet–16 Décembre 1985, Musée de la Révolution française, Château de Vizille.* Vizille: Le Musée, 1985.

Myrdal, Jan. *Franska Revolutionens Bilder: Jean-Louis Prieurs teckningar med kommentarer samt Partiska ställningstaganden av år 1989.* Stockholm: Askelin & Hägglund, 1989.

Rand, Richard, ed. *Intimate Encounters: Love and Domesticity in Eighteenth-Century France.* Hood Museum of Art, Dartmouth College. Princeton, N.J.: Princeton University Press, 1997.

Representing Revolution: French and British Images, 1789–1804. Amherst, Mass.: Mead Art Museum of Amherst College, 1989.

Tableaux des révolutions de Paris depuis le mois de juillet 1789, dessinées et gravés par A.-F. Sergent, avec un précis historique. Première livraison dédiée à la Société de la Révolution de Londres. Paris, n.d.

Tableaux historiques de la Révolution française ou Analyse des principaux événements qui ont eu lieu en France depuis la première assemblée des notables tenue à Versailles en 1787. Designed and etched by J. Duplessi-Bertaux. Paris, 1817.

Vovelle, Michel. *La Révolution française: Images et récit, 1789–1799*. 5 vols. Paris: Editions Messidor, Livre Club Diderot, 1986.

Eighteenth-Century (and Earlier) Published Writings

Annales patriotiques et littéraires

Archives parlementaires de 1787 à 1860: Recueil complet des debats législatifs & politiques des chambres francaises. lst ser. Paris: Librairie Administrative Paul Dupont, 1879.

Arsène, Alexandre. *La Société des Jacobins: Recueil de Documents*. Vol. 5 (January 1793–March 1794). Paris: Quantin, 1895.

Berquin. *Pygmalion; scène lyrique de J.-J.Rousseau. Illustrations de Moreau le Jeune; suivi d'une idylle par Berquin*. Reproduction of original edition of 1775. Paris: J. Lemonnyer, 1883.

Burke, Edmund. *Reflections on the Revolution in France*. Garden City, N.Y.: Doubleday, 1961.

Cabanis, Pierre Jean Georges. *On the Relations between the Physical and Moral Aspects of Man*. Edited by George Mora; translated by Margaret Duggan Saidi. 2 vols. Baltimore: Johns Hopkins University Press, 1981.

———. *Rapports du physique et du moral de l'homme*. Paris: Crapart, Caille et Ravier, Year X–XIII (1802–5).

Condillac, Etienne Bonnot, abbé de. *Essai sur l'origine des connaissances humaines*. In *Oeuvres*, vol. 3. Paris: F. Dufart, 1795–1801.

———. *Essay on the Origin of Human Knowledge*. In *Philosophical Writings of Etienne Bonnot, Abbé de Condillac*. 2 vols. Translated by Franklin Philip. Hillsdale, N.J.: Lawrence Erlbaum, 1982.

Condorcet, Jean-Antoine-Nicolas de Caritat, marquis de. *Esquisse d'un tableau historique des progrès de l'esprit humain*. In *Oeuvres complètes de Condorcet*, vol. 6, edited by A. Condorcet O'Connor and M. F. Arago. Paris, 1947.

———. "Essai sur l'admission des femmes au droit de cité (1790)." In *Oeuvres*, vol. 10, facsimile of Paris edition, 1847–49. Stuttgart-Bad Cannstatt: Friedrich Fromann Verlag, 1968.

———. *Sketch for a Historical Picture of the Human Mind*. Translated by June Barraclough. New York: Noonday Press, 1955.

Courier national, politique, et littéraire

David, Jacques-Louis. *Rapport sur la fête héroique pour les honneurs du Panthéon à décerner aux jeunes Barra & Viala*. Séance du 23 Messidor, Year II de la Republique. Imprimé par ordre de la Convention Nationale.

"Déclaration des droits de l'homme et du citoyen (1789–1791)." In *La Révolution des droits de l'homme*, edited by Marcel Gauchet. Paris: Gallimard, 1989.

Desmoulins, Camille. *Oeuvres*. 10 vols. Preface by Albert Soboul. München: Kraus Reprint, 1980.

Encyclopédie ou Dictionnaire raisonné des sciences, des arts et des métiers, par une société de gens de lettres. 3d ed. Paris: a'Livourne, 1751–65.

Hobbes, Thomas. *Leviathan*. Edited by C. B. Macpherson. Harmondsworth, England: Penguin, 1968.

Journal de la Cour et de la ville

Journal de Perlet

Mirabeau, Honoré Gabriel Riqueti, comte de. *Discours de Monsieur Mirabeau l'Aîné, sur l'éducation nationale.* Paris: L'Imprimerie de la veuve Lejay, 1791.

Le Moniteur Universel

Révolutions de France et de Brabant

Révolutions de Paris

Ripa, Cesare. *Iconology; or, a Collection of Emblematical Figures.* [Selected by] George Richardson. 2 vols. New York: Garland, 1979.

Robespierre, Maximilien, *Lettres à Ses Commetans.* Edited by G. Laurent. Oeuvres Complèts, vol. 5. Gap. Louis Jean, 1961.

Rousseau, Jean-Jacques. *Emile, or on Education.* Translated by Allan Bloom. New York: Basic, 1979.

———. "Letter to M. d'Alembert on the Theatre." In *Politics and the Arts; Letter to M. d'Alembert on the Theatre,* translated by Alan Bloom. Ithaca, N.Y.: Cornell University Press, 1960.

———. *Oeuvres complètes.* 5 vols. Edited by Bernard Gagnebin and Marcel Raymond. Paris: Gallimard, 1959–69.

———. *On the Social Contract, with Geneva Manuscript and Political Economy.* Edited by Roger D. Masters; translated by Judith R. Masters. New York: St. Martin's Press, 1978.

Roussel, Pierre. *Système physique et moral de la femme.* Paris: Vincent, 1775.

Sade, Marquis de. *Opuscules et lettres politiques.* Paris: Union génerale d'éditions, 1979.

Vaughan, C. E., ed. *The Political Writings of Jean Jacques Rousseau.* New York: John Wiley, 1962.

Vinci, Leonardo da. "Paragone: Of Poetry and Painting." In *Treatise on Painting (Codex urbanus latinus 1270),* translated and annotated by A. Philip McMahon. Princeton, N.J.: Princeton University Press, 1956.

Wildenstein, Daniel, and Guy Wildenstein. *Documents complémentaires au catalogue de l'oeuvre de Louis David.* Paris: Fondation Wildenstein, 1973.

Selected Secondary Writings

Adhémar, Jean. *Graphic Art of the Eighteenth and Nineteenth Century.* London: Thames and Hudson, 1964.

Agulhon, Maurice. *Marianne into Battle: Republican Imagery and Symbolism in France, 1789–1880.* Translated by Janet Lloyd. Cambridge: Cambridge University Press, 1981.

———. "Politics, Images, and Symbols in Post-Revolutionary France." In *Rites of Power: Symbolism, Ritual, and Politics since the Middle Ages,* edited by Sean Wilentz. Philadelphia: University of Pennsylvania Press, 1985.

Agulhon, Maurice, and Pierre Bonte. *Marianne: Les Visages de la République.* Paris: Gallimard, 1992.

Anderson, Benedict. *Imagined Communities: Reflections on the Origin and Spread of Nationalism.* Rev. ed. London: Verso, 1991.

Andriès, Lise. *La Bibliothèque bleue au dix-huitième siècle: Une Tradition éditoriale.* In *Studies on Voltaire and the Eighteenth Century,* vol. 270. Oxford: Voltaire Foundation at the Taylor Institution, 1989.

———. *Les Contes bleues.* Paris: Montalba, 1983.

———. *Le Grand Livre des sécrets: Le Colportage en France aux 17e et 18e siècles.* Paris: Imago, 1994.

Applewhite, Harriet B., and Darline Levy, eds. "Women, Radicalization, and the Fall of the French Monarchy." In *Women and Politics in the Age of the Democratic Revolution.* Ann Arbor: University of Michigan Press, 1990.

Arnheim, Rudolf. *Art and Visual Perception: A Psychology of Perception.* Berkeley: University of California Press, 1954.

Arsène, Alexandre. *L'Art du rire et de la caricature.* Paris: Quantin, Librairies-imprimeries réunies, 1892.

Aulard, F.-A. *Le Culte de la raison et le culte de l'être suprême (1793–1794): Essai historique.* Paris: Félix Alcan, 1904.

Babcock, Barbara, ed. *The Reversible World: Symbolic Inversions in Art and Society.* Ithaca, N.Y.: Cornell University Press, 1978.

Badinter, Elisabeth. *Mother Love: Myth and Reality.* New York: Macmillan, 1981.

Badinter, Elisabeth, and Robert Badinter. *Condorcet (1743–1794): Un intellectuel en politique.* Paris: Fayard, 1988.

Baecque, Antoine de. "The Allegorical Image of France, 1750–1800: A Political Crisis of Representation." *Representations* 47 (Summer 1994): 111–43.

———. *The Body Politic: Corporeal Metaphor in Revolutionary France, 1770–1800.* Translated by Charlotte Mandell. Stanford, Calif.: Stanford University Press, 1997.

Baker, Keith Michael. *Inventing the French Revolution: Essays on French Political Culture in the Eighteenth Century.* Cambridge: Cambridge University Press, 1990.

———. "Representation Redefined." In *The French Revolution and the Creation of Modern Political Culture,* vol. 1, *Political Culture of the Old Regime,* edited by Keith Michael Baker. Oxford: Pergamon Press, 1987.

Bakhtin, Mikhail. *Rabelais and His World.* Translated by Hélène Iswolsky. Cambridge, Mass.: MIT Press, 1968.

Barker-Benfield, Ben. *The Culture of Sensibility: Sex and Society in Eighteenth-Century Britain.* Chicago: University of Chicago Press, 1992.

Benjamin, Walter. *The Origin of German Tragic Drama.* Translated by John Osborne. London: NLB, 1963.

———. "The Work of Art in the Age of Mechanical Reproduction." In *Illuminations,* edited by Hannah Arendt; translated by Harry Zohn. New York: Schocken, 1968.

Berezin, Mabel. "Political Belonging: Emotion, Nation, and Identity in Fascist Italy." In *State/Culture: State Formation after the Cultural Turn,* edited by George Steinmetz. Ithaca, N.Y.: Cornell University Press, 1997.

Berger, John. *Ways of Seeing.* London: British Broadcasting Corporation, 1989.

Betterton, Rosemary. "How Do Women Look? The Female Nude in the Work of Suzanne Valadon." In *Visibly Female: Feminism and Art: An Anthology,* edited by Hilary Robinson. London: Camden, 1987.

Bloch, Marc. *The Royal Touch: Sacred Monarchy and Scrofula in England and France.* Translated by J. E. Anderson. London: Routledge, 1973.

Blum, Carol. *Rousseau and the Republic of Virtue: The Language of Politics in the French Revolution.* Ithaca, N.Y.: Cornell University Press, 1986.

Bonnet, Jean-Claude, ed. *La Carmagnole des muses; l'homme de lettres et l'artiste dans la Révolution.* Paris: Armand Colin, 1988.

——, ed. *La Mort de Marat.* Paris: Flammarion, 1986.

Bordes, Philippe, and Régis Michel, eds. *Aux armes et aux arts! les arts de la Révolution, 1789–1799.* Paris: Adam Biro, 1988.

Bourdieu, Pierre. *The Field of Cultural Production: Essays on Art and Literature.* Edited by Randal Johnson. Cambridge: Polity Press, 1993.

——. *Outline of a Theory of Practice.* Translated by Richard Nice. Cambridge: Cambridge University Press, 1977.

Boureau, Alain. *Le Simple Corps du roi: L'Impossible Sacralité des souverains français.* Paris: Editions de Paris, 1989.

Brooks, Peter. *Body Work: Objects of Desire in Modern Narrative.* Cambridge, Mass.: Harvard University Press, 1993.

——. *The Melodramatic Imagination: Balzac, Henry James, Melodrama, and the Mode of Excess.* New Haven, Conn.: Yale University Press, 1995.

——. "The Revolutionary Body." In *Fictions of the French Revolution*, edited by Bernadette Fort. Evanston, Ill.: Northwestern University Press, 1991.

Brown, Frederick. *Theater and Revolution: The Culture of the French Stage.* New York: Viking Press, 1980.

Brown, Norman O. *Love's Body.* New York: Vintage, 1966.

Brubaker, Rogers. *Citizenship and Nationhood in France and Germany.* Cambridge, Mass.: Harvard University Press, 1992.

Bryant, Lawrence M. *The King and the City in the Parisian Royal Entry Ceremony: Politics, Ritual, and Art in the Renaissance.* Geneva: Librairie Droz, 1986.

Bryson, Norman. *Word and Image: French Painting of the Ancien Régime.* Cambridge: Cambridge University Press, 1981.

Bryson, Norman, Michael Ann Holly, and Keith Moxey, eds. *Visual Culture: Images and Interpretation.* Hanover, N.H.: Wesleyan University Press/University Press of New England, 1994.

Burke, Peter, ed. *New Perspectives on Historical Writing.* University Park: Pennsylvania State University Press, 1992.

Cameron, Vivian. "The Challenge to Rule: Confrontations with Louis XVI." *Art Journal* 48, no. 2 (Summer 1989): 150–54.

——. "Political Exposures: Sexuality and Caricature in the French Revolution." In *Eroticism and the Body Politic*, ed. Lynn Hunt. Baltimore: Johns Hopkins University Press, 1991.

Castle, Terry. *The Female Thermometer: Eighteenth-Century Culture and the Invention of the Uncanny.* New York: Oxford University Press, 1995.

Censer, Jack R. "The Political Engravings of *The Révolutions de France et de Brabant*, 1789–1791." *Eighteenth-Century Life* 5, no. 4 (Summer 1979): 105–44.

Censer, Jack R., and Lynn Hunt. *Liberty, Equality, Fraternity: Exploring the French Revolution*. University Park: Pennsylvania State University Press, forthcoming.

Certeau, Michel de. *The Practice of Everyday Life*. Translated by Steven Rendall. Berkeley: University of California Press, 1984.

Chartier, Roger. *The Culture of Print: Power and the Uses of Print in Early Modern Europe*. Translated by Lydia G. Cochrane. Princeton, N.J.: Princeton University Press, 1989.

———. "The World as Representation." In *Histories: French Constructions of the Past*, edited by Jacques Revel and Lynn Hunt; translated by Arthur Goldhammer and others, pp. 544–58. New York: New Press, 1995.

Church, William. "France." In *National Consciousness, History, and Political Culture in Early-Modern Europe*, edited by Orest Ranum. Baltimore: Johns Hopkins University Press, 1975.

Clark, Kenneth. *The Nude: A Study in Ideal Form*. Garden City, N.Y.: Doubleday, 1959.

Clark, T. J. "Painting in the Year Two." *Representations* 47 (Summer 1994): 13–63.

Colley, Linda. *Britons: Forging the Nation, 1707–1837*. New Haven, Conn.: Yale University Press, 1992.

Colwill, Elizabeth. " 'Just Another *Citoyenne*'? Marie-Antoinette on Trial, 1790–1793." *History Workshop* 28 (1989): 63–87.

———. "Pass as a Woman, Act Like a Man: Marie-Antoinette as Tribade in the Pornography of the French Revolution." In *Homosexuality in Modern France*. New York: Oxford University Press, 1996.

Corbin, Alain. "The Secret of the Individual." In *A History of Private Life*. Vol. 4, *From the Fires of Revolution to the Great War*, edited by Michelle Perrot; translated by Arthur Goldhammer. Cambridge, Mass.: Harvard University Press, 1990.

Crow, Thomas. *Emulation: Making Artists for Revolutionary France*. New Haven, Conn.: Yale University Press, 1995.

———. *Painters and Public Life in Eighteenth-Century Paris*. New Haven, Conn.: Yale University Press, 1985.

Darnton, Robert. *The Forbidden Best-Sellers of Pre-Revolutionary France*. New York: W. W. Norton, 1995.

———. *The Literary Underground of the Old Regime*. Cambridge, Mass.: Harvard University Press, 1982.

———. *Mesmerism and the End of the Enlightenment in France*. Cambridge, Mass.: Harvard University Press, 1968.

———. "Trends in Radical Propaganda on the Eve of the French Revolution (1782–1788)." Ph.D. dissertation. Oxford: Oxford University, 1964.

Davis, Natalie Zemon. "Women on Top." In *Society and Culture in Early Modern France*. Stanford, Calif.: Stanford University Press, 1975.

Denby, David. *Sentimental Narrative and the Social Order in France, 1760–1820*. Cambridge: Cambridge University Press, 1994.

Desan, Suzanne. " 'Constitutional Amazons': Jacobin Women's Clubs in the French Revolution." In *Re-creating Authority in Revolutionary France*, edited by Bryant T. Ragan, Jr., and Elizabeth A. Williams. Brunswick, N.J.: Rutgers University Press, 1992.

Duncan, Carol. "Happy Mothers and Other New Ideas in Eighteenth-Century French Art."

In *Feminism and Art History: Questioning the Litany*, edited by Norma Broude and Mary D. Garrard, pp. 201–20. New York: Harper & Row, 1982.

Duprat, Annie. "La Dégradation de l'image royale dans la caricature révolutionnaire." In *Les Images de la Révolution française,* edited by Michel Vovelle. Paris: Sorbonne, 1988.

Elias, Norbert. *The Court Society.* Translated by Edmund Jephcott. New York: Pantheon, 1983.

Fauré, Christine. *Democracy without Women: Feminism and the Rise of Liberal Individualism in France.* Translated by Claudia Gorbman and John Berks. Bloomington: Indiana University Press, 1991.

Feher, M., ed. *Fragments for a History of the Body.* 3 vols. New York: Zone, 1989.

Fort, Bernadette, ed. *Fictions of the French Revolution.* Evanston, Ill.: Northwestern University Press, 1991.

Foucault, Michel. *The Archaeology of Knowledge.* Translated by A. M. Sheridan Smith. New York: Pantheon, 1972.

——. *The Birth of the Clinic: An Archaeology of Medical Perception.* Translated by A. M. Sheridan Smith. New York: Pantheon, 1973.

——. *Discipline and Punish: The Birth of the Prison.* Translated by Alan Sheridan. New York: Vintage, 1977.

Fraisse, Geneviève. Preface to *Opinions de Femmes: De la Veille au lendemain de la Révolution française.* Paris: Côte-Femmes, 1989.

——. *Reason's Muse: Sexual Difference and the Birth of Democracy.* Translated by Jane Marie Todd. Chicago: University of Chicago Press, 1994.

Fried, Michael. *Absorption and Theatricality: Painting and Beholder in the Age of Diderot.* Berkeley: University of California Press, 1980.

Furet, François. *Interpreting the French Revolution.* Translated by Elborg Forster. Cambridge: Cambridge University Press, 1981.

Furet, François, and Jacques Ozouf. *Reading and Writing: Literacy in France from Calvin to Jules Ferry.* Cambridge: Cambridge University Press, 1982.

Furet, François, and Mona Ozouf, eds. *A Critical Dictionary of the French Revolution.* Cambridge, Mass.: Harvard University Press, 1989.

Garaud, Marcel (with Romuald Szramkiewicz). *La Révolution française et la famille.* Paris: Presses universitaires de France, 1978.

Gauchet, Marcel. *La Révolution des droits de l'homme.* Paris: Gallimard, 1989.

——. *La Révolution des pouvoirs: La Souveraineté, le peuple, et la répresentation, 1789–1799.* Paris: Gallimard, 1995.

Geggus, David. "Racial Equality, Slavery, and Colonial Secession during the Constituent Assembly." *American Historical Review* 94, no. 5 (December 1989): 1290–1308.

Germani, Ian, and Robin Swales, eds. *Symbols, Myths, and Images of the French Revolution: Essays in Honour of James A. Leith.* Regina, Saskatchewan: Canadian Plains Research Center, University of Regina, 1998.

Gierke, Otto. *Political Theories of the Middle Ages.* Translated by Frederic William Maitland. Boston: Beacon Press, 1958.

Giesey, Ralph E. *Cérémonial et puissance souveraine: France, XVe–XVIIe siècles.* Paris: Armand Colin, 1987.

———. *The Royal Funeral Ceremony in Renaissance France.* Geneva: E. Droz, 1960.

Godineau, Dominique. *The Women of Paris and Their French Revolution.* Translated by Katherine Streip. Berkeley: University of California Press, 1998.

Goldmann, Lucien. *The Hidden God: A Study of Tragic Vision in the Pensées of Pascal and the Tragedies of Racine.* Translated by Philip Thody. London: Routledge and Kegan Paul, 1964.

Gombrich, E. H. "The Dream of Reason: Symbolism of the French Revolution." *British Journal for Eighteenth Century Studies* 2, no. 3 (1979): 187–205.

———. "*Icones Symbolicae*: Philosophies of Symbolism and Their Bearing on Art." In *Symbolic Images: Studies in the Art of the Renaissance.* London: Phaidon, 1978.

———. "Image and Code: Scope and Limits of Conventionalism in Pictorial Representation." In *Image and Code*, edited by Wendy Steiner. Ann Arbor: University of Michigan Press, 1981.

Greenfield, Liah. *Nationalism: Five Roads to Modernity.* Cambridge, Mass.: Harvard University Press, 1992.

Guicciardi, Jean-Pierre. "Between the Licit and the Illicit: The Sexuality of the King." In *'Tis Nature's Fault: Unauthorized Sexuality during the Enlightenment*, edited by Robert Parks Maccubbin; translated by Michael Murray. Cambridge: Cambridge University Press, 1985.

Gutwirth, Madelyn. *The Twilight of the Goddesses: Women and Representation in the French Revolutionary Era.* New Brunswick, N.J.: Rutgers University Press, 1992.

Habermas, Jürgen. *The Structural Transformation of the Public Sphere: An Inquiry into a Category of Bourgeois Society.* Translated by Thomas Burger. Cambridge, Mass.: MIT Press, 1989.

Hanley, Sarah. *The Lit de Justice of the Kings of France: Constitutional Ideology in Legend, Ritual, and Discourse.* Princeton, N.J.: Princeton University Press, 1983.

Harris, Jennifer. "The Red Cap of Liberty: A Study of Dress Worn by French Revolutionary Partisans, 1789–1794." *Eighteenth-Century Studies* 14, no. 3 (1981): 283–312.

Harten, Elke, and Hans-Christian Harten. *Femmes, culture, et révolution.* Paris: Des femmes, 1989.

Harth, Erica. "The Salon Woman Goes Public . . . or Does She?" In *Going Public: Women and Publishing in Early Modern France*, edited by Elizabeth C. Goldsmith and Dena Goodman. Ithaca, N.Y.: Cornell University Press, 1995.

Hegel, G. W. F. *Phenomenology of Spirit.* Translated by A. V. Miller. Oxford: Oxford University Press, 1977.

Herding, Klaus, and Rolf Reichardt. *Die Bildpublizistik der Französischen Revolution.* Frankfurt am Main: Suhrkamp, 1989.

Hertz, Neil. "Medusa's Head: Male Hysteria under Political Pressure." *Representations* 4 (Fall 1983): 27–54.

Hesse, Carla. "Kant, Foucault, and Three Women." In *Foucault and the Writing of History*, edited by Jan Goldstein. Oxford: Basil Blackwell, 1994.

———. *Publishing and Cultural Politics in Revolutionary Paris, 1789–1810*. Berkeley: University of California Press, 1991.

———. "Revolutionary Histories: The Literary Politics of Louise de Kéralio (1758–1822)." In *Culture and Identity in Early Modern Europe (1500–1800): Essays in Honor of Natalie Zemon Davis*, edited by Barbara B. Diefendorf and Carla Hesse. Ann Arbor: University of Michigan Press, 1993.

Higham, John. "The Indian Princess and Roman Goddess: The First Female Symbols of America." *Proceedings of the American Antiquarian Society* 100 (1990): 45–79.

Higonnet, Patrice. "'Aristocrate,' 'Aristocratie': Language and Politics in the French Revolution." In *The French Revolution, 1789–1989: Two Hundred Years of Rethinking*. Special issue of *The Eighteenth Century: Theory and Interpretation*, edited by Sandy Petrey. Lubbock: Texas Tech University Press, 1989.

———. *Class, Ideology, and the Rights of Nobles during the French Revolution*. Oxford: Oxford University Press, 1981.

———. *Goodness beyond Virtue: Jacobins during the French Revolution*. Cambridge, Mass.: Harvard University Press, 1998.

Hollander, Anne. *Seeing through Clothes*. New York: Viking, 1980.

Honour, Hugh. *The Image of the Black in Western Art*. Vol. 4, parts 1 and 2, *From the American Revolution to World War I*. Cambridge, Mass.: Harvard University Press, 1976.

Huet, Marie-Hélène. *Mourning Glory: The Will of the French Revolution*. Philadelphia: University of Pennsylvania Press, 1997.

———. *Rehearsing the Revolution: The Staging of Marat's Death, 1793–1797*. Berkeley: University of California Press, 1982.

———. "Le Sacre du printemps: Essai sur le sublime et la Terreur." *MLN* 103, no. 4 (September 1988): 782–99.

Hunt, Lynn. "Engraving the Revolution: Prints and Propaganda in the French Revolution." *History Today* 30 (1980): 11–17.

———, ed. *Eroticism and the Body Politic*. Baltimore: Johns Hopkins University Press, 1991.

———. *The Family Romance of the French Revolution*. Berkeley: University of California Press, 1992.

———. "Freedom of Dress in Revolutionary France." In *From the Royal to the Republican Body: Incorporating the Political in Seventeenth- and Eighteenth-Century France*, edited by Sara E. Melzer and Kathryn Norberg, pp. 224–50. Berkeley: University of California Press, 1998.

———. "Hercules and the Radical Image in the French Revolution." *Representations* 1, no. 2 (Spring 1983): 95–117.

———, ed. *The New Cultural History*. Berkeley: University of California Press, 1989.

———. *Politics, Culture, and Class in the French Revolution*. Berkeley: University of California Press, 1984.

——. "Pourquoi la république est-elle une femme? La Symbolique républicaine et l'opposition des genres, 1792–1799." In *République et révolution: L'Exception française*, edited by Michel Vovelle. Paris: Kimé, 1994.

Idzerda, Stanley J. "Iconoclasm during the French Revolution." *American Historical Review* 60 (1954):13–26.

Jackson, Richard A. *Vive le Roi! A History of the French Coronation from Charles V to Charles X.* Chapel Hill: University of North Carolina Press, 1984.

Jacobus, Mary. "Incorruptible Milk: Breast-feeding and the French Revolution." In *Rebel Daughters: Women and the French Revolution*, edited by Sara Melzer and Leslie W. Rabine. New York: Oxford University Press, 1992.

Johannesson, Lena. "Le Yo-Yo, David, et Madame Tussaud: Notices sur l'iconographie de la Révolution." *L'Art et les révolutions, Section I: L'Art au temps de la Révolution française.* Strasbourg: Société alsacienne pour le développement de l'histoire de l'art, 1992.

Jordan, David P. *The King's Trial: Louis XVI vs. the French Revolution.* Berkeley: University of California Press, 1979.

Jordanova, Ludmilla. *Sexual Visions: Images of Gender in Science and Medicine between the Eighteenth and Twentieth Centuries.* Madison: University of Wisconsin Press, 1989.

Jourdan, Annie Renée Michèle. *Les Monuments de la Révolution française: Le Discours des images dans l'espace parisien, 1789–1904.* Amsterdam: Universiteit van Amsterdam, 1993.

Jouve, Michel. *L'Age d'or de la caricature anglaise.* Paris: Presses de la Fondation Nationale des Sciences Politiques, 1983.

——. "L'Image du sans-culotte dans la caricature politique anglaise: Création d'un stéréotype pictural." *Gazette des Beaux Arts* (November 1978): 187–96.

Julia, Dominique. *Les Trois couleurs du tableau noir: La Révolution.* Paris: Belin, 1981.

Kantorowicz, Ernst. *The King's Two Bodies: A Study in Medieval Political Theology.* Princeton, N.J.: Princeton University Press, 1957.

——. "*Pro Patria Mori* in Medieval Political Thought." In *Selected Studies.* Locust Valley, N.Y.: J. J. Augustin Publisher, 1965.

Kates, Gary. *The Cercle Social, the Girondins, and the French Revolution.* Princeton, N.J.: Princeton University Press, 1985.

——. "Jews into Frenchmen: Nationality and Representation in Revolutionary France." In *The French Revolution and the Birth of Modernity*, edited by Ferenc Fehér. Berkeley: University of California Press, 1990.

Kelly, George Armstrong. *Mortal Politics in Eighteenth-Century France.* Waterloo, Ontario: University of Waterloo Press, 1986.

Kennedy, Emmett. *A Cultural History of the French Revolution.* New Haven, Conn.: Yale University Press, 1989.

Kerber, Linda. *Women of the Republic: Intellect and Ideology in Revolutionary America.* Chapel Hill: University of North Carolina Press, 1980.

Kittay, Eva Feder. "Woman as Metaphor." *Hypatia* 3, no. 2 (Summer 1988): 63–85.

Klaits, Joseph. *Printed Propaganda under Louis XIV: Absolute Monarchy and Public Opinion.* Princeton, N.J.: Princeton University Press, 1976.

Knight, Isabel Frances. *The Geometric Spirit: The Abbé de Condillac and the French Enlighten-ment*. New Haven, Conn.: Yale University Press, 1968.

Lajer-Burcharth, Ewa. *Necklines: The Art of Jacques-Louis David after the Terror*. New Haven, Conn.: Yale University Press, 1999.

Landes, Joan B. "Habermas's Public Sphere: A Feminist Retrospective." *Praxis International* 12, no. 1 (April 1992): 106–27.

——. "Political Imagery of the French Revolution." In *Representing Revolution: French and British Images, 1789–1804*. Amherst, Mass.: Mead Art Museum of Amherst College, 1989.

——. "Representing the Body Politic: The Paradox of Gender in the Graphic Politics of the French Revolution." In *Rebel Daughters: Women and the French Revolution*, edited by Sara E. Melzer and Leslie W. Rabine. Oxford: Oxford University Press, 1992.

——. *Women and the Public Sphere in the Age of the French Revolution*. Ithaca, N.Y.: Cornell University Press, 1988.

Le Doeuff, Michelle. *The Philosophical Imaginary*. Stanford, Calif.: Stanford University Press, 1989.

Leith, James A. *The Idea of Art as Propaganda in France, 1750–1799: A Study in the History of Ideas*. Toronto: University of Toronto Press, 1969.

——. *Media and Revolution: Moulding a New Citizen in France during the Terror*. 1968. Toronto: CBC Publications, 1974.

——. *Space and Revolution: Projects for Monuments, Squares, and Public Buildings in France 1789–1799*. Montreal: McGill-Queen's University Press, 1991.

Leppert, Richard. *Art and the Committed Eye: The Cultural Functions of Imagery*. Boulder, Colo.: Westview Press, 1996.

——. *Music and Image: Domesticity, Ideology, and Socio-cultural Formation in Eighteenth-Century England*. Cambridge: Cambridge University Press, 1988.

——. *The Sight of Sound: Music, Representation, and the History of the Body*. Berkeley: University of California Press, 1993.

Levy, Darline Gay, and Harriet B. Applewhite. "Women and Militant Citizenship in Revolutionary Paris." In *Rebel Daughters: Women and the French Revolution*, edited by Sara E. Melzer and Leslie W. Rabine. Oxford: Oxford University Press, 1992.

Levy, Darline Gay; Harriet Branson Applewhite; and Mary Durham Johnson, eds. *Women in Revolutionary Paris, 1789–1795: Selected Documents Translated with Notes and Commentary*. Urbana: University of Illinois Press, 1979.

Liris, Elizabeth, and Jean Maurice Bizière, eds. *La Révolution et la mort*. Toulouse: Presses Universitaires du Mirail, 1991.

Lusebrink, Hans-Jürgen, and Rolf Reichardt. "La Bastille: Dans l'imaginaire social de la France à la fin du XVIIIe siècle (1774–1799)." *Revue d'histoire moderne et contemporaine* 30 (1983): 196–234.

——. *The Bastille: A History of a Symbol of Despotism and Freedom*. Translated by Norbert Schürer. Durham, N.C.: Duke University Press, 1997.

Marin, Louis. "The King's Body." In *Food for Thought*, translated by Mette Hjort. Baltimore: Johns Hopkins University Press, 1989.

——. *Portrait of the King.* Translated by Martha M. House. Minneapolis: University of Minnesota Press, 1988.

Mason, Laura. "*Ça ira* and the Birth of the Revolutionary Song." *History Workshop* 28 (Autumn 1989): 22–38.

——. *Singing the Revolution: Popular Culture and Politics, 1787–1799.* Ithaca, N.Y.: Cornell University Press, 1996.

Mayr, Otto. *Authority, Liberty, and Automatic Machinery in Early Modern Europe.* Baltimore: Johns Hopkins University Press, 1986.

Maza, Sarah. *Private Lives and Public Affairs: The Causes Célèbres of Prerevolutionary France.* Berkeley: University of California Press, 1993.

May, Gita. *Madame Roland and the Age of Revolution.* New York: Columbia University Press, 1970.

McClintock, Anne. "Family Feuds: Gender, Nationalism, and the Family." *Feminist Review* 44 (Summer 1993): 61–79.

Melzer, Arthur M. *The Natural Goodness of Man: On the System of Rousseau's Thought.* Chicago: University of Chicago Press, 1990.

Melzer, Sara E., and Kathryn Norberg, eds. *From the Royal to the Republican Body: Incorporating the Political in Seventeenth- and Eighteenth-Century France.* Berkeley: University of California Press, 1998.

Merrick, Jeffrey. "Impotence in and at Court." In *Studies in Eighteenth-Century Culture,* vol. 25, edited by Syndy M. Conger and Julie C. Hayes. Baltimore: Johns Hopkins University Press, 1996.

——. "The Marquis de Villette and Mademoiselle de Raucourt: Representations of Male and Female Sexual Deviance in Late Eighteenth-Century France." In *Homosexuality in Modern France,* edited by Jeffrey Merrick and Bryant T. Ragan, Jr. New York: Oxford University Press, 1996.

Michaud, Stéphane. *Muse et madone: Visages de la femme de la Révolution française aux apparitions de Lourdes.* Paris: Seuil, 1985.

Mignolo, Walter D. *The Darker Side of the Renaissance.* Ann Arbor: University of Michigan Press, 1995.

Miles, Margaret. *Image as Insight: Visual Understanding in Western Christianity and Secular Culture.* Boston: Beacon Press, 1985.

——. "The Virgin's One Bare Breast: Nudity, Gender, and Religious Meaning in Tuscan Early Renaissance Culture." In *The Expanding Discourse: Feminism and Art History,* edited by Norma Broude and Mary D. Garrard. New York: IconEditions, 1992.

Mirzoeff, Nicholas. *Bodyscape: Art, Modernity, and the Ideal Figure.* London: Routledge, 1995.

——. "Revolution, Representation, Equality: Gender, Genre, and Emulation in the Académie Royale de Peinture et Sculpture, 1785–93." *Eighteenth-Century Studies* 31, no. 2 (1997–98): 153–174.

——, ed. *The Visual Culture Reader.* London: Routledge, 1998.

Mitchell, Claudine. "Spectacular Fears and Popular Arts: A View from the Nineteenth-

Century." In *Reflections of Revolution: Images of Romanticism*, edited by Alison Yarrington and Kelvin Everest, pp. 159–81. London: Routledge, 1993.

Mitchell, W. J. T. *Iconology: Image, Text, Ideology.* Chicago: University of Chicago, 1986.

——. *Picture Theory: Essays on Verbal and Visual Representation.* Chicago: University of Chicago Press, 1994.

Montrose, Louis Adrian. "'Shaping Fantasies': Figurations of Gender and Power in Elizabethan Culture." *Representations* 1, no. 2 (Spring 1983): 61–94.

Mosse, George. *Nationalism and Sexuality: Middle-Class Morality and Sexual Norms in Modern Europe.* Madison: University of Wisconsin Press, 1985.

Mukerji, Chandra. *From Graven Images: Patterns of Modern Materialism.* New York: Columbia University Press, 1983.

——. *Territorial Ambitions and the Gardens of Versailles.* Cambridge: Cambridge University Press, 1997.

Mulvey, Laura. "Visual Pleasure and Narrative Cinema." *Screen* 16, no. 3 (1975): 6–18.

Nora, Pierre, ed. *Realms of Memory: The Construction of the French Past.* Vol. 3, *Symbols*, edited by Lawrence D. Kritzman; translated by Arthur Goldhammer. New York: Columbia University Press, 1998.

Norton, Anne. *Reflections on Political Identity.* Baltimore: Johns Hopkins University Press, 1988.

Olson, Lester C. *Emblems of American Community in the Revolutionary Era: A Study in Rhetorical Iconology.* Washington, D.C.: Smithsonian Institution Press, 1991.

Orr, Linda. *Headless History: Nineteenth-Century French Historiography of the Revolution.* Ithaca, N.Y.: Cornell University Press, 1990.

Outram, Dorinda. *The Body and the French Revolution: Sex, Class, and Political Culture.* New Haven, Conn.: Yale University Press, 1989.

Ozouf, Mona. *Festivals and the French Revolution.* Translated by Alan Sheridan. Cambridge, Mass.: Harvard University Press, 1988.

Pardailhé-Galabrun, Annik. *The Birth of Intimacy: Privacy and Domestic Life in Early Modern Paris.* Translated by Jocelyn Phelps. Philadelphia: University of Pennsylvania Press, 1991.

Parker, Andrew; Mary Russo; Doris Sommer; and Patricia Yeager, eds. *Nationalisms and Sexualities.* New York: Routledge, 1992.

Pateman, Carole. *The Disorder of Women: Democracy, Feminism, and Political Theory.* Stanford, Calif.: Stanford University Press, 1989.

——. *The Sexual Contract.* Stanford, Calif.: Stanford University Press, 1988.

Paulson, Ronald. *Representations of Revolution, 1789–1820.* New Haven, Conn.: Yale University Press, 1983.

——. "The Severed Head: The Impact of French Revolutionary Caricatures on England." In *French Caricature and the French Revolution, 1789–1799*, edited by James Cuno. Los Angeles: University of California, Grunwald Center for the Graphic Arts, Wight Art Gallery, 1988.

Philippe, Robert. *Political Graphics: Art as a Weapon.* New York: Abbeville Press, 1980.

Pitkin, Hanna Fenichel. *The Concept of Representation.* Berkeley: University of California Press, 1972.

——. *Fortune Is a Woman: Gender and Politics in the Thought of Niccolò Machiavelli.* Berkeley: University of California Press, 1984.

Pocock, J. G. A. *The Machiavellian Moment: Florentine Thought and the Atlantic Republican Tradition.* Princeton, N.J.: Princeton University Press, 1976.

——. *Virtue, Commerce, and History : Essays on Political Thought and History, Chiefly in the Eighteenth Century.* Cambridge: Cambridge University Press, 1985.

Pointon, Marcia. *Naked Authority: The Body in Western Painting, 1830–1908.* Cambridge: Cambridge University Press, 1990.

Pommier, Édouard. *L'Art de la liberté: Doctrines et débats de la Révolution française.* Paris: Gallimard, 1991.

Popkin, Jeremy. *Revolutionary News: The Press in France, 1789–1799.* Durham, N.C.: Duke University Press, 1990.

Potts, Alex. "Beautiful Bodies and Dying Heroes." *History Workshop* 30 (Autumn 1990): 1–21.

——. *Flesh and the Ideal: Winckelmann and the Origins of Art History.* New Haven, Conn.: Yale University Press, 1994.

Proctor, Candace. *Women, Equality, and the French Revolution.* New York: Greenwood Press, 1990.

Pye, Christopher. "The Sovereign, the Theater, and the Kingdome of Darknesse: Hobbes and the Spectacle of Power." In *Representing the English Renaissance,* edited by Stephen Greenblatt. Berkeley: University of California Press, 1988.

Ramaswamy, Sumathi. "Body Language: The Somatics of Nationalism in Tamil India." *Gender and History* 10, no. 1 (April 1998): 78–109.

——. "Virgin Mother, Beloved Other: The Erotics of Tamil Nationalism in Colonial and Post-Colonial India." *Thamyris* 4, no. 1 (Spring 1997): 9–39.

Ravel, Jeffrey. *The Contested Parterre: Public Theater and French Political Culture, 1680–1791.* Ithaca, N.Y.: Cornell University Press, 1999.

——. "Seating the Public: Spheres and Loathing in the Paris Theaters, 1777–1788." *French Historical Studies* 18, no. 1 (Spring 1993): 173–210.

Reid, Roddey. *Families in Jeopardy: Regulating the Social Body in France, 1750–1910.* Stanford, Calif.: Stanford University Press, 1993.

Renouvier, Jules. *Histoire de l'art pendant la Révolution: Considéré principalement dans les estampes.* Paris: Jules Renouard, 1863.

Rétat, Pierre, ed. *La Révolution du journal, 1788–1794.* Paris: Editions du Centre National de la Récherche Scientifique, 1989.

Revel, Jacques. "Marie-Antoinette and Her Fictions: The Staging of Hatred." In *Fictions of the French Revolution,* edited by Bernadette Fort. Evanston, Ill.: Northwestern University Press, 1991.

Riot-Sarcey, Michelle. *La Démocratie à l'épreuve des femmes: Trois figures critiques du pouvoir, 1830–1848.* Paris: Albin Michel, 1994.

Roche, Daniel. *The People of Paris: An Essay in Popular Culture in the 18th Century.* Translated by Marie Evans and Gwynne Lewis. Berkeley: University of California Press, 1987.

Rosanvallon, Pierrre. *Le Sacre du citoyen: Histoire du suffrage universel en France.* Paris: Gallimard, 1992.

Roudinesco, Elisabeth. *Théroigne de Méricourt: A Melancholic Woman during the French*

Revolution. Translated by Martin Thom. London: Verso, 1991.

Rubin, James H. "Disorder/Order: Revolutionary Art as Performative Representation." In "The French Revolution, 1789–1989: Two Hundred Years of Rethinking." Special issue of *The Eighteenth Century: Theory and Interpretation*, edited by Sandy Petrey. Lubbock: Texas Tech University Press, 1989.

Russo, Mary. *The Female Grotesque: Risk, Excess, and Modernity*. New York: Routledge, 1994.

Sahlins, Peter. *Boundaries: The Making of France and Spain in the Pyrenees*. Berkeley: University of California Press, 1989.

Schama, Simon. *Citizens: A Chronicle of the French Revolution*. New York: Alfred A. Knopf, 1989.

Schiebinger, Londa. *The Mind Has No Sex? Women in the Origins of Modern Science*. Cambridge, Mass.: Harvard University Press, 1989.

Schmidt-Linsenhoff, Viktoria, ed. *Sklavin Oder Bürgerin? Französische Revolution und Neue Weiblichkeit, 1760–1830*. Frankfurt: Historiches Museum Frankfurt; Marburg: Jonas Verlag, 1989.

Sewell, William H., Jr. "*Le citoyen/la citoyenne*: Activity, Passivity, and the Revolutionary Concept of Citizenship." In *The Political Culture of the French Revolution*, edited by Colin Lucas. Oxford: Pergamon Press, 1988.

——. *A Rhetoric of Bourgeois Revolution: The Abbé Sieyes and "What Is the Third Estate?"* Durham, N.C.: Duke University Press, 1994.

Sheriff, Mary D. *The Exceptional Woman: Elisabeth Vigée-Lebrun and the Cultural Politics of Art*. Chicago: University of Chicago Press, 1996.

——. "Letters: Painted/Penned/Purloined." In *Studies in Eighteenth-Century Culture*, vol. 26, edited by Syndy M. Conger and Julie C. Hayes. Baltimore: Johns Hopkins University Press, 1998.

Silverman, Kaja. "Liberty, Maternity, Commodification." In *New Formations* 5 (Summer 1988): 69–90.

Singer, Brian C. J. *Society, Theory, and the French Revolution: Studies in the Revolutionary Imaginary*. New York: St. Martin's, 1986.

Singham, Shanti. "Betwixt Cattle and Men: Jews, Blacks, and Women and the Declaration of the Rights of Man." In *The French Revolution and the Idea of Freedom: The Old Regime and the Declaration of Rights of 1789*, edited by Dale Van Kley. Stanford, Calif.: Stanford University Press, 1994.

Skinner, Quentin. "Meaning and Understanding in the History of Ideas." *History and Theory* 7 (1969): 3–53.

Sledziewski, Elisabeth G. *Révolutions du sujet*. Paris: Meridiens Kincksieck, 1989.

Smith, Anthony D. *National Identity*. Reno: University of Nevada Press, 1991.

Smith-Rosenberg, Carroll. "Domesticating 'Virtue': Coquettes and Revolutionaries in Young America." In *Literature and the Body: Essays on Population and Persons*, edited by Elaine Scarry. Baltimore: Johns Hopkins University Press, 1988.

Soboul, Albert. *Le Procès de Louis XVI*. Paris: Collection Archives Juillard, 1966.

Solomon-Godeau, Abigail. "Male Trouble: A Crisis in Representation." *Art History* 16, no. 2

(June 1993): 186–312.

———. *Male Trouble: A Crisis in Representation.* London: Thames and Hudson, 1997.

Sommer, Doris. *Foundational Fictions: The National Romances of Latin America.* Berkeley: University of California Press, 1991.

Stafford, Barbara Maria. *Artful Science: Enlightenment Entertainment and the Eclipse of Visual Education.* Cambridge, Mass.: MIT Press, 1994.

———. *Body Criticism: Imaging the Unseen in Enlightenment Art and Medicine.* Cambridge, Mass.: MIT Press, 1991.

———. "The Eighteenth-Century: Towards an Interdisciplinary Model." *Art Bulletin* 70, no. 1 (March 1988): 6–24.

———. *Good Looking: Essays on the Virtue of Images.* Cambridge, Mass.: MIT Press, 1996.

Stallybrass, Peter, and Allon White. *The Politics and Poetics of Transgression.* Ithaca, N.Y.: Cornell University Press, 1986.

Starobinski, Jean. *Jean-Jacques Rousseau: La Transparence et l'obstacle, suivi de sept essais sur Rousseau.* Paris: Gallimard, 1971.

Stewart, Philip. *Engraven Desire: Eros, Image, and Text in the French Eighteenth Century.* Durham, N.C.: Duke University Press, 1992.

Sussman, George D. *Selling Mothers' Milk: The Wet-Nursing Business in France, 1715–1914.* Urbana: University of Illinois Press, 1982.

Tanner, Tony. *Adultery in the Novel: Contract and Transgression.* Baltimore: Johns Hopkins University Press, 1979).

Terdiman, Richard. *Discourse/Counter-Discourse: The Theory and Practice of Symbolic Resistance in Nineteenth-Century France.* Ithaca, N.Y.: Cornell University Press, 1985.

Thomas, Chantal. "L'Héroïne du crime: Marie-Antoinette dans les pamphlets." In *La Carmagnole des Muses: L'Homme de lettres et l'artiste dans la Révolution française*, edited by Jean-Claude Bonnet. Paris: A. Colin, 1988.

———. "Heroism in the Feminine: The Examples of Charlotte Corday and Madame Roland." In *The French Revolution, 1789–1989: Two Hundred Years of Rethinking.* Special issue of *The Eighteenth Century: Theory and Interpretation*, edited by Sandy Petrey. Lubbock: Texas Tech University Press, 1989.

———. *The Wicked Queen: The Origins of the Myth of Marie-Antoinette.* Translated by Julie Rose. New York: Zone, 1999.

Trumbach, Randolph. *Sex and the Gender Revolution.* Vol. 1, *Heterosexuality and the Third Gender in Enlightenment London.* Chicago: University of Chicago Press, 1998.

Tulard, Jean; Jean-François Fayard; and Alfred Fierro, eds. *Histoire et dictionnaire de la Révolution française, 1789–1799.* Paris: Robert Laffont, 1987.

Turner, Bryan. *The Body and Society.* Oxford and New York: Basil Blackwell, 1984.

Turner, Victor. *From Ritual to Theater: The Human Seriousness of Play.* New York: Performing Arts Publications, 1982.

Vallery-Radot, Jean. *L'Estampe satirique et burlesque en France, 1500–1800.* Paris: [La Bibliotheque],1950.

Vaughan, William, and Helen Weston, eds. *Jacques-Louis David's Marat.* Cambridge:

Cambridge University Press, 2000.

Vovelle, Michel, ed. *Les Images de la Révolution française*. Paris: Publications de la Sorbonne, 1988.

——, ed. *L'Image de la Révolution française: Communications présentées lors du Congrès Mondial pour le Bicentenaire de la Révolution, Sorbonne, Paris, 6–12 Juillet 1989*. 3 vols. Paris: Pergamon Press, 1989.

Waldinger, Renée; Philip Dawson; and Isser Woloch, eds. *The French Revolution and the Meaning of Citizenship*. Westport, Conn.: Greenwood Press, 1993.

Walzer, Michael. "The King's Trial and the Political Culture of the Revolution." In *The French Revolution and the Creation of Modern Political Culture*, vol. 2, *The Political Culture of the French Revolution*, edited by Colin Lucas. Oxford: Pergamon Press, 1988.

——, ed. *Regicide and Revolution: Speeches at the Trial of Louis XVI*. Translated by Marian Rothstein. London: Cambridge University Press, 1974.

Warner, Marina. *Monuments and Maidens: The Allegory of the Female Form*. New York: Atheneum, 1985.

Watt, Tessa. *Cheap Print and Popular Piety, 1550–1640*. Cambridge: Cambridge University Press, 1991.

Yalom, Marilyn. *A History of the Breast*. New York: Ballantine, 1997.

Index